INTERNATIONAL BUSINESS TRAVEL
IN THE GLOBAL ECONOMY

Transport and Mobility Series

Series Editors: Professor Brian Graham, Professor of Human Geography, University of Ulster, UK and Richard Knowles, Professor of Transport Geography, University of Salford, UK, on behalf of the Royal Geographical Society (with the Institute of British Geographers) Transport Geography Research Group (TGRG).

The inception of this series marks a major resurgence of geographical research into transport and mobility. Reflecting the dynamic relationships between socio-spatial behaviour and change, it acts as a forum for cutting-edge research into transport and mobility, and for innovative and decisive debates on the formulation and repercussions of transport policy making.

For further information about this series, please visit www.ashgate.com

International Business Travel
in the Global Economy

Edited by

JONATHAN V. BEAVERSTOCK
University of Nottingham, UK

BEN DERUDDER
Ghent University, Belgium

JAMES FAULCONBRIDGE
Lancaster University, UK

FRANK WITLOX
Ghent University, Belgium

Routledge
Taylor & Francis Group
LONDON AND NEW YORK

First published 2010 by Ashgate Publishing

Published 2016 by Routledge
2 Park Square, Milton Park, Abingdon, Oxon OX14 4RN
711 Third Avenue, New York, NY 10017, USA

Routledge is an imprint of the Taylor & Francis Group, an informa business

British Library Cataloguing in Publication Data
International business travel in the global economy. --
   (Transport and mobility series)
   1. Business travel. 2. Business travel--Economic aspects.
   3. Business travel--Social aspects. 4. Aeronautics,
   Commercial--Passenger traffic.
   I. Series II. Beaverstock, Jonathan V.
   910.8'865-dc22

Library of Congress Cataloging-in-Publication Data
International business travel in the global economy / by Jonathan V. Beaverstock ... [et al.].
      p. cm. -- (Transport and mobility)
   Includes bibliographical references and index.
   ISBN 978-0-7546-7942-4 (hardback) -- 1. Business
travel. 2. Globalization--Economic aspects. I. Beaverstock, Jonathan V.
   G156.5.B86I58 2009
   387.7'42--dc22

                                                              2009033607

ISBN 9780754679424 (hbk)

Contents

PART 3 THE PRODUCTION AND MEANING OF BUSINESS TRAVEL

List of Figures

List of Tables

Notes on Contributors

Jonathan V. Beaverstock is Professor of Economic Geography at the University of Nottingham, UK, and was instrumental in the development and co-directorship of the 'Globalization and World Cities' Research Network. He obtained his BA from the University of Wales (Lampeter) and PhD from the University of Bristol, under the supervision of Professor Nigel Thrift. His current research focuses on: globalization and world cities; international financial centres, particularly London, Frankfurt and Singapore; the globalization of professional services; and, expatriation and business travel in a digital age. He has published widely in Human Geography (for example, in the *Annals of the Association of American Geographers*; *Environment and Planning A*; *Geoforum*; *Transactions of the Institute of British Geographers*; *Urban Studies*) and frequents the geographical conference circuits in North America, Europe and Asia. From 2007-2010, he has been appointed a Honorary Professor in Geography at the University of Otago, New Zealand.

John Bowen is Assistant Professor of Geography at Central Washington University, USA. His research interests include transport, economic development, and Asia. He has written about the role of air transport in development, airline industry liberalization and the integration of air cargo services in global production networks. In addition to having published on air transportation themes, John also has real-world experience in aviation, having worked for several years for Singapore Airlines in Singapore.

Lucy Budd is a Lecturer in Transport Studies in the Department of Civil and Building Engineering at Loughborough University, UK, specializing in commercial aviation. Lucy's main research interests include the geographies of airspace, air traffic management, and the socio-environmental impacts of aircraft operations at a variety of scales. She has worked on a number of major research projects including, most recently, climate-related air traffic management, and the environmental consequences of European airspace charging regimes. Her work has been published in a wide range of academic and industry journals.

Jon Martin Denstadli is Senior Research Economist at the Institute of Transport Economics, Norway. He holds a PhD in marketing and marketing research from Norwegian School of Economics and Business Administration. Professional interests include research methods, aviation and analysis of travel behaviour, with a special focus on business travel. He has conducted extensive research in the area of business communication and managers' perceptions of face-to-face meetings and ICT. Studies include large scale surveys of Norwegian industry and commerce as well as case studies of industrial enterprises.

Ben Derudder is Lecturer in Human Geography at the Department of Geography, and Associate Director of the 'Globalization and World Cities' Research Network (GaWC). His research focuses on: (1) the conceptualization and empirical analysis of transnational urban networks; (2) the (persisting) importance of business travel in the space economy; and (3) spatial modelling techniques. He teaches courses on human geography, global city-formation, and methods and techniques in geographical research.

Lomme Devriendt is Research Assistant at the Geography Department of Ghent University and a Research Fellow of the 'Globalization and World Cities' Research Network (GaWC). He holds an MA in Geography and Land Surveying (Ghent University). His PhD research is funded by the Flemish Fund for Scientific Research (FWO), and deals with the conceptualization and empirical assessment of the digital and physical accessibility of cities in the global economy. He is a member of the editorial board of Aerlines Magazine and AGORA.

James Faulconbridge is a Lecturer in Economic Geography at Lancaster University, UK. His work examines a range of issue relating to the globalization of professional service firms with particular focus upon the way knowledges and practices are reproduced and transformed within firms as they move across space. He has published articles relating to this in *Geoforum*, *Global Networks*, the *Journal of Economic Geography* and *Urban Studies*. His current research projects develop these interests by first exploring the use of training in global law firms as part of strategies to manage cultural coherency across countries, and second by analysing the way knowledges about sustainability are produced and circulated within the architecture profession and in global architecture firms.

Brian Graham is Emeritus Professor of Human Geography at the University of Ulster. He is a Chartered Geographer of the Royal Geographical Society and was formerly Chair of its Transport Geography Research Group from which he received the 2008 Alan Hay Award for contributions to Transport Geography. Brian Graham is a member of the editorial boards of *Journal of Transport Geography* and *Transport Reviews*, and has published widely on many aspects of air transport. His present research interests focus on the interconnections between air transport, economic development and the environment. He is the author of *Geography and Air Transport* (1995), has acted as an advisor on aviation matters to government departments in Northern Ireland, and was formerly a director of Air Route Development (NI) Ltd.

Mattias Gripsrud is a Media and Communication Research Scientist at the Institute of Transport Economics, Norway. His main research interest areas lie within new communication patterns, new media technology and the manifold forms of interplay between transport and communication. As a former research scientist for the telecom company Telenor, he has an extensive background in user gratification studies, customer insight and in the development of service concepts for broadband and mobile technologies. He has also served as New Media Adviser for the Norwegian media regulatory authorities.

Phil Hubbard is an urban social geographer with interests in the changing form of the late capitalist city under conditions of contemporary globalization. This has been manifest in studies of the changing places of the sex industry; leisure spaces and consumption patterns and the urban geographies of asylum seeking, and migrant groups. He is author/editor of a number of recent books, including *The Sage Companion to the City*; *Key Thinkers on Space and Place*; *Key Concepts in Geography – the City*, and the *International Encyclopedia of Human Geography*.

Andrew Jones lectures at Birkbeck College, University of London. Primarily an economic geographer, his research interests span a range of economic, urban and sociological issues. His research focus has for some time been on globalization, transnational firms and the knowledge economy. This work has spanned a range of business service industries including legal services, consultancy and architecture, and has recently focused, in particular, on the globalization of working practices. His policy work includes research into the globalization of voluntary work and international skilled labour mobility. He is author of over 20 journal articles and book chapters, as well as three books including *Management Consultancy and Banking in an Era of Globalisation* (Palgrave Macmillan, 2003).

Aharon Kellerman is Emeritus Professor of Geography at the University of Haifa, Israel. He is President of Zefat Academic College, Israel, and he further serves as Vice-President of the International Geographical Union (IGU). His current fields of interest are the geography of information and mobilities. Prof. Kellerman received his PhD at Boston University, US (1976). Over the years he also worked for the University of Miami, University of Maryland, Bar-Ilan University, and Oxford University. At the University of Haifa he served as Vice-President for Administration (1995-2004). He has published five books and is a Fulbright Alumnus. In 2000 he established the IGU Commission on the Geography of the Information Society and chaired it until 2008.

Sven Kesselring is the director of research of the mobil.TUM – interdisciplinary project group on mobility and transport at the Technische Universität München. In the summer of 2008, he was a visiting professor for sociological theory at the University of Kassel. Sven holds a PhD from the Ludwig Maximilians Universität München. His PhD on 'Mobile Politik' was published in 2001. He recently received a grant from the Erich-Becker-Stiftung (Frankfurt Airport Foundation) for his work on airports and globalization. He is the speaker of the international Cosmobilities Network (www.cosmobilities.net) which is funded by the Deutsche Forschungsgemeinschaft (DFG). He has published extensively in the field of interdisciplinary mobilities research, and co-edited *Aeromobilities* (London: Routledge, 2009) with Saulo Cwerner and John Urry. In 2008 he published *Tracing Mobilities. Towards a Cosmopolitan Perspective* (Aldershot: Ashgate) with Weert Canzler and Vincent Kaufmann (eds).

Claus Lassen is Associated Professor at the Department of Development and Planning, and Director of the Centre of Mobility and Urban Studies (C-MUS), Aalborg University, Denmark. His research interests include (aero)mobility, air travel, work, airports, cities, knowledge industries and travel management. His main focus has been to analyse various forms of social relations in the light of international air travel and he has published several works in the fields of aeromobility and work.

John Salt (Professor of Geography, UCL 1996-2007; Emeritus Professor 2008-present), is Director of the Migration Research Unit, UCL (1989-present); Co-Director of the Leverhulme Programme on Migration and Citizenship (2003-present), and Consultant to: OECD (1985-present), EU (1995-97; 2000-2002), Council of Europe (1991-2006), Australian government (2003, 2005-2006), UK Home Office (1999-present), National Audit Office (2004), and the Office for National Statistics (2002-present). He is an Advisory Board Member of the ONS Centre for Demography (2006-present). His current research foci are the migration of expertise within corporate global labour markets, international students, and the UK graduate labour market.

Nathalie Van Nuffel was Research Assistant at the Department of Geography of Ghent University. She holds a degree in Spatial Planning (Ghent University) and a PhD in Geography (Ghent University) on regionalization of the residential market in North Belgium. Her research interests include spatial planning, housing, commuting and migration. She worked on the BELSPO (Belgian Science Policy) project 'ISEEM', which aims at developing and implementing an integrated spatio–economic–ecological modelling approach.

Alessandra Vecchi is a Research Fellow based in the School of Business and in the International Institute of Integration Studies at Trinity College, Dublin. She is working on the SMART Project which aims to support intelligent business networking and consumer services based on effective and efficient information/ knowledge sharing and collaboration across supply chain partners, capitalizing on the fact that products are uniquely identified with the use of the RFID technology. She teaches at the undergraduate and graduate level in the areas of International Business and Globalization Studies.

Gerlinde Vogl is a sociologist, and holds a PhD from the Technical University, Munich. She works currently as a researcher at the Chair of Sociology on the project 'New Mobility Regimes' (with Sven Kesselring). Her main research interests are: mobility, work and technology, and social network analysis. Important publications include: *Selbstständige Medienschaffende in der Netzwerkgesellschaft* (Verlag Werner Hülsbusch: Boizenburg, 2008); in collaboration with Kesselring, 'Networks, Scapes and Flows – Mobility Pioneers between First and Second Modernity', in Canzler, Weert, Vincent Kaufmann, Sven Kesselring (2008), *Tracing Mobilities. Towards a Cosmopolitan Perspective in Mobility Research* (Aldershot: Ashgate, pp. 163-180).

James Wickham is Director of the Employment Research Centre (ERC) in the Department of Sociology at Trinity College, Dublin, where he is also Head of the School of Social Sciences and Philosophy. His PhD from the University of Sussex (UK) was a social history of working class politics in Weimar, Germany; he then researched and published on Irish industrialization and labour market issues, especially the electronics industry. In 1998 he was awarded a Jean Monnet Personal Chair in European Labour Market Studies. He has studied urban transport and sustainability, and has published *Gridlock: Dublin's Transport Crisis and the Future of the City* (Dublin, 2006). His current research focuses on employment and different forms of mobility, from migration to business air travel. He is particularly interested in new forms of high skill migration and is directing a project on 'Migrant Careers and Aspirations' within the Trinity College Immigration Initiative, Dublin.

Frank Witlox is Professor of Economic Geography at the Geography Department of Ghent University, and Associate Director of the 'Globalization and World Cities' Research Network (GaWC). He is also a senior researcher at the University of Antwerp's Department of Transport and Regional Economics and a visiting professor at the Institute of Transport and Maritime Management Antwerp. Frank Witlox holds a PhD in Urban Planning (Eindhoven University of Technology), an MA in Applied Economics, and an MA in Maritime Sciences (both University of Antwerp). He teaches social and economic geography, transport geography, urban geography, spatial modelling techniques, geography of the world economy, and maritime economic geography. His research focuses on transport economics and geography, economic geography, spatial modelling techniques, (city) logistics, world cities and globalization, and urban planning.

Foreword:
Business Travel in the Global Economy

Brian Graham

Introduction

The chapters collected in this volume reflect upon the complexities of the causes, motivations for and measurement of business travel. There is, of course, the interconnection between travel and the differentiated geographies and networks of globalization, but readily apparent, too, are the behavioural and cultural practices and processes involved in business travel. The network at the core of the discussions in this book is that of the international air transport industry, a prime characteristic of which lies in its market segmentation. While premium-class air travel (first- and business-class) accounts for, perhaps, no more than ten per cent of airline passengers, this is by far the highest-yield market segment, even though it is also the highest-cost sector for the airlines. It is fair to say that the configurations and even scheduling of long-haul aircraft are determined by the needs and aspirations of premium-class passengers and that airlines compete vigorously in responding to this market.

Simultaneously, however, airlines are also dealing with the demands of an increasingly globalized economy, albeit constrained by their origins in national contexts and the geopolitics of international air travel which still militate against free trade in transport. International (sometimes referred to as network) airlines therefore, generally have a dual role. Their domestic networks are vested in national circumstances, but also feed the international networks that provide the global linkages. These latter, however, are likely to be partial, still reproducing the national in that, for example, diasporic connections are at the heart of many airline networks. These also reproduce connections of language, international relations and tourism consumption patterns as well as those of globalizing economic networks. Therefore, for airlines, responding to the demands for business travel in the global economy is a multi-layered and not necessarily consistent process of attempting to reconcile different and perhaps conflicting motivations and markets, meanwhile constrained by the legacy of their national origins and aviation geopolitics. The aim of this forward is to say something about this complexity of air transport global networks and how they interact in different ways with other manifestations of the network economy which are contributing to the newly emerging typologies of business space explored throughout this book.

On Network Models

At a global scale, air transport networks are increasingly being defined by two trends which are often depicted as contradictory but, equally, may be complementary. Firstly, is the hub-and-spoke system which was defined by the deregulation of aviation markets that began in the 1970s. Secondly, this seemingly contrasts with the fragmentation model, advocated for more than a decade by Boeing, which promotes a proliferation of point-to-point connections between a greater number of city-pairs (Graham and Goetz 2008).

The initial response by network (or legacy) carriers in the US internal market to the threat of start-up competition after deregulation in 1978 lay in the creation of hub-and-spoke networks. Strictly speaking, a hub is an integrated air transport interchange through which (normally) a single carrier operates synchronized banks – or waves – of flights. In these, the hub-arrival times of aircraft, originating from cities at the ends of numerous spokes, are co-ordinated into a short time period. After the minimum interval necessary to redistribute passengers and baggage, an equally large number of aircraft departs to the spoke cities. This pattern is repeated several times during the day (Dennis 1994, Graham 1995, Vowles 2006). The role of a hub is to concentrate business and leisure traffic and origin/destination-connecting traffic in one aircraft. The split between business and leisure traffic varies but – as a rule of thumb – stands around a ratio of 25-30 to 70-75 per cent (remembering that much business traffic is actually accommodated in economy class). Hub dominance has also been regarded as a large incumbent's most effective defensive tactic in a liberalized market because, especially when combined with airport congestion and linked to an alliance strategy, it offers the real possibility of pre-empting – or at least controlling – competition at a particular airport. The model, however, no longer offers a 'fortress' to the network carriers, such '… barriers [to market entry] protect[ing them] only from market entrants that plan to imitate their principal business market' (Lindstädt and Fauser 2004: 28). Efficient hub operation is dependent upon available runway and terminal capacity to handle the peaks, combined with extensive feeder connections that often employ smaller aircraft operated by regional airlines. The US hub-and-spoke model, with its dominant carriers and dedicated terminals and gates, has not been replicated fully elsewhere, largely because of factors such as existing restrictions on airport capacity, political fragmentation and environmental constraints although the hubs more recently established in the United Arab Emirates (UAE) display similar traits of dominance.

At a global scale, the dominant intercontinental traffic axes interlink Europe, North America, and the Asia–Pacific region. Consequently, the demand for, and provision of, air transport has a pronounced east-west bias, the basic network interconnecting some 20 or so of the world cities that serve as the gatekeepers of the global service economy (Zook and Brunn 2006). Metropoles such as London, New York, Chicago, Tokyo, Singapore and Hong Kong constitute a set of commercial and financial nodes, joined by a series of linkages including virtual and physical transport flows. Inevitably, they have become the key locations for the global airline networks. North-south routes into South America, Africa and the South-west Pacific are effectively little more than capillaries, connecting Buenos Aires, Johannesburg and Sydney to the other world cities. But this basic pattern is also modified by the interplay between the two essential spatial characteristics of hubs – centrality and intermediacy (Fleming and Hayuth 1994). As Derudder et al. (2007a), observe, the role of global cities as prime, central, nodal switching points in air transport flows has increasingly been supplemented by other sites which have the quality of intermediacy and thus of re-routing traffic rather than being origin and destination cities in their own right.

Despite the importance of concentration, the future strategic domination of the mega-hub has been questioned because of an apparently contradictory trend towards dispersal or 'fragmentation' on long-haul routes with smaller aircraft like the Boeing (B)767/777 or Airbus (A)A330 being used to serve a much larger number of point-to-point city-pairs as traffic flowing between two regions breaks into ever smaller flows as the total grows over time. Simultaneously however, this reflects a growth in total traffic between two regions over time, which means that there are two complementary trends. Even as traffic fragments, the original stream continues to grow, reflecting the relatively fixed and static nature of much price elastic air transport demand – leisure, visiting friends and relations (VFR) and migrant labour. For example, the United Kingdom Government has promoted the development of long-haul services from regional airports to counteract congestion in South-east England (Graham 2008), but despite this being a successful strategy, 'the proportion of London long-haul traffic connecting from domestic services has actually increased' (Civil Aviation Authority 2007: 3).

Fragmentation occurred first in the transatlantic market and then on trans-Pacific routes and is now apparent in many Asian markets, especially routes into China (Boeing 2007). To some extent, the process is a reflection of the ways in which globalization encourages long-distance interaction, thereby elongating supply lines and demanding the use of smaller vehicles. As Castells (1996) argues, cities are no longer exclusively identifiable for their stable embeddedness in a given territorial milieu, but act as nodes in networks at myriad scales of which air transport is one. As the enlargement and deepening of the global economy is increasingly focused on cities rather than states, transport demand in general for both passengers and freight is becoming more customized as global activity is dispersed away from the top-ranked global cities (O'Connor 2003). Moreover, despite real-time information and communications technology (ICT), the continuing demand for face-to-face contact requires more low-density routings.

The Geopolitics of Global Air Transport

Although it can be difficult to determine the direction of cause-effect relationships, globalization would simply not be possible without air transportation. Likewise, the airline industry would be much less significant without concomitant global expansion. For example, it is estimated that about 40 per cent of global freight trade by value (if only 2 per cent by weight) is moved by air (Bowen and Leinbach 2006). Airline freight operations are shared between integrators such as FedEx and UPS, both of which have global networks, and combination carriers which use dedicated freighters, but also the considerable belly-hold freight capacity of wide-bodied passenger aircraft (Bowen 2004).

The historical regulation of air transport does, however, still impose significant constraints on the sector's ability to respond to globalization and fragmentation requires the implementation of liberalized air service agreements (ASAs) which is why it first occurred on the North Atlantic and is only now increasingly apparent in other markets. Many cities of more than 6m population have remarkably few direct international air services (Boeing 2007). Derudder et al. (2007b) concluding that in the world city network, less important cities are not only less connected, but on average, their connections are likely to be more regional that international. At the international scale, air service provision between countries was controlled historically by bilateral agreements, negotiated between pairs of governments. These governed the applicability of the nine so-called 'freedoms' of civil aviation (Graham and Goetz 2008). The basic principle of all bilaterals is reciprocity or equivalency, the agreements covering fares, capacity, frequency, number of carriers and routes flown. Since domestic airline deregulation in 1978, the US government has pursued a global policy – congruent with US national interests – to liberalize international bilaterals. Most recently, it has sought so-called 'open-skies' bilaterals, allowing unrestricted market entry and code-sharing alliances (in which one service is operated under the flight codes of two airlines). This version of 'open skies' has been accompanied by the offer of anti-trust immunization for various airline alliances and mergers.

The logical outcome of full 'open skies' is the replacement of bilateral with multilateral agreements, in which groups of like-minded countries permit any airline virtually unlimited access to any market within their boundaries. This has occurred *within* regional markets such as the European Union (EU) and the North American Free Trade Area and is now increasingly the focus of inter-bloc negotiations as in the EU–US transatlantic Open Skies agreement, the first imperfect stage of which was implemented in 2008. This will permit more carriers to serve more gateways and promote, inevitably, further fragmentation on the North Atlantic as, for example, has already occurred in the UK where – as observed above – a number of regional airports now sustain direct US services. Indeed, the US legacy carriers like Delta and Continental are aggressively exploiting such opportunities, switching medium-sized aircraft to point-to-point or hub-spoke international routes in an attempt to counteract loss of revenues incurred by competition with low-cost carriers (LCCs) in the US domestic market. Other countries such as Singapore, New Zealand, Australia and the UAE with quality airlines, but small and finite domestic markets, are also in favour of liberalized ASAs which allow airlines to operate 5th and 6th freedom services (the rights to carry passengers between two countries by an airline from a third country). Although 'liberalization in international markets is a global phenomenon' (Boeing 2007: 15), nevertheless, both passenger and freight air transport between many individual countries still remains constrained by bilaterals (for example, Singapore Airlines (SIA) is the largest carrier on the Kangaroo route out of Australia to Europe, but all its flights change codes at Singapore as it does not have 6th freedom rights). Continuing restrictions on foreign ownership of airlines (not least within the United States) also act as barriers to merger, acquisition and firm consolidation. The major network carriers thus tend to remain firmly fixed into a nation-state framework despite the dispersal inherent in globalized network economies, one reason why national capitals also tend to be the pre-eminent national hubs.

The result is that no one airline could ever mount a global operation without recourse to partners (Goetz and Graham 2004). This has led to the creation of global airline alliances which, at one level, provide a means of circumventing at least some of the restrictions on international services and may offer the possibility of *de facto* consolidation and 'seamless' interlining. There are three principal groupings, Star Alliance, oneworld (sic) and Sky Team. Each alliance is based on core members in the key air transport regions, supplemented by affiliate carriers in less strategic markets. Crucially, therefore, hubs – both central and intermediate – while usually dominated by a single carrier, are also sites at which alliance traffic is concentrated through long-haul connections from other alliance hubs. To an extent, alliances reflect that the globalized world, paradoxically, still remains a bounded and sovereign space in which historical processes of localized economic development continue to influence the location of economic activity. Despite the revolution in air transport and other communications technologies, all economic activity is grounded in specific locations, 'both physical[ly], in the form of sunk costs, and less tangibl[ly] in the form of localized social relationships' (Dicken 1998: 11). One consequence is noted by Zook and Brunn (2006) who adapt Goetz's 'pockets of pain' concept (2002) – those places that 'lost out' in US deregulation – to the global context. They argue that there are similar 'forgotten places', actively being forged as a result of processes of inclusion and exclusion in the global economy.

Airbus and Boeing

Airbus and Boeing, the two companies that dominate global aircraft manufacturing, have long advanced seemingly diametrically opposed arguments on hub-and-spoke versus fragmentation. Boeing favours point-to-point or one-stop connecting services over a single hub as alternatives to multi-sector journeys. In this network strategy which requires airlines to 'maintain or reduce airplane size to provide frequent, non-stop service', albeit serving thinner, but higher-yield routes (Boeing 2003: 11). To serve this model, the company developed various variants of the B777 and, more recently, the carbon-titanium B787 'Dreamliner'. Seen as the ultimate 'fragmenter', it was intended that this aircraft would enter service in 2008, but by year's end, it had yet to fly and most airlines expect around two years delay on initial deliveries.

Airbus, conversely, argues that 'in response to increasingly severe cost pressures, established airlines will be driven even further to improve the efficiency of their route networks and to use low-unit-cost aircraft'. This will involve the replacement of point-to-point systems by 'lower-cost, lower-fare "hub" systems' (Airbus 2002: 13, 17). Thus the company has developed the (nominal capacity 550-seat) A380 as a low-cost people carrier catering for the bulk of long-haul passengers concentrated in the world's major centres of population and being moved across hubs. According to Airbus (2006, 2008), half of the top 100 fastest-growing city-pairs involve a hub at both ends and all, but one, has a hub city at one end. Thirty-two top hub cities account for 80 per cent of passengers while 25 per cent of passengers on routes longer than 2,000km are flying hub-to-hub and no less than 77 per cent want to fly to or from one of these cities.

Consequently, the demand is there, but the moot question is, however, whether or not this will deliver profits for the airlines because size does not necessarily equate with sustainable yields. Mason (2007) cites evidence from British Airways (BA) that a change in gauge on North Atlantic services from B747-400s to smaller B777-200s actually led to increased profitability from fewer passengers because of the elimination of non-profitable traffic carried on a marginal revenue basis. Not surprisingly, Boeing and Airbus aircraft market outlooks differ significantly for the period out to c. 2025. Boeing predicts that 84 per cent of new aircraft will be single or twin-aisle, allowing more people to go more directly to their destinations. It predicts a 'niche' market of around 1,000 units for B747 and larger aircraft (including freighters). Although the predictions are not directly comparable, Airbus projects around 1,700 large aircraft and freighters, and downplays the smaller twin-aisle market.

Both companies have, however, qualified their positions and, as Mason (2007: 10) observes, neither 'is prepared to unilaterally cede any part of the wide-body market to its competitor'. Airbus now acknowledges that high-yield business traffic will demand direct, frequent non-stop point-to-point flights and, faced with the market success of the twin-engined 777 and 787 (894 orders by end October 2008, prior to service entry), has developed its own A350XWB which had more than 458 orders and commitments by the end of October 2008 (although it will not be in service until 2013 if all goes to plan). Despite its adherence to the fragmentation model, Boeing which sees large aircraft being flown only 'on dense routes by a limited number of airlines', an argument seemingly vindicated by the 192 sales of the A380 (end October 2008), has not abandoned the large airliner market entirely and launched the B747-8 in 2005. Tellingly, only 20 passenger variants had been sold by the end of 2007, the outcome of a rather whimsical decision by Lufthansa to operate both the A380 and B747-8. Thus it does seem to be the case that most growth in the world's airlines will be manifested as 'increased frequencies, more nonstops, and new city pairs served by small- and intermediate-size airplanes' such as the B787 (Boeing 2003: 14), a model that is seemingly more compliant with the dispersal apparent in network economies. Both companies do agree that economic growth is the primary driver for aircraft orders and that Asia–Pacific (including China and India) is the key market.

International Business Travel in the Global Economy

It is against this context that international business travel in the global economy and the various chapters in this book can be located. First, business travel can be visualized as a set of practices and processes related not only to the articulation of the global economy, but also to culture, behaviour, status and even leisure mobilities. The privilege attached to this form of travel is also underlined by the continued use of the term, 'class', which, more generally, has fallen into disfavour as a means of socio-economic demarcation in a world of neo-liberal politics and economics. Business travel comprises a complex set of mobilities that are part of a wider 'aeromobility' that reflects lifestyle as much as economics. Business travel is certainly, in John Bowen's telling phrase, for 'a people set apart', some sufficiently so that even the most elitist form of scheduled air travel is insufficient for their needs. Instead, the wealthiest and most privileged can afford to employ executive jets for private business travel. Business travel also carries a raft of motivations in which the distinction between leisure and business and between managers and managed is blurred and open to markedly different negotiations.

Secondly, however, mobile workers are logged into other spatial and technological networks as they travel. Thus business travel is also about interconnections, both between these various networks and also in terms of spatialities. Technological alternatives to travel do exist as with video-conferencing and real-time virtual communications. But the need for co-presence or face-to-face meetings seems to remain a consistent motivation for corporate mobility, no doubt partly because of the blurring of motives and the indistinct boundary between business and leisure involved in that form of travel. These complex intermeshing motivatory layers – which reflect, perhaps, the conceptualization of globalization as a set of overlapping economic, political and social networks – also produce complex spatialities of business travel although it can be difficult to capture these from official data sources. One result, however, is that, paralleling the social hierarchies of business travel, there is also a hierarchy of places stemming from the differentiation of business-class flows.

In sum, therefore, the ostensibly straightforward term, 'business travel', opens up a window into the complexities of understanding mobility in the global economy. This book is a truly interdisciplinary endeavour in the sense that a raft of different academic perspectives is required to elicit an understanding of business travel. First, we need to appreciate how the individual layers – business, culture, society, politics – overlap in producing a raft of motivations and demands for business travel. Secondly, we then need to work out how these intersect with the different economic and political networks and their constraints. Prime among these is the international aviation industry which is the principal facilitator of mobility in the global economy. *International Business Travel in the Global Economy* provides that measure of interdisciplinarity at a time when, perhaps perversely, the global credit crisis and possibly impending recession make the suppliers of mobility even more dependent on maintaining the demand for business travel.

References

Airbus 2002. *Global Market Forecast, 2001-2020*. Blagnac: Airbus S.A.S.

Airbus 2006. *The Future of Flying: Global Market Forecast, 2006-2025*. Blagnac: Airbus S.A.S.

Airbus 2008. *Flying by Nature: Global Market Forecast, 2007-2026*. Blagnac: Airbus S.A.S.

Boeing 2003. *Current Market Outlook 2003*. Seattle: Boeing.

Boeing 2007. *Current Market Outlook 2007*. Chicago: Boeing.

Bowen, J.T. 2004. The geography of freighter aircraft operations in the Pacific Rim. *Journal of Transport Geography*, 12, 1-11.

Bowen, J.T. and Leinbach, T. 2006. Competitive advantage in global production networks: Air freight services and the electronics industry in Southeast Asia. *Economic Geography*, 82, 147-166.

Castells, M. 1996. *The Rise of the Network Society*. Oxford: Blackwell.

Civil Aviation Authority 2007. *Connecting the Continents – Long Haul Passenger Operations from the UK, CAP 771*. London: CAA.

Dennis, N. 1994. Strategic strategies for airline hub operations. *Journal of Air Transport Management,* 12, 131-144.

Derudder, B., Devriendt, L. and Witlox, F. 2007a. Flying where you don't want to go: An empirical analysis of hubs in the global airline network. *Tijdschrift voor Economische en Sociale Geografie*, 98, 307-324.

Derudder, B., Witlox, F. and Taylor, P.J. 2007b. United States cities in the world city network: Comparing their positions using global origins and destinations in airline passengers. *Urban Geography*, 28, 74-91.

Dicken, P. 1998. *Global Shift*. Third edition. London: Sage.

Fleming, D.K. and Hayuth, Y. 1994. Spatial characteristics of transportation hubs: Centrality and intermediacy. *Journal of Transport Geography*, 41, 3-18.

Goetz, A.R. 2002. Deregulation, competition and antitrust implications in the U.S. airline industry. *Journal of Transport Geography*, 10, 1-18.

Goetz, A.R. and Graham, B. 2004. Air transport globalization, liberalization and sustainability: Post-2001 policy dynamics in the United States and Europe. *Journal of Transport Geography*, 12, 265-276.

Graham, B. 1995. *Geography and Air Transport*. Chichester: John Wiley.

Graham, B. 1998. UK air travel: Taking off for growth?, in *Traffic Jam: Ten Years of 'Sustainable' Transport in the UK*, edited by I. Docherty and J. Shaw. Bristol: Policy Press, 139-160.

Graham, B. and Goetz, A.R. 2008. Global air transport, in *Transport Geographies*, edited by R.D. Knowles, I. Docherty and J. Shaw. Oxford: Blackwell, 137-155.

Lindstädt, H. and Fauser, B. 2004. Separation or integration? Can network carriers create distinct business streams on one integrated production platform? *Journal of Air Transport Management*, 10, 23-31.

Mason, K.J. 2007. Airframe manufacturers: Which has the better view of the future? *Journal of Air Transport Management*, 13, 9-15.

O'Connor, K. 2003. Global air travel: Towards concentration or dispersal. *Journal of Transport Geography*, 11, 83-92.

Vowles, T.M. 2006. Geographic perspectives of air transportation. *The Professional Geographer*, 58, 12-19.

Zook, M.A. and Brunn, S.D. 2006. From podes to antipodes: Positionalities and global airline geographies. *Annals Association of American Geographers*, 96, 471-490.

Chapter 1

International Business Travel and the Global Economy: Setting the Context

Jonathan V. Beaverstock, Ben Derudder,
James Faulconbridge and Frank Witlox

International travel remains at the heart of international business. (Welch and Worm 2005: 284)

Non-expatriates [Business travellers] … tend to be the forgotten group, yet for many firms they may comprise the largest contingent of employees involved in international business. (Dowling and Welch 2004: 128)

The role of international business travel and the functionality of the business traveller have been persistently overlooked in a broad sweep of literature which embraces international human resource management, international business, the sociology of work and labour, mobilities, transient migration and travel, for example. Welch and Worm (2005: 284) find such a dearth in the literatures 'somewhat curious', because they argue that the nature of the contemporary globalizing firm, characterized by geographical dispersion, global production divisions and complex sub-contracting/ supplier networks, provides the impetus and need for physical travel, especially if the corporate employee wishes to be an effective executive, manager or sales person. As we reach the end of the first decade of the Twenty-First Century, business travel remains an important mode of production in firms with, amongst other things, travel being used to: attend firm meetings or training sessions; visit clients to close deals, pitch for business or provide product support; attend trade fairs/conferences; and visit sub-contractors and suppliers to monitor quality control or negotiate new business. For many workers, business travel is now a normal everyday reality of the working day or night, involving what can be best described as persistent or mundane travel, which can have many downsides like separation from the family, travel stress, health concerns (including jet-lag) (DeFrank et al. 2000). But, for some, especially relatively younger corporate professionals, business travel remains a 'perk' or welcomed, persistent lifestyle choice which enhances personal career paths and brings much job satisfaction and variety to the working week (Welch and Worm 2005).

It is perhaps not surprising, then, that 'mobility' has become a primary discourse in geographical and sociological debates, particularly in relation to globalization, because of the ever growing forms of hyper-mobility that define the lives of many workers. Indeed, whilst mobility in the late twentieth and early twenty-first century takes many forms, including tourism and family-related travel, in economic terms business travel now appears to be the fundamental production process in constructing and reproducing the 'Network Society' and the global, knowledge-based economy that have come to be the hallmarks of contemporary capitalism. Explanations for such compulsions of mobility include clients' expectations of the delivery of expertise, advice, and one-off solutions through face-to-face encounters, the internal/external labour markets of Transnational Corporations (TNCs) and the mobility associated with maintaining various forms of stretched, social management practices, control and relationships. In addition to intra-national travel, cross-border business travel has, therefore, become a significant global flow within and generator of corporate networks. It is, therefore, surprising that to date relatively little time has been devoted to the study of business travel, both as an economic practice and a facet of contemporary mobility. Amongst a broad array of work on mobility and travel (see for example Urry [2003, 2007], Larsen, Axhausen and Urry [2006] and Nowica [2006]), we find much theoretical relevance that can help us explain the nature of business travel, but few empirical investigations that truly unpack the intricacies of this now daily and omnipresence practice (although see Lassen [2006] and Laurier [2004] for notable exceptions).

The formative aim of this edited volume is to address this research lacuna and explore some of the most important contemporary debates associated with the role, nature and effects of business travel in the twenty-first century. More specifically, through the contributions of a number of international experts from different backgrounds, the purpose of this book is to advance understanding of international business travel so as to address major academic, practitioner and policy debates. In particular, the different chapters of the book provide insight into a range of issues and investigate:

1. The role of the airline industry in international business travel and the changing nature of provision. A number of chapters feature in-depth discussions of the relationships between airlines and business travellers, including analyses of the changing form of the airline industry and the effects of this on business travel.
2. The role of mobility in international business activities. Much has been written about the need for mobility and the role of face-to-face contact in business. Yet how the insights in these literatures can be used to theorize business travel has not been addressed head-on. A number of chapters push these debates forward by offering a focused discussion of the way the need for, organization of and costs/benefits of business travel influence the operation of major companies.
3. The sociology of international business travel and its role in and effects on the global economy. The book offers one of the first focused interpretations of the affects of an increasing preponderance to business travel on the sociology of work in contemporary organizations. This will help develop

debates across the social sciences about the nature, organization and space of work in the twenty-first century.

This book emanates from an international workshop held at Ghent University, Belgium in January 2008. This workshop was partly sponsored by the Flemish Fund for Scientific Research (FWO) and we are grateful for their contribution. One of the key priorities of the workshop was to provide a space for multidisciplinary dialogue, with presentations give by researchers from Economics, Geography and Sociology. We believe that this deliberate strategy has allowed us to bring together a diverse range of leading researchers in the field so as to offer an integrative and wide-ranging analysis of international business travel. The chapters presented here are not, however, transcripts of the conference presentations – this book is not a publication of proceedings. Rather each author has revised and developed their papers to aid the editors in creating an integrated whole.

Structure and Summary

Largely mirroring the three core objectives of this book, the different chapters are divided into three sections: (1) geographies and modes of business travel; (2) business travel and mobility regimes in firms; and (3) business travel in question: the causes and consequences of business travel in twenty-first century commerce. Similar to all such divisions, the allocation of the different chapters is somewhat arbitrary: the different authors tackle complex topics that cannot easily be pigeon-holed into simple categories. Our approach has been to group together chapters on the basis of what we think to be the main thrust of their contribution to the literature.

The relevance of this division is also based on the foreword by Brian Graham. In this preface, he reminds us of the fact that – despite being an ostensibly straightforward term – 'business travel' opens up a window into the complexities of understanding mobility in the global economy. This is because business travel can be conceptualized as a set of practices and processes related to the articulation of the global economy, but also to culture, behaviour, status and even leisure mobilities. Furthermore, mobile workers are logged into other spatial and technological networks such as video-conferencing and real-time virtual communications before, after and as they travel. The three parts of the book reflect Brian Graham's observations through a focus on (1) the forms and spatialities of business travel; (2) the role of mobility in twenty-first century firms; and (3) the causes of travel, the consequences and the myriad ways in which 'business travel' interacts with other technologies (e.g. ICT) and travel motivations (e.g. leisure travel), forcing us to adopt far more sophisticated approaches when considering the nature, form and function of corporate mobility.

In line with this structuring of the book, the chapters in the first section deal with some of the most notable features of the modes and geographies of business travel. The chapters by Derudder, Witlox and Van Nuffel and by Beaverstock and Faulconbridge take the issue of the actual geographies of corporate mobility literally and present an overview of the geographies of business travel in Europe and to/from the UK respectively. Derudder, Witlox and Van Nuffel examine the validity of 'business class air travel' data for examining the geography of 'business travel' at large, and present an analytical framework that allows for meaningful comparisons of the spatiality of different types of travel flows. Beaverstock and Faulconbridge report on some of the most notable and important characteristics of the patterns of overseas residences' business visits to the UK and UK residences' business visits abroad from the late 1970s onwards. They supplement these 'official' data of business visit trends by analysing 'unofficial' data sources on business travel in order to add depth to the dearth of available data on this form of international labour mobility. The final two chapters in the first section of the book combine an analysis of the geographies of business travel with analysis of the way geography also relates to mode of travel. John Bowen notes that, given the importance of business class services (on average, these account for over 25 per cent of a legacy carriers' revenues), it is surprising that so little attention has been given to their spatial development and current articulations. He therefore considers the social stratification of transportation systems and the different geographies of travel that emerge when different stratums of travellers of analysed and mapped. Budd and Hubbard, in turn, focus on a new form of business travel: they note that for the truly super-rich, a private jet rather than business class air travel is the preferred mode of aeromobility. They explore the reasons for the growth of this 'bizjet' market and document the possible implications of private flight for the networked geographies of the global economy.

The second part of the book focuses on characteristics and consequences of corporate mobility. John Salt locates business travel within broader portfolios of mobility developed by large international companies. His analysis shows that business travel is one of an interlinked set of mobilities used by international companies, where it fulfils a number of roles, including career development, project planning and implementation, and attendance at a wide range of meetings. Wickham and Vecchi, in turn, present a case study of business travel in the Irish software industry in an attempt to reduce the gap between theorizing and empirical investigation in the study of business travel. They sketch the social structure of the Irish software industry, focusing on the importance of professional and technical workers, and use this to develop a taxonomy of business travellers. This taxonomy is then used to explore the extent of autonomy enjoyed by different groups of travellers, which leads them to the conclusion that business travel replicates rather than destabilizes managerial hierarchies. The impact of business travel on individuals is also the core theme in the chapter of Kesselring and Vogl. In this chapter, the authors examine the social consequences of the intensification and extensification of corporate travel activities for employees. This theme is often neglected in analysis and planning of corporate mobility regimes and, therefore, the impacts of travel in terms of social cohesion within companies and the work/life balance of the workforce are too often forgotten by academics and those managing travel in firms. Kesselring and Vogl's empirical study suggests that negotiations about the conditions of work and travelling are usually the responsibility of the individual workers rather than part and parcel of a genuine corporate policy, something which identifies a major issue that deserves academic scrutiny in future research. Most of chapters in the first two parts of the book sidestep crucial questions about whether business travel is necessary or indeed useful in an era of global e-communication. The chapter by Salt is an exception in that it also examines the particular role in corporate knowledge transfer played by business travel and the degree to which there is substitution between it and virtual mobility in an era of concern about carbon emissions.

The chapters in the third part book, therefore, focus on questions about the cause, need and potential for minimising business travel. Aharon Kellerman sets the scene by comparing business and leisure travel at the international level from several basic perspectives: motivations and goals, relative magnitude, spatial patterns, and interrelationships between both types of travellers. From this basic overview, it becomes clear that it is very problematic to posit a clear-cut distinction between both types of travel. This observation is fleshed out in more detail by Lassen, who bemoans the tendency to conceptualize business travel as a structural output of work and business. Drawing on a study that explores international business travel among knowledge workers in two Danish knowledge-intensive organizations, he shows that the travel of international professionals needs to be understood in conjunction with a number of social obligations and compulsions of face-to-face meeting. Furthermore, knowledge workers are also members of an individualised labour market in which a number of non-work related compulsions of proximity function as important rationalities for travelling internationally. Taken together, this suggests that research into business travel needs a much stronger focus on the individual social motives for business travel if it is to acquire a more in-depth understanding of the motivations for corporate mobility.

The observation that the motives for international business travel are much more complex than an amorphous set of 'work requirements' is taken up by Jones, who sets out to examine the nature, form and function of mobility in the professional business service sector. Like Lassen, this dose of 'rethinking' allows us to gain more insight in the extent to which claims about the high degree of mobility amongst business service sector employees are generally applicable. Jones notes that the nature of business travel and employee mobility is complex to say the least because travel varies hugely and cannot be effectively demarcated from other forms of globalized working practice sustained by ICT technologies. Jones' analysis clearly shows that separating pure 'business travel' from wider forms of global working is, therefore, problematic. ICT may substitute for some forms of business travel, but the evidence also suggests it may also lead to an increased level of mobility as it increases the capacity of professional service firms to deliver existing and new services to global client markets. The latter observation is systematically discussed in the concluding chapter by Denstadli and Grisprud. The authors' purpose is to assess the qualities of video conferencing as a communication technology and evaluate how it fits with modern business practices in general, and business travel in particular. In line with the expectations of Jones, they emphasize that ICT technologies such as video conferencing have thus far had minor impacts on travel. Although disaggregated substitution effects can be found (from the individual or company perspective there is clearly a question of travel replacement), aggregate analyses are fairly conclusive that industries demand for transportation and telecommunications follows parallel tracks, so that the net effect for the economy as a whole is complementarity.

Future Agendas:
Business Travel, the Credit Crunch and Global Economic Recession

We do not claim that the different chapters of this book provide a completely comprehensive analysis of international business travel in the early twenty-first century; that would be impossible in one volume. But, the chapters in this book do represent an unusually rich range of empirics, concepts, theories and ideas which can help us develop a more advanced understanding of the contemporary nature and role of business travel in firms. To our knowledge, there has not yet been any other attempt to bring together such a wide range of research on this topic in one collection. Whether we have indeed been able to produce a benchmark collection of essays only time will tell, but we are confident that we have put together a state of the art book on understanding international business travel under conditions of contemporary globalization.

One thing is for sure though: this book comes at a crucial moment for business travel as a corporate practice. As we write this introduction to the book, we are in the depths of what some have been calling the worst global recession since the Great Depression of the 1930s. The events of this period have been truly dramatic: the collapse of leading international banks, redundancies affecting everything from retail to financial services, shipping to education; severe market contraction in China and other emerging markets; major corporate restructurings as firms fight to maintain profitability in a period of falling demand. And the same time, desperate efforts to reduce levels of business travel. During tough economic times it is unsurprising that firms seek to reduce costs, with the cost of travel often being one of the first to come under scrutiny. As a result, we are in the midst of a real-time experiment in which firms find out just what type of business travel is essential, what is desirable, and what impacts reduced travel has on their operations. The airlines are, of course, inevitably suffering as the number of business class travellers declines, by up to 25 per cent in the case of some leading airlines, and we might be witnessing a re-configuration of business mobility regimes/portfolios. This is not the first time such a re-configuration has seemed possible; the SARS epidemic of the early 2000s led to a similar, albeit short-term, reduction in international business travel, as did the September 11th attacks in 2001. But, today virtual communications are much more advanced than in the past and might, and we stress might, lead to a more long-term and fundamental change in business travel regimes. It is pure speculation to say more at this point, however, what current events do mean is that understanding the status quo in terms of business travel leading up to the current financial turmoil, something the chapters in this book allow, will be important in the future as we chart changes in international business travel habits and the causes and effects of these changes.

References

DeFrank, R.S., Konospaske, R. and Ivancevich J.M. (2000), Executive travel stress: Perils of the 'road warrior'. *Academy of Management Executive*, 14(2), 58-71.

Dowling, P. and Welch, D. (2004), *International Human Resource Management: Managing People in a Multinational Context*. Thomson: London.

Larsen, J., Axhausen, K.W. and Urry, J. (2006), Geographies of social networks: Meetings, travel and communications. *Mobilities*, 1(2), 261-283.

Laurier, E. (2004), Doing office work on the motorway. *Theory, Culture & Society*, 21(4/5), 261-277.

Nowicka, M. (2006), *Transnational Professionals and their Cosmopolitan Universes*. Frankfurt/New York: Camous Verlag.

Urry, J. (2003), Social networks, travel and talk. *British Journal of Sociology*, 54(2), 155-175.

Urry, J. (2007), *Mobilities*. Cambridge: Polity.

Welch, D.E. and Worm, V. (2005), International business travellers: A challenge for IHRM, in Stahl, G. and Bjorkman, I (eds) *Handbook of Research in International Human Resource Management*. Cheltenham: Edward Elgar., 283-301.

PART 1
Geographies and Modes of Business Travel

Chapter 2

A People Set Apart:
The Spatial Development of
Airline Business Class Services

John T. Bowen, Jr.

Introduction

Who are the skies for? AirAsia has one answer to that question. The carrier, one of the most successful new entrant low-cost carriers (LCCs) emblazons the following motto upon every one of its Boeing 737 and Airbus A320 aircraft: 'Now everyone can fly'. It is certainly undeniable that LCCs like AirAsia have helped to democratize air travel; and like most other LCCs, AirAsia offers only one class of service: economy class. So not only can everyone fly, but they do so with an equality uncharacteristic of air passenger travel. Yet concurrent with the emergence of LCCs has been the further development and elaboration of business-class services – the most recent manifestation of which is the flurry of all business-class services. In this chapter, I plot the historic trajectory of business class, plot its contemporary geography and peer into its future.

Only about 12 per cent of air travellers fly in business class, but they generate 28 per cent of airline revenues (Mason 2005). The consultancy Forrester Research estimates that airlines make five times as much profit on a business class seat as on one in economy class (Shein 2008). Indeed, despite some success on the part of LCCs in attracting business traffic away from full service network carriers (FSNCs), business passengers remain crucial to the vitality of the latter. Accordingly, FSNCs have engaged in a unrelenting competition, especially on transatlantic and transpacific routes, to outdo one another in the opulence and diversity of the amenities offered in business class in the air, and in business lounges on the ground.

Given the importance of business class services, it is surprising that so little attention has been given to their spatial development and current articulation. In general, transportation geographers have neglected class; yet the social stratification of transportation systems is not only enduring, in the case of commercial aviation at least, it seems to be deepening. The results include different geographies – at a variety of scales, from the body to the globe – for different strata of travellers. In particular, business class passengers are, to a growing degree – in a world of their own. This chapter is about that world.

Space, Class, and Transportation Systems

The separation of classes in the air mirrors their separation on the ground where the class-based organization of space is ancient indeed. In his book *Postmetropolis*, Ed Soja (2000) examines the role of class in shaping cities all the way back to Ur in Mesopotamia. In Ur as in airliners, preferred spaces carried both functional and symbolic advantages. Functionally, space near the centre of Ur and at the front of an airliner lowers interaction costs. For the favoured denizens of Ur, being near the centre of town meant being near one of the community's principal marketplaces. For the favoured denizens of airspace, a seat in business class or first class means travelling in greater comfort and arriving better prepared for work on the ground. Symbolically, certain spaces on the ground and in the sky connote status and power and serve to reinforce social advantage.

Yet residential segregation in urban areas has generated far more academic inquiry than segregation in transportation systems. The only real exception has been research on urban transportation (Deka 2004) where the socially uneven costs and benefits of urban expressway construction have, for instance, been examined in a wide variety of settings.

Although the topic has been largely overlooked, long-haul transportation systems are also rife with class divisions and have been for a long time. The railroad was hailed initially for its democratizing effects, but only a few decades into the Railway Age, Prussian lines had as many as five separate classes (Faith 1990). Interestingly, more democratic societies had less rigidly divided railways. Norway's railroads never had more than one class, for instance. Still, that was the exception. At sea, the sheer size of ocean liners in the nineteenth and early twentieth centuries offered broad scope to spatially differentiate the classes. A 1925 *New York Times* editorial observed,

> For many years the ocean liner has served as an example of the working out of the caste system. Class distinctions were not more clearly drawn in Hindustan. On shipboard, the lines were fixed and taut. Captain, staff and crew made up the bureaucracy, the first cabin the aristocracy, the second cabin the *bourgeoisie*, and the steerage the proletariat. (*New York Times* 1925, quoted in Brinnin 1971)

So when first airlines were formed in the twentieth century, they emerged amidst a fundamentally undemocratic transportation system. The earliest carriers had only one class, of course, by virtue of the small size of early aircraft and the extremely high airfares. Air travel was an extension and a reflection of the class divisions on the ground; for only the very rich could afford to fly with any regularity. Indeed, in the 1930s, airfares were still much higher on most routes than for first-class rail or ocean liner travel and aircraft cabins were fitted with accoutrements befitting high quality surface transportation. By the 1940s, however, commercial aircraft were large enough and the costs of air travel low enough to permit the encroachment of class-divided travel aloft. Capital Airlines' Nighthawk between New York and

Chicago became the first 'tourist class' service by a US carrier in 1948 (*New York Times* 1948).

By the late 1950s, as aircraft grew even larger and the cost of air transport fell still further, transatlantic carriers offered as many as four different classes: deluxe first-class sleeperette, first class, tourist class, and now economy class. Interestingly, the new economy class had a seat pitch so low that the *New York Times* described it as 'an austerity class, with seats set as close together as those in a bus, if not closer' (Friedlander 1958). And yet the seat pitch of 34 inches in the new economy class was as generous as the most generous airline's economy class today, even though today's travellers are taller. In fact, AirAsia and several other LCCs have seat pitches as low as 29 inches.

The Creation of Business Class

In 1978, Pan Am became the first airline in the world to introduce business class (Table 2.1). Pan Am's Clipper Class was a separate cabin with product features positioned between economy class and first class. Within a matter of months, about a dozen other transcontinental and intercontinental carriers launched their own business class products (Grimes 1980). Like Pan Am, the other airlines tried to create a strong brand identity to distinguish the new in-between service from economy class. So TWA crafted Ambassador Class, El Al offered King Solomon Service, and Cathay Pacific introduced Marco Polo Class. The emphasis on business class branding, then and now, was testament to a dilemma associated with the new service. On the one hand, business class was clearly second-class; but no airline could market it as such.

Table 2.1 Early airline business class products

Airline	Business class product
Pan Am	Clipper Class
TWA	Ambassador Class
Delta	Medallion Class
Cathay Pacific	Marco Polo Class
El Al	King Solomon Class
British Airways	Club
Iberia	Ronda Executive Class
SAS	Euroclass

Source: Contemporary news accounts, especially Grimes (1980).

The emergence of business class in the late 1970s is no accident, of course. Deregulation had opened some markets to new competitors, pushed down economy-class fares, and encouraged a greater emphasis on price discrimination. Neither is it any accident that the aircraft most associated with business class in the early years was the 747. The huge size of the jumbo jet lent itself to partition – much like the voluminous piston-engine flying boats of the 1930s and 1940s – and furthermore, the democratization of air travel engendered by the 747 was a problem to full-fare passengers for whom the creation of business class was a partial remedy.

The features that defined business class at the beginning included a wider seat pitch, fewer seats per row, better in-flight catering, free drinks, shorter check-in lines, an increased baggage allowance, and access to airline club rooms. Since then, there have been two basic changes in business class. First, airlines have engaged in a never-ending contest to top one another in developing better, roomier seats. As an example, Singapore Airlines (SIA) business (Raffles) class on its A380 services features seats with an upright seat pitch of 55 inches and which can be converted into a fully flat bed 80 inches long. Second, a wider range of ever-more engaging and diverse electronic entertainment has been integrated into each business class seat. SIA, for instance, offers business class passengers 1,000 choices on in its Krisworld in flight entertainment system as well as a power outlet at each seat to permit a passenger to work on his or her laptop.

Generally speaking, US carriers have lagged behind their European and Asian counterparts in business class, primarily because the repeated financial crises and revolving bankruptcies in the American airline industry have curtailed investments in airline cabins. In 2006, for instance, critics panned American Airlines' new business class seat, lamenting that it was one to two generations behind state-of-the-art Asia–Pacific and European carriers. For instance, American's new seats were equipped a 10.5-inch in-flight entertainment screen while Singapore Airlines' redesigned Raffles Class seat came equipped with a 15.4-inch screen. And American's seats, while advertised as lie-flat, did not meet the newer and more demanding standard of 'true lie-flat'. Rather, American's seats when converted to a bed were not parallel to the floor but angled; the configuration saved space, but some passengers complained of a tendency to slip down on the bed towards their feet (Table 2.2).

In its early years, business class was available primarily on transatlantic and to a lesser extent transpacific routes. In shorter-haul markets, it took much longer for the new class to take hold. For instance, although Pan Am and TWA introduced business class on the New York-Los Angeles route in the early 1980s, American, United, and Delta did not follow suit until a decade later. The new business class offerings then were spurred by two circumstances: first, the recession of the early 1990s, which reduced corporate customer appetites for first-class travel and, second, the proliferation of frequent flyer programs. Business class created an opening into which economy class frequent flyers could be upgraded while protecting the first-class passenger. Similar factors, along with the more general increase in business travel, have fuelled the expansion of business class services in most other markets, too. Today, even some short-haul markets served by regional jets have separate business class compartments.

Table 2.2 Business class seat type for the largest* airlines, mid-2008

1	American Airlines	Angled lie-flat seats**
2	Air France-KLM	Angled lie-flat seats**
3	United Airlines	Old style seats
4	Delta Air Lines	Angled lie-flat seats**
5	Continental Air Lines	Angled lie-flat seats
6	Northwest Airlines	Angled lie-flat seats**
7	British Airways	Lie-flat seats
8	Lufthansa	Angled lie-flat seats**
9	Southwest Airlines	No business class
10	US Airways	Angled lie-flat seats**
11	Japan Airlines	Angled lie-flat seats**
12	Singapore Airlines	Lie-flat seats and angled lie-flat seats
13	Qantas	Lie-flat seats and angled lie-flat seats
14	Emirates	Lie-flat seats and angled lie-flat seats
15	Air Canada	Lie-flat seats and angled lie-flat seats
16	Cathay Pacific Airways	Angled lie-flat seats
17	China Southern Airlines	Angled lie-flat seats**
18	Air China	Angled lie-flat seats**
19	All Nippon Airways	Angled lie-flat seats**
20	Thai Airways	Angled lie-flat seats**

Note: * Airlines ranked by passenger-kilometers; ** Some aircraft only.
Source: www.flatseats.com.

Business class is now available almost world-wide and has become the most profitable service class for many carriers. And yet, more than twenty-five years after business class was first introduced, the airline industry may be poised on the threshold of an important change in business travel. In the past few years, there has been a small flurry of all-business class services, especially across the Atlantic. So far, the number of seats offered in such services is very small but the growth of such services, along with related developments on the ground, point to the deepening of aviation's caste system.

The Geography of Scheduled Business Class Services

Before turning to all business class services, I would like to examine the geography of scheduled business class services more generally. The primary data source for these analyses is the March 2003 edition of OAG Max, a CD-ROM containing schedule data for virtually every airline in the world. More specifically, OAG Max contains the breakdown between first, business and economy class capacity for every scheduled flight. I should emphasize however that this database contains no information on flown traffic, so the perspective I offer is strictly supply-side.

In early 2003, the world's scheduled airlines offered approximately 49 million seats weekly. Of these, only 4 per cent were in business class cabins and a little more than 2 per cent were in first class. Of course, the significance of business class travel varies spatially and it is that variation that I want to examine. To begin with, there is a clear association between the per cent of seats in business class and stage length. While only 6 per cent of all scheduled airline seats in 2003 were on flights more than 6,000 kilometers in length, fully 15 per cent of business class seats were (Table 2.3).

Table 2.3 Business class share by stage length

	Business class seats per week (000s)	All seats per week (000s)	BCL share (%)
0-2,000 kilometers	1,347	38,495	3.5
2,001-4,000 kilometers	294	6,148	4.8
4,001-6,000 kilometers	118	1,455	8.1
6,000-8,000 kilometers	139	1,535	9.1
8,001 or more kilometers	175	1,491	11.8
Total	**2,074**	**49,125**	**4.2**

Source: Author's analysis of schedules contained in the OAG Max March 2003.

The greater importance of business class on long-haul routes is evident in the variation in the importance of this product by aircraft type. The Boeing 747-400 ranked first in terms of the total number of business class seats offered in 2003 and in the number of business class available seat-kilometers (Table 2.4). Indeed, the world's six hundred 747-400s made up just over three per cent of all aircraft in the world's jet fleets in 2003 yet they produced a staggering 29 per cent of all business class ASKs. The 747, of course, was the airliner upon which business class got its start and the long-haul capabilities of the -400 (nicknamed the 'Longreach' by Qantas) are consonant with the spatiality of the globe-trotting transnational capitalist class.

The decisions that airlines have made in how to segment the 747-400 in terms of first, business, and economy class seats vary widely. The four largest -400 operators are British Airways, Japan Airlines, United and Singapore Airlines. Whereas BA operates some of its -400s with as few as 38 Club class seats, United's are equipped with a minimum of 73 Business Class seats. And Japan Airlines operates -400s on its Narita-JFK route with 99 Executive seats. Somewhat surprisingly, the number of business class seats on SIA's 747-400s has been repeatedly cut since the airliner was launched in the late 1980s. Initially, SIA equipped its -400s with 65 business class seats. In the late 1990s, that was reduced to 58, and the aircraft are now fitted with just 50 business class seats. In fact, despite having what is widely hailed as among the best business class products, the number of business class seats on SIA's 747-400s is substantially lower than that on some of its less well-regarded rivals – a consequence in part of the adoption of lie-flat bed-seats. Not for nothing does SIA call its business class seats 'Spacebeds'.

Table 2.4 Business class share by aircraft type

Aircraft type	Business class seats per week (000s)	All seats per week (000s)	BCL share (%)
Boeing 747	311	2,717	11.4
Boeing 767	231	2,972	7.7
Other Wide-body	477	6,394	7.5
Total Wide-body	1,019	12,083	8.4
Airbus A320	375	7,218	5.2
Boeing 737	354	14,831	2.4
Other Narrow-body	326	14,993	2.2
Total Narrow-body	1,055	37,042	2.8
Total	**2,074**	**49,125**	**4.2**

Source: Author's analysis of schedules contained in the OAG Max March 2003.

Nevertheless, wide-body aircraft like the 747 remain dominant in terms of available seat-kilometers in business class. Similarly, in terms of the proportion of seats, there is a clear association between wide-body aircraft and business class seating capacity. The business class proportion of seats on all flights operated with wide-body aircraft was 8.4 per cent, versus just 2.8 per cent on flights operated by narrow-body aircraft.

The 747-400 has been called the 'Pacific airliner' and routes across the Pacific Ocean flown by that jet did have very high numbers of business class seats. In fact, among major markets, the share of business class seats was greatest in the markets where this product began: the North Pacific ranked first and the North Atlantic second (Figure 2.1). Conversely, within North America, fewer than 2 per cent of seats were in business class. Indeed, first class seats outnumbered business class seats by a more than two-to-one margin in the region.

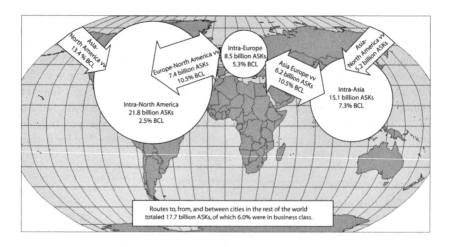

Figure 2.1 Business class seats by route/region
Source: Author's analysis of schedules contained in the OAG Max March 2003.

Among very heavily travelled city-pairs (more than 2,000 total seats – all classes combined – each direction per day), the business class share of seats was high on some of the key spans in the architecture of the global economy – like New York-Tokyo, Paris-New York, and London-Tokyo. Yet city-pairs like Auckland-Wellington, Madrid-Paris, and Ottawa-Toronto also appear in the top 30 city-pairs ranked by business class share (Table 2.5). Of course, the quality of business class on short-haul routes tends to be quite different from that on long-haul routes. British Airways' Club World product, for instance, is distinctly superior to its Club Europe product, and these shorter routes are fed to some degree by longer-haul traffic. Still the predominance of short-haul routes in Table 2.5 is a reflection of persistent distance decay in business relations – even in a globalized economy. That said, it is important to reiterate that this ranking is based on 2003 data. In Europe especially, the rapid growth of low cost carriers and high speed rail since then have likely diminished business class flows on some short-haul routes.

Turning now to the nodes of the economy rather than its linkages, there were 141 cities with large air traffic volumes – defined as having an average of more than 10,000 scheduled seats per day – in 2003. Among these, London, Tokyo, Paris, Hong Kong, and Madrid ranked at the top in terms of total business class seats; and Vienna, Auckland, Lisbon, Singapore, and Zurich ranked first through fifth in terms of the share of business class seats (Table 2.6). At the other end of the spectrum, a number of low cost carrier-dominated American cities (Sacramento, Oakland, St. Louis, Santa Ana, Nashville, and Ontario, California) had virtually no business class seats.

Table 2.5 Leading city-pairs by business class share of total seats

City 1	City 2	Seats per week	Share of seats by service class		
			First	Business	Economy
Paris	Vienna	14,580	0.0	29.7	70.3
London (GB)	Vienna	16,125	0.0	28.0	72.0
Frankfurt	Vienna	18,592	0.0	21.7	78.3
Chicago	Tokyo	17,024	4.6	20.5	74.9
Atlanta	Fort Myers	28,098	0.0	19.3	80.7
New York	Tokyo	28,838	3.3	19.1	77.6
Lisbon	Madrid	23,156	0.0	18.1	81.9
Amsterdam	Zurich	14,522	0.0	17.9	82.1
London (GB)	Tokyo	29,318	5.6	17.5	76.8
Los Angeles	Sydney (AU)	19,810	3.6	17.2	79.3
Barcelona (ES)	Seville	15,964	0.0	16.9	83.1
Auckland	Wellington	39,228	0.0	16.6	83.4
Auckland	Christchurch	39,206	0.2	16.6	83.2
Paris	Tokyo	23,832	4.0	16.5	79.5
Honolulu	Tokyo	35,934	1.7	16.3	81.9
Hong Kong	San Francisco	15,778	5.0	16.1	78.9
Canberra	Melbourne (AU)	17,262	0.0	16.1	83.9
Boston	London (GB)	23,814	5.9	15.9	78.2
New York	Paris	32,762	6.4	15.6	78.0
Los Angeles	Tokyo	37,832	3.8	15.6	80.6

Source: Author's analysis of schedules contained in the OAG Max March 2003.

Table 2.6 Leading cities by business class share of total seats

Rank	Route	Weekly Business class seats per week	BCL share (%)
1	Vienna	29,571	20.9
2	Auckland	15,643	13.8
3	Lisbon	14,714	12.0
4	Singapore	45,333	10.9
5	Hong Kong	51,330	10.9
6	Zurich	25,541	10.9
7	Madrid	46,771	10.5
8	Mumbai	19,654	10.2
9	Bangkok	44,774	10.0
10	Sydney	30,809	10.0

Source: Author's analysis of schedules contained in the OAG Max March 2003.

To make sense of this variation, this set of cities with large traffic volumes was broken into two subsets: the first included all of the so-called world-cities (New York, London, and Tokyo in the first tier; nine cities in the second tier; and 21 cities in the third tier) (classification based on Knox and Marston 2003: 438); and the second included all of the other cities. The difference in business class shares among these two groups was tested using a Mann-Whitney U test. The result was statistically very significant. Interestingly, however, tier one cities did not have especially high shares. London ranked 24th, Tokyo 26th, and New York 36th. The sheer size of these metropolitan areas makes them major economy class traffic generators, too. Moreover, no one airline dominates any of these markets and the resulting mixture of carriers and their strategies moderates the business class share of total seats.

Indeed, the strategies of locally dominant airlines do affect the composition of capacity in smaller markets. Among large carriers (those with more than a billion dollars in revenue), Austrian ranked first in the proportion of seats in business class. Austrian has emphasized the carriage of business traffic over a network that mediates the linkages between Eastern Europe and the rest of the world. That strategy helps to account for Vienna's high proportion of business class seats.

Interestingly, the greatest absolute number of business seats in 2003 was offered by Iberia. Like Austrian, Iberia is well-positioned to mediate business traffic between Western Europe and a developing, middle-income region – Latin America in the case of Iberia. The Spanish flag carrier offered approximately the same proportion of business class seats – about 15 per cent – across a variety of stage lengths (Table 2.7). Conversely, British Airways offered virtually no business class seats on flights of less than 2,000km, but 15 per cent of seats on flights more than 4,000km in length were in business class. Even more interestingly, Austrian offered a greater proportion of business class seats on short-haul flights than on long-haul ones – where the carrier's services to destinations like Tokyo offered no great advantage compared to those of larger European rivals. In 2006, Austrian decided to abandon much of its long-haul network (Flottau 2006).

Table 2.7 **Business class importance by stage length for several carriers (per cent business class)**

Carrier	2000 km or fewer	2,001–4,000 km	4,001–6,000 km	6,001–8,000 km	8,000 km or more
Austrian	38.6	32.3	4.7	8.1	4.5
British Airways	0.5	3.8	15.0	15.1	14.7
Iberia	15.5	17.3	15.9	13.8	14.8

Source: Author's analysis of schedules contained in the OAG Max March 2003.

There have been two, seemingly contradictory directions in the development of long-haul services with respect to class. On the one hand, some carriers have shifted to a two-class service on some routes; on the other hand, some carriers have not only retained the conventional three-classes, but have inserted a fourth class. In fact, both of these developments can be credited to the relentless upward creep in the size and accoutrements of business class seats. The result has been a narrowing of the gap between first and business class so that some carriers have decided to eliminate the former and the widening of the gap between business and economy class into which other carriers have inserted a new economy plus service (Shifrin 2006).

To complicate matters further, several large carriers now pursue a mixture of geographically varying class strategies. In 2005, for instance, Air France announced that it would split its long-haul fleet, increasing the number of business class seats and simultaneously removing the first class cabin on most long-haul routes, while retaining the three-class configuration on others – particularly its CIO (Caribbean – Indian Ocean) routes (Shifrin 2005). A particularly interesting case is SIAs' transpacific services to the United States. The carrier introduced its ultra-long-haul A340-500 nonstop services to the US in 2004 with 64 lie-flat Spacebeds in its Raffles business class and 117 Executive Economy seats; as discussed in the next section, SIA later converted the A340-500s to a 100-seat business class only configuration. In contrast, the carrier's Boeing 747-400 transpacific services to the US, which stop Hong Kong or Tokyo en route, are operated with 12 First Class, 50 Raffles Class, and 313 Economy Class seats.

Meanwhile, as noted above, a growing number of carriers have inserted a less expensive and less luxurious economy plus class between rock-bottom economy and business class. On its Boeing 777-300s, for instance, British Airways offers World Traveller Plus with a seat pitch of 38 inches between World Traveller (31 inches) and Club (73 inches). Interestingly, there were four classes across the Atlantic in the 1950s, too, but the disparities among them, both with respect to service quality and airfares, were much smaller. It is striking that, after adjusting for inflation, economy class travel across the Atlantic is far less expensive today than half a century ago, but first class travel – at least on the best airlines – is more costly (Table 2.8). The huge range of air fares today corresponds to the huge range of services on board as evident in, for instance, the 47 inch gap in the seat pitch between BA's First and World Traveller classes. So the caste system deepens.

The gap between the upper and lower classes is more pronounced on BA than on some of its rivals. On United Airlines, for example, there is just a 20 inch difference between the seat pitch in business and economy class on its 747-400s (Table 2.9); but United, like all long-haul full-service carriers is under unremitting pressure to improve the quality of its business class product.

Table 2.8 Transatlantic seat pitch and fare comparison, 1958 and 2008

1958*	Fare (US dollars)	Real fare** (US dollars, 2008)	Seat pitch (inches)
First, sleeperette	485	2,900	–
First	435	2,600	42
Tourist	315	1,900	39
Economy	252	1,500	34
2008*			
First	16,337	16,337	78
Club World	4,028	4,028	73
World Traveller Plus	1,173	1,173	38
World Traveller	698	698	31

Note: * IATA approved; ** Converted to year 2008 dollars using the price deflator data available from the Federal Reserve Bank of St. Louis (research.stlouisfed.org) and an estimate of 3% inflation in 2008; *** For travel on British Airways between New York-JFK and London-LHR, departing October 24, 2008 and returning October 31, 2008 with a one-month advance purchase.
Source: Friedlander (1958), www.britishairways.com.

Table 2.9 Common seat configurations on the Boeing 747-400 for six airlines

Airline		Economy	Economy Plus	Business	First
British Airways	Seats	227	36	52	14
	Pitch	31"	38"	73" full-flat bed	78" full-flat pod
Cathay Pacific	Seats	324	0	46	9
	Pitch	32"	–	74" full-flat bed	81" full-flat bed
Japan Airlines	Seats	201	0	91	11
	Pitch	30-31"	–	62" flat bed*	78" full-flat bed
Qantas	Seats	315	0	50	14
	Pitch	31"	–	79" full-flat bed	79" full-flat pod
United Airlines	Seats	172	88	73	14
	Pitch	31"	34-36"	55" recliner	78" full-flat bed
Virgin Atlantic	Seats	228	62	54**	
	Pitch	32"	38"	79" full-flat bed	

Note: * 160 degrees of recline; ** Virgin Atlantic's Upper Class is positioned between Business and First class.
Source: www.seatguru.com, 15 September 2008.

Indeed, the competition on the ground and in the sky is only likely to tighten (Pilling 2007). The history of business class begins around the same time as deregulation and some of the new entrants that have emerged in the airline industry since then have become formidable players in the long-haul business class market – most notably Virgin Atlantic, but also EVA, Asiana, and China Southern. More generally, deregulation has increased the intensity of competition on many routes. With low-cost carriers continuing to gain market share in the economy-class, short-haul market, the dependence of full-service carriers upon the long-haul market, especially business travellers, is likely to grow.

All-Business Class Services

One of the newest developments in this arena has been the advent of all-business class international services. These have taken two forms. First, several FSNCs have launched all-business class flights among a very small set of points. Second, a handful of all-business class airlines began plying long-haul routes in the early years of this decade. Although none survived the harsh market realities that developed in 2007 and 2008, in the longer term, this type of niche carrier might prove enduring and important.

All-business class services by full service network carriers

Among FSNCs, Lufthansa led the way in the development of scheduled all-business class services. In June 2002, Lufthansa joined with Geneva-based Privatair to launch an all-business class service between Newark and Dusseldorf. Lufthansa had operated a three-class Airbus A340 on the route but suspended that service in response to poor loads after the September 11, 2001 terrorist attacks. The all business-class service allowed Lufthansa to lower its costs while simultaneously retaining a foot in the lucrative business market on this sector (according to Lufthansa, 40 out of Europe's 100 largest companies are based in the Dusseldorf area) (Bond 2002, Sarsfield 2004). Lufthansa later withdrew the Dusseldorf-Newark service, but by late 2008, Privatair was operating three routes for the German flag carrier: Munich-Boston, Munich-Dubai, and Frankfurt-Pune.[1]

Inspired no doubt by Lufthansa's success with this concept, Swiss International and KLM have also contracted with Privatair for all-business class services between Zurich and Newark and between Amsterdam and Houston, respectively. The latter service is directed specifically at the oil industry (Airline Business 2005).

---

1 Pune was added to Lufthansa's network following the liberalization of Lufthansa's air services agreement with India, but the airport at the west Indian city will be unable to accommodate the wide-body aircraft Lufthansa normally deploys on Indian routes before 2009 or 2010 (United News of India 2008).

Meanwhile, two Asian airlines have also adopted the all-business class configuration. In September 2006, ANA launched all business class Boeing 737-700ER services between Tokyo and Mumbai (Sanchanta 2007). The suffix on the airliner gives one clue to the role of technology as an enabling factor in the emergence of these services. Extended range versions of the Boeing 737 and Airbus A319 (Privatair flies Boeing Business Jets and Airbus A319LRs) have allowed FSNCs to operate long-haul all-business class services that are 'right-sized' to match market demand (Sarsfield 2004). Another enabling factor has been liberalization. The new ANA service, for instance, was made possible when air services between Japan and India were further liberalized in 2006 as part of a broader effort by the two countries to forge closer economic ties.

Finally, in 2008, SIA converted its A340-500 services from Singapore to Newark and Los Angeles to a full business class configuration. Each aircraft is outfitted with 100 of the airline's full lie-flat seats. The SIA flights are the first all-business class transpacific services (Figure 2.2).

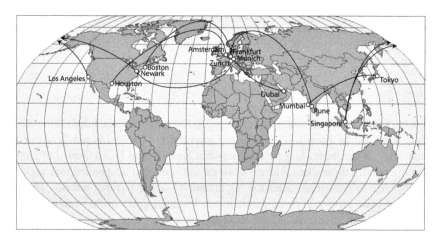

**Figure 2.2   All-business class services operated by full service network
carriers, mid-2008**
Source: www.privatair.com and media accounts.

Geographically, most of the all-business class services operated by FSNCs fit a certain profile: point-to-point operations linking important business centres and bypassing, at least to some degree, traditional routings. SIA's services, for example, bypass the usual stop in Europe or Northeast Asia on routes linking Southeast Asia and the United States. And Swiss International's Zurich–Newark service complements the carrier's conventional services which arrive at John F. Kennedy International rather than Newark.[2] More direct head-to-head competition between an airline's mainline services and its all business class services would risk cannibalizing very high yield traffic from the former, undermining their profitability.

All-business class airlines

The risks for Lufthansa, Swiss, KLM, and even ANA and SIA in launching these new services are small. Each operates hundreds of flights per day, and so the success or failure of these specialized services is unlikely to strongly affect their bottom lines. Conversely, the handful of all business class startups that emerged early in this decade pursued a far riskier strategy, and none survived for long as an independent entity. Despite their failure, they merit attention because this type of airline might prove to have a long-term future.

The idea of an all-business class airline is not new. In the 1980s, Houston-based Ultrair and St. Louis-based Air One launched all-business class services (Salpukas 1983, Hayes 1992). Air One, for instance, commenced service with a fleet of four Boeing 727s equipped with 76 business class seats each over a network that linked St. Louis to Newark, Washington, Dallas-Ft. Worth, and Kansas City. These ventures proved fleeting, however, stymied by too few frequencies and an inability to match the fare-cutting of the major networks carriers.

Two decades after those failed domestic US ventures, several new all-business class airlines emerged in the transatlantic market. The first of these was Eos, which commenced all-business class Boeing 757 services between London-Stansted and New York-JFK in October 2005. In November 2005, MAXjet followed suit on the same route albeit with Boeing 767s. It is noteworthy that the first two all-business class scheduled international airlines targeted the same route linking the world's premiere financial centers. Although both flew from JFK in the New York metro area, they served Stansted instead of Heathrow because the then-prevailing US-UK air services agreement limited the number of carriers at Heathrow (Fiorino 2006).

Eos and MAXjet exemplified two different strategies available to all-business class airlines (Wingfield 2007). Eos went for the 'super-luxury' route, essentially trying to out-pamper travellers – including some of those who formerly had flown the Concorde. Each of Eos' 757s was equipped with just 48 'pods' (Fiorino 2006). Passengers, who were given cashmere blankets and champagne cocktails after boarding, likened flying Eos to flying a corporate jet (Moline 2006). MAXjet, conversely, took its cue from the LCCs in trying to provide a service comparable to that already offered by the full-service carriers but at a lower cost. MAXjet seated 102 on its 767s. MAXjet's fares were certainly one reason that 15 per cent of the carrier's customers were drawn from economy class on other carriers (Fiorino 2006) (Table 2.10).

---

2   Somewhat similarly, in 2009 British Airways will commence all-business class operations between London City Airport and New York City (the specific destination airport had not been determined when the service was announced in 2008).

Table 2.10 New York–London business class airfares, 2007

Airline	Fare (USD)	Routing(s)
Maxjet	2,356	JFK-STN
Air India	2,634	JFK-LHR
Eos	4,927	JFK-STN
American	4,995	JFK-LHR
Continental	5,124	EWR-LGW
Virgin	8,062	EWR-LGW, EWR-LHR, JFK-LHR
British	8,072	JFK-LHR, EWR-LHR

Note: For roundtrip travel 28 February to 7 March 2007 with one week advance purchase. EWR = Newark Liberty International Airport, JFK = New York John F. Kennedy International Airport, LGW = London Gatwick Airport, LHR = London Heathrow Airport, and STN = London Stansted Airport.
Source: www.travelocity.com.

MAXjet's business model was more easily extended and so it is perhaps unsurprising that it rather than Eos which expanded geographically. Before its demise MAXjet flew to Las Vegas, Los Angeles, and Washington-Dulles, while Eos never escaped its debut sector. In the same vein, two later all business class carriers bore more resemblance to MAXjet than Eos. In January 2007, L'Avion began flying between Paris-Orly and Newark and Silverjet commenced services between Luton Airport and Newark.

It is important to put these four carriers into perspective. Together, at their peak, they offered just 33 roundtrip transatlantic flights per week (Figure 2.3). All other airlines together had more than 2,500 weekly frequencies in this market. British Airways alone had 75 roundtrips per week between London and New York. Likewise, Silverjet's daily flight between London and Dubai represented a tiny share of the capacity between Europe and the Middle East.

Moreover, while several of the all business class carriers (ABCCs) emulated the LCCs to some degree, there were always significant impediments to taking the LCC model far in business class travel. To begin, the latter have emphasized rapid turnaround times on short-haul routes as a primary means of achieving cost-savings. The ABCCs, by contrast, operated long-haul international routes with typically long turnaround times. MAXjet's 767s, for instance, remained on the ground for more than three hours in Stansted and nearly six hours in JFK between flights. Second, the low fares offered by the LCCs have compelled passengers to adjust their travel behaviour – with respect to departure and arrival times, choice of airport, and willingness to wait at intermediate stops. Business travellers are not as flexible; and related to this point, the low frequency of ABCC operations was a significant liability in their pursuit of business travellers. In the same vein, frequent flyer programs are more important to the typical business class than economy class traveller; and, therefore, the limited FFPs offered by both the LCCs and the ABCCs – particularly compared to FSNCs integrated into global alliances – was a greater obstacle to the ABCCs' success. Third, because LCCs target a much larger market segment, the number and variety of city-pairs into which they can expand is huge and certainly much larger than those where the ABCCs could prosper.

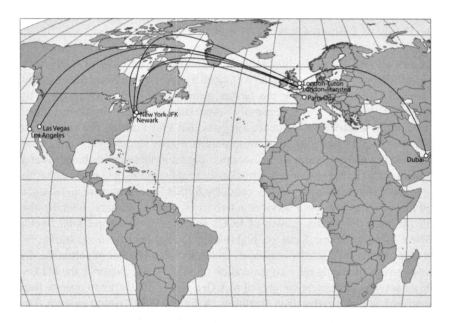

Figure 2.3 Services operated by all-business class carriers, late 2007
Source: Websites of defunct airlines and media accounts.

In the end, none of the transatlantic ABCCs endured the punishing airline market that set in after 2007 and 2008. The carriers were affected by the same high fuel prices and weaker travel demand that caused misery throughout the industry, but the upstarts were also undermined by the difficulty of raising new capital in the midst of a galloping banking crisis. As a result of these and other adversities, MAXjet stopped flying in December 2007, Eos in April 2008, and Silverjet in May 2008 (Werdigier 2008). That left only L'Avion still in the air, but the French carrier was acquired by British Airways in July 2008. The former ABCC became Open Skies (60 per cent of whose seats are in business class), a new subsidiary established by BA to fly between Paris and New York under the auspices of the new US-European Union Open Skies agreement (Stoller 2008).

The failure of all four of the ABCCs compelled some industry observers to disparage the very concept as unsound. One airline consultant quoted in *USA Today* (Stoller 2008) offered this advice, 'The all-business class model doesn't work. For a new independent brand, the first thing at the time of start-up is to hire a CEO, and the second thing is to send the retainer to the bankruptcy attorney'. Such sarcasm and pessimism may seem well warranted by the experience of this decade; yet it is worth emphasizing that the failures of 2007 and 2008 occurred amid an especially lethal market for start-ups. The future could be kinder.

The Future of Business Class

The outlook for business class services, including all-business class flights is generally bright, though the horizon is clouded by several significant uncertainties. Among the factors favouring the further growth of this class of travel is the growth of business travel generally, especially long-haul business travel. Interestingly, a variety of evidence suggests that globalization has engendered wider levels of income inequality while simultaneously stretching the linkages of everyday life across continents and oceans. Together, these trends have fostered a proportionately larger global transnational capitalist class, the target market for long-haul business class services. Second, the further liberalization of air transport will fuel new business class services in two ways. On the one hand, liberalization will facilitate the further growth of LCCs and other new competitors, forcing FSNCs to tighten their focus on high-yielding, long-haul business traffic. On the other hand, liberalization will open additional international opportunities for niche carriers including the next generation of ABCCs. For example, the old US-UK air services agreement compelled MAXjet, Eos and Silverjet to operate from Luton and Stansted rather than Heathrow. A future ABCC would enjoy a freer choice of gateways to London and some other metropolitan areas. Third, further technological innovation by Boeing, Airbus, other aircraft manufacturers and their suppliers will create further opportunities for innovation in business class services. Certainly, the advances made in seats and the electronic paraphernalia with which they are fitted are unlikely to abate. More fundamentally, smaller long range and ultra-long-range jets permit new services between business centres that, like KLM's Amsterdam-Houston link, bypass traditional hubs.

Countering these positive forces are several dangers that might bring business class services back down to earth, figuratively speaking. Obviously, the price of fuel will powerfully affect the future trajectory of aviation. In the case of Silverjet, for instance, crude oil prices hovered near $55 when the airline took off in January 2007 and were approaching $130 when it was grounded in May 2008. Oil prices have fallen sharply since oil prices peaked in the summer of 2008, but if grim forecasts of $200 per barrel oil were to be realized, the result would be a smaller airline industry, including fewer business class seats. Furthermore, higher fares (whether due to radically higher oil prices or due to taxes intended to curtail aviation's environmental burden) could push more business travellers out of business class seats. Already, there is evidence that LCCs have captured some business traffic, and, indeed, a handful of such carriers are trying to parlay the convenience of their high frequency, low-fare services into a stronger presence in the business travel market.[3] To the degree that that trend gathers momentum, it could dim both the importance and the opulence of FSNC business class cabins.

The success of LCCs in business travel points to a broader threat to the future of business class services: namely that they will lose their rationale. The fragmentation of business travellers among the various classes on board FSNC services, LCCs, niche carriers (including perhaps ABCCs again), private business jets, and competing modes (especially high-speed rail within Europe) weakens the primacy of the conventional business class services. According to British Airways, only 15 per cent of short-haul business travellers flew in business or first class, and there is broader evidence that many business travellers regard business class as a poor value-for-money proposition (Mason 2005). Will airlines continue to make the massive investments in leapfrogging service amenities that have produced such lavish travelling conditions for the favoured?

For now at least, the answer is yes. In July 2008, with airlines across much of the world reeling from peaking oil prices, Emirates debuted its first A380. Although the showers available to passengers travelling in the airliner's first class suites attracted the greatest media attention, Emirates did not neglect its business class passengers. The 76 full-flat seats in business class are fitted with 17" digital television screens, 1,000 choices of in-flight entertainment, and a built-in minibar. The Emirates A380, which made its commercial debut between Dubai and New York City, was one more bit of evidence that business class services remain crucial to the industry (though their geography is changing). Having permitted economy class travel to be turned into a commodity, major network carriers cannot countenance the same in business class much less first class. So long as at least some of those carriers remain financially healthy, the battle to gain an advantage in the competition for high-yield traffic will persist, particularly in the established corridors of power across the Atlantic and Pacific and the new corridors such as those linking the oil-rich Middle East to the world's primary financial centers.

References

Airline Business 2005. *KLM kicks off all-business class service*. October, 20.

Bond, D. 2002. Lufthansa sees BBJ limits, but looks for opportunities. *Aviation Week & Space Technology*, May 27, 44.

Brinnin, J.M. 1971. *The Sway of the Grand Saloon: A Social History of the North Atlantic*. New York: Delacorte Press.

---

3   However, the efforts of LCC Air Berlin to expand into business class services were stymied by high fuel prices in 2008. The carrier was forced to withdraw from long-haul mixed class services between Germany and China.

Deka, D. 2004. Social and environmental justice issues in urban transportation, in *The Geography of Urban Transportation*. Third edition, edited by S. Hanson and G. Giuliano. New York: The Guilford Press, 332-355.

Faith, N. 1990. *The World the Railways Made*. New York: Carroll & Graf.

Fiorino, F. 2006. Business not as usual. *Aviation Week & Space Technology*, July 31, 50.

Flottau, J. 2006. Shorting long-haul. *Aviation Week & Space Technology*, November 13, 40.

Friedlander, P. J. 1958. Economy air fares; Austerity service to be introduced on Atlantic flights on April 1. *New York Times*, February 2, 1.

Grimes, P. 1980. The case for business class. *New York Times*, April 13, 25.

Hayes, T.C. 1992. New airline in Houston announced. *New York Times*, November 12, D4.

Knox, P. and Marston, S. 2003. *Places and Regions in Global Context*. Second edition. Upper Saddle River: Prentice Hall.

Mason, K.J. 2005. Observations of fundamental changes in the demand for aviation services. *Journal of Transport Geography*, 11, 19-25.

Moline, J. 2006. Flying in style. *Entrepreneur*, September.

New York Times 1925. Classes at sea. September 10, 24.

New York Times 1948. 'Tourist' service by air is started. November 4, 59.

Pilling, M. 2007. Flat out. *Airline Business*. January, 46-8.

Salpukas, A. 1983. Wooing the business flier, Air One's new service. *New York Times*, June 4, 29.

Sanchanta, M. 2007. ANA all business about Mumbai. *The Financial Times*, February 7, 10.

Sarsfield, K. 2004. Right on schedule. *Flight International*, May 18, 50.

Shein, E. 2008. Riding high; Business-class travel is growing more luxurious and costly. Is it worth it? CFO.Asia.com, September 2008.

Shifrin, C. 2005. Comfort zone. *Airline Business*, February, 62.

Shifrin, C. 2006. A class apart. *Airline Business*, January, 48-9.

Soja, E. W. 2000. *Postmetropolis, Critical Studies of Cities and Regions*. Malden, Massachusetts: Blackwell.

Stoller, G. 2008. All-business class airlines take off despite past failures; Sector hasn't seen success, yet backers keep trying. *USA Today*, May 29, 7A.

United News of India 2008. Lufthansa commences Pune-Frankfurt direct service. July 2.

Werdigier, J. 2008. Loss of a backer grounds a business-class airline. *The New York Times*, May 31, C3.

Wingfield, K. 2007. A dogfight in business class. *Wall Street Journal*, January 25, A19.

Chapter 3

Geographies of Business Air Travel in Europe

Ben Derudder, Lomme Devriendt, Nathalie Van Nuffel and Frank Witlox

Introduction

This chapter presents a quantitative analysis of the geography of business air travel in Europe. In this respect, our formative aim is to help fill some of the 'gaping holes' in our knowledge about business travel patterns and trends (see Faulconbridge et al. 2009). To this end, we draw upon an information source that has not yet been regularly used in social science research, a dataset devised by the Association of European Airlines (AEA). The AEA is a non-profit-making organization that brings together 35 major European airlines (mostly so-called 'legacy carriers') and represents them at relevant European and international organizations within the aviation value chain. The AEA-dataset contains information on the connections of its member airlines, and features for each connection data on – inter alia – carrier, origin and destination, number of passengers, and travel class. Obviously, in the context of this volume, it is the information on the passengers' travel class (with the distinction between economy and business class) that is the most interesting feature of this dataset. In this chapter, we use this particular distinction to sketch some of the main features of the spatiality of business air travel in Europe.

This chapter discusses two separate, but interrelated issues. In the first section, we present an overview of the geography of business air travel in Europe. This is done by interrogating some of the basic patterns emerging from our AEA-dataset, and by using these results as the backdrop for a discussion of the validity of 'business class travel' data for examining the geography of 'business travel' at large. The second section, in turn, has a more conceptual purpose, and outlines an analytical framework that allows for meaningful longitudinal analyses/comparisons of the spatiality of economy class and business class traffic in the face of overall changes in aviation networks. Put differently: the analytical framework presented here allows us to obtain meaningful comparisons between networks with different numbers of nodes and connections, which opens up possibilities for – amongst other things – thorough longitudinal analyses of the decentralization/concentration of business travel between European cities.

Basic Features of the Geography of Business Air Travel between European Cities

You are the way you fly:
Conceptual relations between 'business class travel' and 'business travel'

In the aviation industry, business class is generally understood as being a 'high quality travel class'. A detailed overview of the major features and developments in business class air travel can be found in Bowen (this volume). In general, the characteristics that define business class include (1) travel flexibility (e.g., tickets can often be changed without an additional cost, less restrictions on baggage allowance); (2) enhanced comfort and associated amenities in the aircraft (e.g., more legroom, better in-flight catering and laptop power ports for each seat); and (3) a business-friendly environment between check-in and the actual flight (e.g., lounges with Internet connections and meeting rooms). Taken together, it is obvious that 'business class' is designed to satisfy the needs of 'business travellers'. However, due to a number of interrelated data problems, examining the geography of business air travel based on business class air travel is far from straightforward. Generally speaking, these difficulties fall into three categories: (1) conceptual problems related to the one-dimensional, clear-cut categorization of 'business travel' (because of the complex connections between travel, work, tourism, and play); (2) empirical problems related to the changing and increasingly blurry division between 'business class' and 'economy class' (principally because of the increased popularity of in-between categories such as 'flexible economy' or 'economy plus'); and (3) the more generic problem of equating 'business class travel' with 'business travel' (e.g., rich tourists may well choose to travel in business class because of enhanced comfort, while business travellers may well fly economy class on short-haul flights because of the short travel time, or because companies adopt – in view of cutting rising travel costs – an economy class travel policy only). We will discuss each of these difficulties in turn.

The first problem relates to the fact that it is becoming increasingly difficult to disaggregate passenger motivations for air travel, because a single trip can assume different roles. Indeed, as most academic conference-goers know from their personal experience, the boundary between work and tourism is sometimes far from clear (see also Kellermann, this volume). As Lassen (2006) has recently pointed out, although regular travel may well be necessary for a number of employees (e.g. having face-to-face meetings across the globe), their travel may at the same time equally involve a number of elements from other spheres of everyday life. Lassen therefore argues that the supposed requirement of work-related travel is not only constructed on the basis of external demands, structures, materialities and expectations, but also on the basis of more individual orientated conditions such as experience, consumption, tourism, health, identities, spare time, family, life style, values, dreams and goals. The latter conditions also influence how business travellers construct and estimate the need for face-to-face contacts and the related air travel (see also Denstadli and Gripsrud, this volume), which implies that it is impossible to work out an unambiguous distinction between business and non-business air travel. In this chapter, however, we proceed under the hypothesis that it is possible to derive meaningful measures of the spatiality of business travel. This stance is based on the observation that, in spite of differential and complexly entangled motivations for undertaking business travel, the prime stimulus for undertaking business travel is somehow to conduct business. From this perspective, an analysis of business travel remains most certainly feasible.

The second problems can be traced back to the lack of readily available data on the geography of business travel at large (Faulconbridge et al. 2009). Most airline data sources feature information on general flow patterns through the aggregation of connections in different fare booking classes. Since very few of the commonly employed airline statistics are able to distinguish between tourist or leisure and business flows, there have been no clear procedures for estimating the amount of business-related traffic in overall air travel. Our AEA-dataset – with its distinction between economy and business class bookings – is a major exception here, but a number of recent trends in the aviation industry make the use of this exceptional information trickier than might be expected. Business class, for instance, has started to disappear from a number of short/medium haul routes. On these routes, seats are the same for all passengers; only the flexibility of the ticket and the food and beverage service differs (e.g. Brussels Airlines currently employs a 'full fare economy' versus 'discount economy' scheme rather than business class versus economy class). On shorter routes, many airlines (such as BMI) have removed business class entirely and offer only one class of service. Furthermore, most low-cost carriers, such as Ryanair in Europe and JetBlue in the United States, do not offer any premium classes of service. As a consequence, business class is now found mostly on international routes and aircraft that are configured for long-haul travel. At the other end of the market, a number of all-business carriers (e.g. MaxJet on the London-New York route) began competing for a share of the lucrative long-haul business class traffic, but high fuel prices and softening demand ultimately made their business model unsustainable. That said, new forms of global aeromobility enjoyed by the so-called 'bizjet set' (such as private flights, see Budd and Hubbard, this volume) clearly show that business class travel organized by legacy carriers gives us a far-from-complete picture of the overall spatiality of business travel.

In addition, even if carriers make a distinction between economy class and business class, the division is becoming increasingly complicated. For instance, some airline carriers (e.g., United Airlines) now offer Premium Economy seats, a separate class of seating and service offering that provides 5-7 inches of extra legroom as well as additional amenities, which can include laptop power ports and premium food service. Importantly, this fuzzy distinction has a spatial dimension in that the disparities in 'business class travel' often relate to different strategies pursued by the so-called legacy carriers. These erstwhile 'national carriers' still largely dominate some 'national airports' (e.g., British Airways at

London Heathrow and KLM at Amsterdam Schiphol), so that carrier strategies are weighing in on the figures for these airports. For instance, as we will see below, Scandinavian airports have until recently enjoyed large proportions of business class travel because dominant regional carrier SAS has long been at the forefront of business class travel. The net effect of this bias is that business class bookings for, say, Copenhagen and Stockholm will be somewhat overvalued when compared to, say, Brussels and Amsterdam.

The third problem requires more explicit interrogation in the context of this chapter, i.e. the more generic issue whether business class bookings actually capture the spatiality of business travel. After all, business travellers do not necessarily travel in business class, while some tourists may well travel in business class because of enhanced comfort (see Alderighi et al. (2005) for a discussion of the use of LCC's for business travel). When combined with the two previously discussed problems, the fundamental question we are asking here is whether measures of business class travel provide us with satisfactory proxies for assessments of business-related travel. At one level distortions are clearly present, but the critical issue is whether the ensuing biases are so strong that they undermine an analysis of business travel on the basis of business class bookings. To address this issue, the next section discusses some basic features of business class travel in Europe.

Business class travel: Temporality and spatiality

The empirical analyses in this chapter are based on AEA-datasets, which we were able to obtain through the cooperation of an airline. The dataset contains information on the connections of its member airlines, and features for each connection data on the carrier, origin and destination (airport, city, country, and region), number of passengers (subdivided into first class, business class, and economy class), freight, mail, number of flights (subdivided into passenger flights and freight flights) and distance between origin and destination. The data is summarized on a monthly basis for the period January 2001 to December 2005, which allows a detailed analysis on recent data. Because of some difficulties with the homogeneity of the data for different years, we will only make use of the data for 2005.[1] The AEA-database includes flights within Europe, as well as flights between Europe and other regions. For our research purposes, we only selected those flights where both the origin and destination are European airports. This airport-to-airport database was then converted into a city-to-city database by summing the number of passengers over all the airports for a given city (e.g. the flows to/from Heathrow, Stansted, Gatwick, City Airport, and Luton are aggregated in a single London measure). And finally, given that we do not know the home-based location of the travellers, we summed the passengers travelling from city A to city B with those travelling in

---

1   Between 2003 and 2004, the number of passengers shows a major increase, mainly caused by a growth in domestic passengers (passengers flying within one country), which is due to a change in the registration procedure.

the opposite direction, and grouped the same connections, resulting in a database of non-directional flows. After these transformations, our 2005 database contains information on the connections of 130,663,329 passengers (of which 90 per cent in economy class and 10 per cent in first and business class), divided over 22 carriers, 35 countries and 183 cities. In principle, the AEA dataset offers the possibility of various analyses and comparisons: the evolution in time (2001-2005), the difference between business class and economy class, and separate analyses per carrier or country.

Obviously, the AEA-data is a very rich source of information. There are, however, two drawbacks that should be taken into account when interpreting the results. The first problem is the fact that no low-cost carriers are member of the AEA. According to the European Low Fares Airline Association (www.elfaa. com), the low cost carrier sector accounted for approximately 30 per cent of intra-European traffic in 2006. A second and arguably more significant disadvantage of the AEA-data, and a potential source of distortions and misinterpretations, is the lack of real origin-destination data: the database records the individual legs of a trip rather than the trip as a whole. For example, a flight from Oslo to Madrid via London will be recorded as two separate flights, one from Oslo to London and one from London to Madrid. Any possible stopovers are not registered as such, which implies that the connectivity of cities with an important hub function, like London and Paris, will be overestimated.

The two features of the AEA-dataset relevant for this section of the chapter relate to the temporality and spatiality of business class travel in 2005. It can be expected that business class travel will primarily (1) peak in non-holiday periods (e.g. March and November) and (2) be orientated towards clear-cut business centres (e.g. Geneva and Düsseldorf). If both patterns are found in reality, then this suggests that the data we use on business class travel does indeed allow for a reasonable assessment of business travel in spite of the limitations discussed in the previous paragraph.

First, there seems to be a straightforward difference in seasonal intensity for both types of booking classes. Figure 3.1 gives an overview of the monthly fluctuations in air travel in 2005 for the entire AEA-database for both booking classes. The monthly variations in connectivity are gauged through z-scores so that inter-booking class comparisons are possible in spite of different passenger volumes. The seasonality of air travel is obviously different for economy and business class bookings. The economy class curve increases from January to July/August, and then decreases again towards the end of the year. The business class curve, in contrast, reaches its lowest levels in major holiday periods (July/August and December/January). The major point here is that the contrasting curves in Figure 3.1 suggest that, in general, air travel in business class does on average capture business travel.

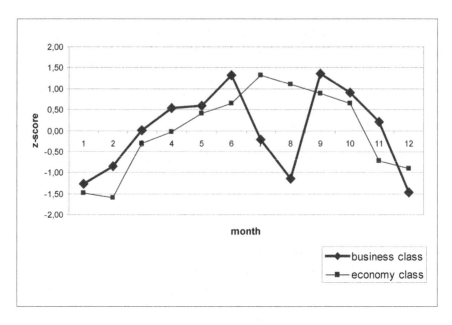

Figure 3.1 Monthly distribution of the number of passengers (z-scores)
Source: AEA, 2005.

Second, the relative proportion of business class travel is indeed higher for major 'business cities' such as Geneva and Düsseldorf. Table 3.1 contains two rankings of European cities according to their connectivity in the European airline network. The first ranking focuses on the absolute importance of business class travel, the second ranking focuses on the relative proportion of business class travel within a city's overall passenger volume. When taking on board that (1) the proportion of business class travellers to/from Scandinavian cities is higher because of the historical legacy of SAS's corporate strategies, and that (2) the proportion of business class travel to/from cities such as London, Paris, Frankfurt and Amsterdam is somewhat relegated because of their function as gateways for rerouting international air travel (Derudder et al. 2007), it becomes clear that business centres do have a higher proportion of business class travel. Once again, this seems to validate our assertion that business class travel does indeed provide us with reasonable proxies for measuring business travel.

The basic rankings in Table 3.1 can be extended by focusing on two further aspects of the geography of business travel. First, rather than restricting the discussion to the absolute and relative dimensions of business travel on a city-by-city basis, we can assess the actual spatiality of business flows between cities. To this end, Figure 3.2 depicts the most important business travel links in 2005 between the most important European cities in terms of the total volume of business class passengers. In the figure, the size of the nodes varies with the total number of incoming or outgoing passengers, while the size of the edges varies with the number of business passengers flying between two cities. For reasons of clarity, only the most important links are shown (>100,000 passengers). In addition to a cohesive business network centred on Stockholm, Oslo and Copenhagen, it is clear that business travel to/from Frankfurt, London, Paris and Amsterdam is dominant. These cities are highly interrelated, while most business travel from/to other major cities is also primarily orientated towards these cities (e.g., each city has well-connected business class flows to London).

**Figure 3.2 Most important nodes and connections in European business
class travel**
Source: AEA, 2005.

Second, we can focus on the spatiality of the relative importance of business travel to/from the most important business centres in 2005 (London, Paris, Frankfurt, and Amsterdam). Table 3.2 summarizes the results of a least squares regression on the logarithms of the volume of economy and business class passengers to/from each of these cities, and lists all cities with a standardized residual with an absolute value larger than 1: large negative residuals indicate that a city has less business class travellers than expected on the basis of the number of economy class passengers, positive residuals point to relatively strong business class connections to London, Paris, Frankfurt, and Amsterdam. Overall, the table reveals that cities with large positive residuals are primarily business centres (e.g. Frankfurt and Zurich), while cities with negative residuals are those that are also major tourist centres (e.g. Rome and Barcelona).

Table 3.1 Ranking of European cities according to their business class connectivity in the AEA-database, 2005

		Total business			**Proportion business**
1	London	3,281,117	1	Geneva	16.26
2	Frankfurt	2,026,604	2	Oslo	16.00
3	Paris	2,019,845	3	Stockholm	14.78
4	Amsterdam	1,737,635	4	Düsseldorf	14.62
5	Copenhagen	1,096,543	5	Frankfurt	13.61
6	Munich	1,080,402	6	London	12.95
7	Stockholm	863,045	7	Zurich	12.77
8	Milan	853,438	8	Copenhagen	11.80
9	Vienna	764,851	9	Munich	11.75
10	Brussels	763,111	10	Vienna	10.75
11	Madrid	759,496	11	Brussels	10.72
12	Oslo	694,255	12	Amsterdam	10.10
13	Geneva	568,867	13	Paris	9.67
14	Rome	514,360	14	Milan	9.32
15	Düsseldorf	461,820	15	Berlin	8.39
16	Prague	419,508	16	Madrid	8.24
17	Zurich	413,365	17	Prague	8.03
18	Barcelona	397,845	18	Helsinki	7.62
19	Istanbul	394,400	19	Athens	7.21
20	Athens	338,843	20	Manchester	7.18
21	Helsinki	332,139	21	Istanbul	7.09
22	Lisbon	310,424	22	Budapest	7.09
23	Budapest	256,799	23	Rome	6.77
24	Hamburg	219,458	24	Lisbon	6.59
25	Manchester	202,300	25	Barcelona	6.16

Table 3.2 **Least squares regression on business and economy class flows in the AEA-database, 2005: Standardized residuals larger than one standard deviation**

London		Paris		Frankfurt		Amsterdam	
City		**City**		**City**		**City**	
positive		*positive*		*positive*		*positive*	
Geneva	3.09	London	3.59	Brussels	2.92	London	5.16
Frankfurt	3.05	Amsterdam	3.30	Zurich	2.86	Paris	3.39
Düsseldorf	2.67	Geneva	2.52	Geneva	2.50	Frankfurt	1.45
Brussels	1.76	Frankfurt	1.71	Basle	1.30		
Zurich	1.01	Düsseldorf	1.18	Milan	1.24		
				Amsterdam	1.00		
negative		*negative*		*negative*		*negative*	
Barcelona	-2.02	Barcelona	-1.59	Barcelona	-1.55	Barcelona	-1.29
Rome	-1.88	Madrid	-1.46	Istanbul	-1.45		
Dublin	-1.74	Rome	-1.22	Madrid	-1.44		
Lisbon	-1.35			Rome	-1.41		
				Lisbon	-1.19		

A New Framework for Analysing the Spatiality of Business Flows

Hierarchical differentiation in networks

The objective of this second section is to outline an analytical framework that allows for an assessment of the (shifting) equilibrium between concentration and dispersal in airline networks (e.g. the different configurations of economy and business class networks). This framework is based on a detailed examination of the degree of 'hierarchical differentiation' in spatial networks, and draws on earlier research carried out with a number of colleagues (Van Nuffel et al. 2009). The 'hierarchical differentiation' concept is borrowed from Pumain (2006), and refers to the ranking of elements from large to small (e.g. the rank size rule for cities). It differs from 'hierarchical organization', which indicates the existence of different levels, with new properties emerging at each level (e.g. a Christaller pattern of central places). Hierarchical differentiation in a spatial network has three features, i.e. (1) dominance (at the nodal level), which relates to the degree to which flows are evenly distributed across the different nodes in the network; (2) connectivity (at the flow level), which relates to the degree to which flows are evenly distributed across the different links in the network; and (3) symmetry (at the flow level), which relates to the degree of reflexivity of the flows. In principle, the analysis of hierarchical differentiation involves the measurement of each of these characteristics, because a network with relatively little hierarchical differentiation in terms of dominance may well exhibit extensive hierarchical differentiation in terms of connectivity and/or symmetry . However, as explained earlier in this chapter, because of data constraints, we are unable to measure symmetry, and our framework therefore exclusively deals with the measurement of connectivity and dominance.

The framework outlined in Van Nuffel et al. (2009) builds on the work of Limtanakool et al. (2007), who introduce a number of spatial interaction indices with the aim of examining the pattern of interaction between Functional Urban Regions (FURs) in France and Germany. Based on the values for these indices, the urban network configuration in both countries was located on the continuum between the archetypal fully monocentric and fully polycentric networks. In our framework, we propose to extend their indices by calculating two additional measures and by normalizing the ratio between the different measures and their corresponding values for a rank size distribution. These extensions are deemed necessary because of possible interpretation problems with the initial framework, which primarily stem from the fact that the clear-cut interpretation of these measures seems to depend on the number of nodes/links in the network, especially when the latter becomes large and complex. The relevance of this extended analytical framework for future research will be shown by applying it to the AEA-data on air passenger flows within Europe. That is, we will use the bifurcation between economy class and business travel connectivity in our dataset to show the relevance of this methodology for future research on this topic. More specifically, to test the relevance of our analytical framework, we will apply it to examine a hypothesis regarding the spatial structure of business travel in the context of the European urban network. Because it can be assumed that not all cities are business centres, we expect business class flows to be more hierarchically differentiated than economy class flows. Or, put differently: the inclusion of a number of major tourist destinations in the dataset implies that we expect economy class flows to be more evenly distributed (and thus less hierarchically differentiated) than business class flows. It is on the basis of this hypothesis that we will assess the empirical merits of our analytical framework elaborated in the next paragraphs.

The remainder of this section is organized as follows. The next paragraph details the context and overall relevance of our measurement framework, i.e. the changing configurations of airline networks. The following paragraph presents the four spatial interaction indices based on the work of Limtanakool et al. (2007), after which some preliminary results are used to call for the extension of this framework. The two next paragraphs focus on the proposed changes and the main results respectively. Obviously, in the context of this chapter, we are primarily interested in how our framework can be used for gauging/comparing the shifting spatiality of business air travel networks, and this will therefore be the focus in our discussion of the results.

Context: The changing configuration of airline networks

Although the world's air transport networks were largely pioneered before the Second World War, the origins of mass air travel date back to no earlier than around 1960. Aggregate growth rates since then have been quite dramatic, although there seems to be an ever-present sense of volatility in the industry. In spite of some intermittent falls in this aggregate growth pattern (such as the industry's slump after '9/11' and the SARS outbreak in Asia) and structural constraints on the development towards evermore connectivity (such as rising fuel costs, negative environmental impacts, and airspace and runway congestion around key metropolises), the aviation industry remains confident about long-term growth. The International Air Transport Association (IATA), for instance, has recently stated that – in spite of seemingly ever-worsening predictions about global economic conditions – growth in air transport will remain strong, albeit that international passenger volume growth has passed its peak level for the current growth cycle. Indeed, IATA expects that international air passenger numbers will continue to grow at an average annual growth rate (AAGR) of 5.1 per cent between 2007 and 2011, which is only slightly lower than the average rate of 7.4 per cent seen between 2002 and 2006. These predictions are based on the assumption that demand growth will be weakened by slower global economic growth, but at the same time boosted by the further liberalisation of markets and the emergence of new routes and services. Furthermore, a significant growth in national connectivity is expected in the Chinese and Indian domestic markets, not in the least in terms of business-related air travel: in these markets domestic passenger numbers are forecast to grow at an AAGR of 5.3 per cent between 2007 and 2011, higher than the average rate of 4.4 per cent seen between 2002 and 2006 (Derudder and Witlox 2008).

These aggregate growth trends obfuscate a number of dramatic changes that have been taking place in the airline industry in the last few decades. Most of these trends are at least in some way related to the increasing deregulation of the global airline market. Historically, at the international scale, air service provision between countries was controlled by strict bilateral agreements that were reciprocally negotiated between governments, which governed the so-called 'freedoms' of civil aviation. Since the deregulation of the American domestic airline market in 1978, the US government has pursued a global policy to liberalize these bilateral agreements. Most recently, it has sought so-called 'open skies' agreements, allowing unrestricted market entry for every carrier. The logical outcome of full open skies will be the replacement of bilateral with multilateral agreements, in which groups of like-minded countries permit any airline virtually unlimited access to any market within their boundaries. This trend towards ever more deregulation has significant impacts on the industry at large. For instance, to circumvent remaining regulatory constraints, airlines have sought to establish strategic global alliances (such as Star Alliance, OneWorld, and SkyTeam), while the need for efficiency and economies of scale in a global marketplace have led to new rounds of mergers and acquisitions. Deregulation, in turn, has led to new forms of air transport such as the well-known low-cost carriers, as well as the new travel classes such as 'Premium Economy'. In the context of the present discussion, however, the most interesting trend induced by recent changes in the airline industry is a series of shifts in the organizational geography of airline networks.

In the US, for instance, the deregulation of the passenger aviation market in 1978 has resulted in a radical reorganization of the airline network. More specifically, agreements between airports and airlines have tended to result in hub-and-spoke configurations in which a small number of key airports (hubs) serve as transfer points where passengers change planes. From these hubs, the spoke flights then take passengers to their final destinations (Burghouwt et al. 2003). The process of deregulation also took place in Europe, albeit in a more gradual way. Three packages of deregulation measures (1987, 1989, 1992) have led to a shifting of power from governments towards the European airlines (Button et al. 1998, Hakfoort 1999). However, because European carriers already showed a very high traffic concentration rate before deregulation, the deregulation process did not result in a restructuring as radical as in the US (Burghouwt et al. 2003). The advantages of such a radial hub-and-spoke configuration, as compared to a point-to-point configuration (Figure 3.3), are obvious: for the same number of destinations, there are fewer routes to serve, which in turn yields the possibility of higher flight frequencies and the use of bigger aircraft (Burghouwt and Hakfoort 2001).

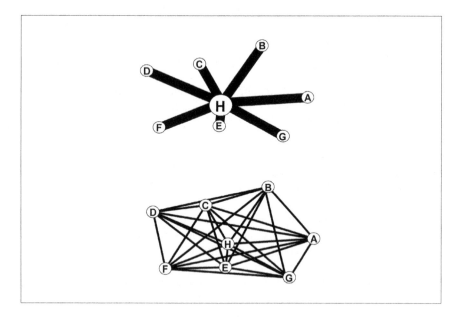

Figure 3.3 'Optimal' point-to-point and hub-and-spoke configurations
Source: AEA, 2005.

Although the gradual deregulation of the airline market may seem to be coupled with a continuous evolution towards hub-and-spoke configurations (further facilitated by mergers and alliance building), a number of important counter tendencies have emerged in the last few years. A first major counter trend is induced by the mounting success of low-cost carriers, which tend to prefer a point-to-point organization to avoid costs associated with the organization of an elaborate transfer system (Alderighi et al. 2005) . This resurgence of point-to-point forms of spatial organization is, however, also apparent in the airline sector more generally; this can for instance be read from the different visions developed by Boeing and Airbus – the world's leading commercial jet producers – as to the future organization of airline networks. Both firms' latest commercial airplane, Boeing's 787 Dreamliner and Airbus's A380, are based on diametrically opposed visions of the future. The Airbus A380 represents the hub-and-spoke model in that it is built around the assumption that airlines will continue to fly smaller planes on shorter routes (spokes) into a few large hubs, then onward to the next hub on giant aircraft. It also presumes that passengers will accept the hassle of changing planes. Boeing's 787, in contrast, represents an alternative in that it does not take the hub-and-spoke model as a given. The company bets on increased point-to-point connectivity, and substantiates this based on the observation that since 1990 the number of city pairs more than 3,000 nautical miles apart served by the world's airlines has doubled. This trend shows no sign of abating, while the average airplane size has actually declined slightly. All this suggests that customers have come to prefer more point-to-point flights on smaller airplanes, and this may well point to a change in the fortune of the point-to-point system at large (Bowen 2002, Graham and Goetz 2007).

The continuous development of the air transport industry leads to a number of questions regarding the changing spatial configuration of airline networks at large. A number of earlier studies have tried to measure this shifting spatial configuration in more detail, by comparing the real network configurations with ideal hub-and-spoke and point-to-point structures (for an overview, see Alderighi et al. 2007). In this section, we propose another approach by situating airline-based networks between both ideal-typical extremes. More specifically, we will do so by examining the degree of hierarchical differentiation in the economy class and business travel networks in the European urban network.

Spatial interaction indices

Our analytical framework is based on the measurement of hierarchical differentiation (Van Nuffel et al. 2009), and consists of an adapted and extended version of the research presented in Limtanakool et al. (2007). As mentioned in the introduction of this section, we will focus on two aspects of hierarchical differentiation, i.e. dominance (at the nodal level) and connectivity (at the link level) . Because the same degree of connectivity in a network can be associated with different levels of dominance (and the other way round), we need to combine indexes for both dimensions. We use a total of four indices, two for measuring dominance and two for measuring connectivity. One of the dominance indices (the overall distribution index based on cities ODI_c) is measured at the level of the overall network; the other (the non-directional dominance index DIT_i) is measured at the level of the individual cities. Similarly, for the connectivity measures, one index is calculated at the level of the overall network (the overall distribution index based on links ODI_l); the other index is calculated at the level of the individual connections or links (the relative strength index RSI_{ij}).

The first index, the overall distribution index based on cities ODI_c, is an entropy measure that measures the extent to which the total interaction is distributed evenly across all cities in the network:

$$ODI_c = - \sum_{i=1}^{I} \frac{(Z_i)\ln(Z_i)}{\ln(I)} \tag{1}$$

where Z_i is the share of passengers associated with city i in the total number of passengers, and I is the number of cities in the network. A value of 1 indicates an equal distribution over the I cities, while small values point to the presence of hierarchical differentiation.

The second index is the non-directional dominance index DIT_i, calculated as the ratio between the sum of the interactions associated with city i and the average size of the interactions associated with the other cities in the network:

$$DIT_i = \frac{T_i}{\sum_{j=1}^{J} \frac{T_j}{J}} \tag{2}$$

where T_i is the total number of passengers associated with city i and $i \neq j$. Cities with a DIT_i value above 1 are considered dominant cities because they are more important than the average of the other cities in the network. 'Large' differences between DIT_i values for different cities indicate a high degree of hierarchical differentiation.

The third index, the overall distribution index based on links ODI_l, is again an entropy index, measuring the extent to which the total interaction is distributed evenly across all links (city-pairs) in the network:

$$ODI_l = - \sum_{l=1}^{L_p} \frac{(Z_l)\ln(Z_l)}{\ln(L_p)} \tag{3}$$

where Z_l is the share of passengers travelling on link l in the total number of passengers, and L_p is the potential number of links in the network. The maximum

ODI_I value of 1 indicates a fully connected structure. Small values point to the presence of hierarchical differentiation.

Finally, the fourth index is the relative strength index RSI_{ij}, which is simply the proportion of interaction on a single link between two cities relative to the total interaction in the network:

$$RSI_{ij} = \frac{T_{ij}}{\sum\limits_{i=1}^{I}\sum\limits_{j=1}^{J} T_{ij}} \tag{4}$$

where T_{ij} is the total number of passengers travelling between city i and city j, and $i \neq j$. The RSI_{ij} values for all links in the network sum to unity, while individual values range from 0 to 1. Similar to the DIT_i measure, 'large' differences between RSI_{ij} values point to the presence of hierarchical differentiation.

Extension of the analytical framework

Prior to applying the analytical framework adapted from Limtanakool et al. (2007) to our airline data, we modified it in two ways. The first modification stems from the fact that intuitively clear notions such as 'small differences' or 'large differences' between the different DIT_i and RSI_{ij} values cannot be interpreted straightforwardly. Such interpretation poses little or no problems when only a small number of nodes is analysed, as is the case in the paper of Limtanakool et al. (8 FURs in Germany, and 6 in France). However, when the number of nodes is large – as is the case in our research – then conclusions about the degree of hierarchical differentiation in terms of the differences between the individual values are not always straightforward to make. We therefore propose to calculate the standard deviations of the values of both indices as a second overall measure of hierarchical differentiation that may be helpful in interpretation of the differences between the values of DIT_i and RSI_{ij}. High standard deviations reflect large differences in the values of the indices and thus point to more dominance and less connectivity. In other words: the higher the standard deviations, the less equally divided passengers are between cities and links. In terms of the bifurcation between economy and business class travel, this implies that we expect to see larger standard deviations for business class travel, because the presence of a number of major business centres in the dataset implies that we expect business class nodes/flows to be less evenly distributed (and thus more hierarchically differentiated) than economy class flows.

The second modification stems from the fact that the measures are sensitive to the number of cities and links. This can be shown by calculating them for rank size distributions. A rank size distribution can be defined as:

$$\sum_{c=1}^{I} T_c = \sum_{r=1}^{I} \frac{1}{r} T'_l \quad \text{(for cities)} \quad \text{and} \quad \sum_{l=1}^{L_p} T_l = \sum_{r=1}^{L_p} \frac{1}{r} T'_l \quad \text{(for links)} \quad (5)$$

where T'_c (T'_l) is the rank-size predicted number of passengers associated with city c (link l) in a rank size distribution, r_c (r_l) is the rank order of that city (link) in the distribution, and $T_{c,max}$ ($T_{l,max}$) is the number of passengers associated with the largest city (link) in the dataset. For instance, in a rank size distribution, the rank-size predicted number of passengers associated with the city ranked 6th in the distribution equals 1/6th of the number of passengers associated with the most important city. The basic advantage of using the rank size distribution as a reference point is that it provides a 'balanced' distribution between both extremes of maximal and minimal hierarchical differentiation. If the actual values T_c and T_l are – on average – higher than the rank-size predicted values T'_c and T'_l, then we are dealing with a relative dearth of hierarchical differentiation. In contrast, if the actual values T_c and T_l are – on average – lower than the rank-size predicted values T'_c and T'_l, then we are dealing with a relative presence of hierarchical differentiation . Details of this normalization procedure can be found in Van Nuffel et al. (2009). The major point here is that in practice we will be working with reconfigured indices of which all values assume a similar interpretation (Table 3.3).

Before turning to the discussion of the results, two final comments should be made. The first comment relates to the way in which the different indices deal with differences from the mean. The entropy measures ODI_c and ODI_l are not very sensitive to changes in the values of the largest cities/links, because the proportions of passengers are multiplied by their logarithm. On the other hand, although the standard deviations treat positive and negative deviations from the mean in the same way, they are more sensitive to higher deviations because of the squaring. Therefore, in interpretations, it is best to combine entropy values and standard deviations.

The second comment relates to the use of the potential links L_p in our actual analysis. In practice, a lot of links feature no passengers at all (e.g., there are at present no direct flights between Brussels and Glasgow), so that Z_l equals 0 for quite a lot of connections. However, because 0 does not have a logarithm, these values cannot be used in the numerator of ODI_l, and in our calculations we have therefore replaced L_p by the total number of 'real links' L_r. As a consequence, in (3) we assume that all potential links are actually existing links, while in (1) there are no cities where Z_i equals 0. In other words: in our calculations, we only employed those links that actually feature passengers, and accordingly make use of a rank size distribution that starts from the number of 'real links'.

Table 3.3 Overview of the measures and their interpretations

Measure	Interpretation
DIT_i	Non-directional dominance index at the city-level
RSI_{ij}	Relative strength index ay the link-level (connectivity)
	$DIT_i > 0$, whereby values > 1 point to important cities
	$RSI_{ij} \in [0, 1]$, whereby large values point to important links
$SD_{RSR}(DIT_i)$	Normalized standard deviation of non-directional dominance index $DITi$ at the level of the individual cities (dominance)
	$SD_{RSR}(DIT_i) \in [0,1]$, with:
	• 0 = completely even distribution (no HD)
	• 1 = all passengers concentrated in one city (maximum HD)
	• $0,5$ = rank size distribution
$SD_{RSR}(RSI_{ij})$	Normalized standard deviation of relative connectivity strength index $RSIij$ at the level of the individual cities (connectivity)
	$SD_{RSR}(RSI_{ij}) \in [0,1]$, with:
	• 0 = completely even distribution (no HD)
	• 1 = all passengers concentrated in one city (maximum HD)
	• $0,5$ = rank size distribution
$ODI_{c,RSR}$	Overall distribution index based on cities ODIc, is an entropy measure that measures the extent to which the total interaction is distributed evenly across all cities in the network (dominance)
	$ODI_{c,RSR} \in [0,1]$, with:
	• 0 = completely even distribution (no HD)
	• 1 = all passengers concentrated in one city (maximum HD)
	• $0,5$ = rank size distribution
ODI_{LRSR}	Overall distribution index based on links ODIl, is again an entropy index, measuring the extent to which the total interaction is distributed evenly across all links (city-pairs) in the network (connectivity)
	$ODI_{c,RSR} \in [0,1]$, with:
	• 0 = completely even distribution (no HD)
	• 1 = all passengers concentrated in one link (maximum HD)
	• $0,5$ = rank size distribution

Note: ODI = overall distribution index (based on either c = cities or l = links); RSI = relative strength index; DIT = non-directional dominance index; HD = hierarchical differentiation; RDS = rank size distribution; SD = standard deviation; RSR = rank size distribution.

Results

Table 3.4 lists the top-5 of the most important cities and links in 2005, divided between business class and economy class connections. From the table, it can be seen that while Frankfurt holds the fourth place for economy class flows, it comes second for business class flows. The analyses with regard to the links show that the fourth and fifth most important links for economy class are the connections of Madrid to Paris and to London. For business class flows on the other hand, places 4 and 5 are taken by Scandinavian capital city-pairs: Oslo-Stockholm and Copenhagen-Stockholm, reflecting the (declining) importance of business class travel in the SAS network. The cumulated RSI_{ij} values (multiplied by 1000) of the five most important connections amount to 61.01 for economy class and to 110.39 for business class, reflecting the more hierarchically differentiated nature of the business class network.

Table 3.4 Top-5 DIT_i and RSI_{ij} values in 2005

	DIT_i (DIT$_i$ value between brackets)		RSI_{ij}	
	Economy class	**Business class**	**Economy class**	**Business class**
Rank	**City**	**City**	**Link**	**Link**
1	London (21.36)	London (25.26)	Amsterdam-London	Amsterdam-London
2	Paris (17.12)	Frankfurt (15.27)	London-Paris	London-Paris
3	Amsterdam (13.74)	Paris (14.11)	Frankfurt-London	Frankfurt-London
4	Frankfurt (12.06)	Amsterdam (12.54)	Madrid-Paris	Oslo-Stockholm
5	Munich (7.34)	Munich (7.82)	London-Madrid	Copenhagen-Stockholm
Cumulated RSI$_{ij}$ value (x 1000)			61.01	110.39

A similar conclusion can be drawn from the normalized entropy values and the standard deviations. These results are summarized in Table 3.5, where the normalized values are shown for economy and business class networks, in addition to flows within the European countries with the largest internal aviation market (i.e. Germany, France, and the United Kingdom). When interpreting these tables, recall that a value larger than 0.5 indicates a distribution that is more hierarchically differentiated than the rank size distribution, while a value smaller than 0.5 indicates a less hierarchically differentiated distribution, it can be noted that – at both the city and the link level – the German aviation network is far less hierarchically distributed than that of France and the United Kingdom. This is logical given the different configurations of their 'national' urban network: the primacy of London and Paris implies that the national networks are more hierarchically differentiated than the German urban network, which is notorious for its more polycentric structure (see e.g. Krätke 2001, Taylor et al. 2006).

To visualise this difference between the spatiality of business class and economy class flows, Figures 3.4a-3.5b summarize the distributions of the number of passengers for both booking classes. The bold line indicates the real values, the dashed thin line the values for the corresponding rank size distribution. The x-axis is made logarithmic to ease interpretation. The corresponding normalized index values are indicated beside the graphs. Once again, the more profound hierarchical differentiation in business class flows reappears here. Because these results do not depend on the number of nodes/links in the network (because of the normalization vis-à-vis the rank-size rule), they can be used in future longitudinal research tracing the nature of changes in air travel networks at large (even when nodes are added and/or disappear).

Table 3.5 Normalized results for 2005

| | # Pass. | Cities | | | Links | | |
		SD DIT$_i$	ODI$_c$	# Cities	SD RSI$_{ij}$	ODI$_l$	# Links
Economy	117,853,550	0.42	0.55	183	0.15	0.40	1088
Business	12,809,779	0.48	0.56	160	0.21	0.43	929
France	17,929,179	0.75	0.60	33	0.50	0.53	98
Germany	13,206,507	0.48	0.54	18	0.32	0.44	47
United Kingdom	9,923,747	0.73	0.60	18	0.53	0.55	36

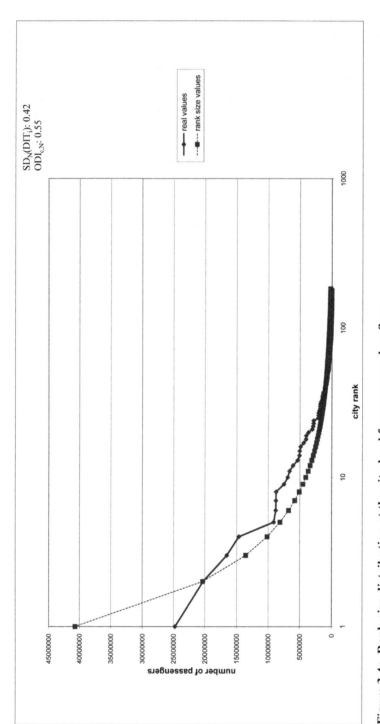

Figure 3.4a Rank-size distribution at the city-level for economy class flows
Source: AEA, 2005.

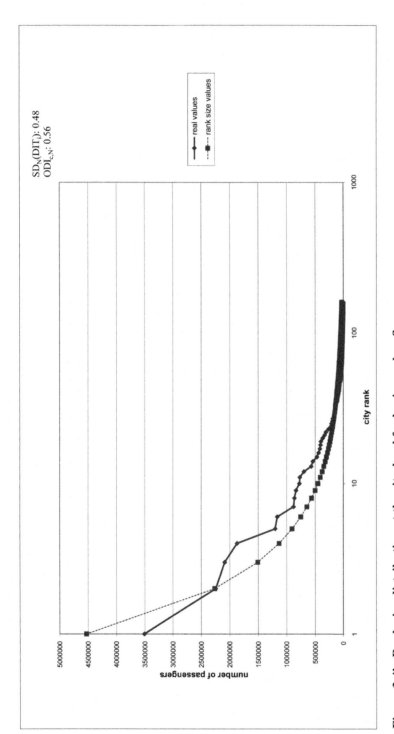

Figure 3.4b Rank-size distribution at the city-level for business class flows
Source: AEA, 2005.

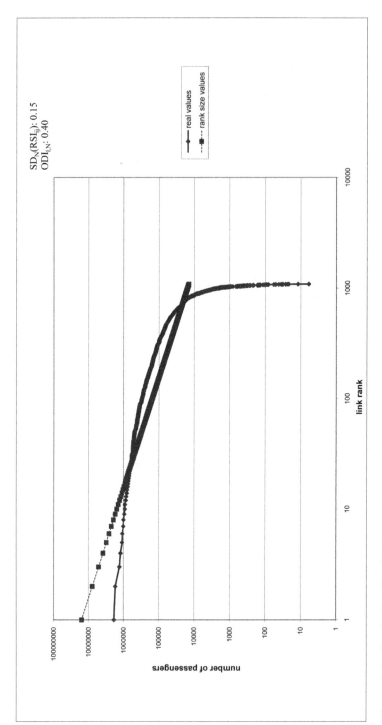

Figure 3.5a Rank-size distribution at the link-level for economy class flows
Source: AEA, 2005.

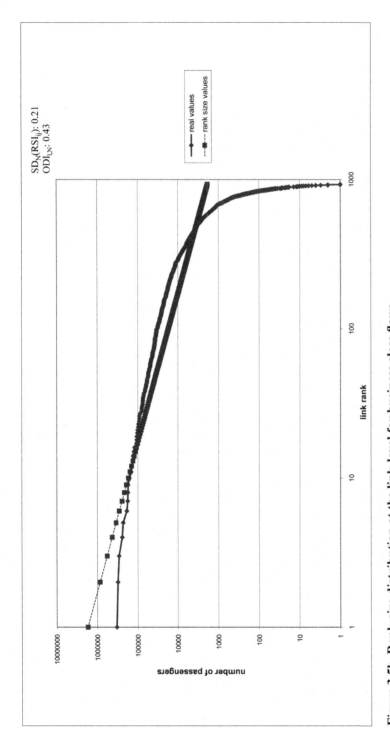

Figure 3.5b Rank-size distribution at the link-level for business class flows
Source: AEA, 2005.

Conclusions

The overall objective of this chapter is twofold. Firstly, based on a straightforward overview of the basic patterns of business class travel in Europe, we have argued that – in spite of a number of conceptual and empirical uncertainties – it is possible to devise a sensible mapping of business air travel based on business class air travel. Secondly, we have outlined a framework that allows for meaningful analyses/ comparisons of the spatialities of different types of travel networks (including meaningful longitudinal analyses). The usefulness of this framework has been shown by focusing on the diverging degrees of hierarchical differentiation in economy class and business class travel networks: the expectations regarding the comparison between both travel classes is that because not all cities are major transnational business centres, we assume business class flows in Europe to be more hierarchically differentiated than economy class flows. Furthermore, the fact that German inter-city relations are less hierarchically differentiated than those in France and the United Kingdom also points in this direction.

The results show that the developed analytical framework can be used to analyse dominance and connectivity in spatial networks (such as travel connections), which opens up possibilities for meaningful longitudinal analyses of the decentralization/concentration of business travel in Europe based on this framework. This appreciation of more 'meaningful' analyses is based on our extension of the framework presented in Limtanakool et al. (2007) aimed at deriving a clear-cut and readily interpretable benchmark for assessing the degree of concentration and/or dispersal in a network. To this end, the initial outline of the analytical framework was altered in two ways. First, the standard deviations of two of the indices (DIT_i and RSI_{ij}) were calculated as additional measures of hierarchical differentiation. Second, because of their sensitivity to the number of cities or links, these standard deviations and the entropy indices ODI_c and ODI_l were normalized by comparing the indicators to their corresponding values for a rank size distribution with the same number of cities/links, which is especially important when dealing with large and/or complex networks.

It should be stressed that our specific analyses of hierarchical differentiation in European air passenger flows was not an objective in and by itself. Rather, it served as a heuristic device to assess the merits of our methodological framework at large. The important point, then, is that it can easily be applied in future research. In particular, studies of the changing spatiality of airline networks in the face of deregulation and other wide-ranging changes in the aviation business may use it for assessing the shifting overall balance between concentration (more hierarchical differentiation) and dispersal (more hierarchical differentiation) in the network at large, rather than having to guesstimate these changes through a series of general indicators at the city level. The major advantage over other indicators is that the normalization of the indicators vis-à-vis the rank-size-rule leads to a straightforward assessment of the concentration/dispersal-continuum irrespective of the number of nodes/links. In this context, its proper application in a longitudinal and/or comparative perspective allows for a detailed assessment of the alleged effects of deregulation on the overall spatiality of airline networks in general, and of those in business class travel flows in particular.

References

Faulconbridge, J.R., Beaverstock, J.V., Derudder, B. and Witlox, F. 2009. Corporate Ecologies of Business Travel in Professional Service Firms: Working towards a Research Agenda. *European Urban and Regional Studies*, 16, 295-308.

Alderighi, M., Cento, A., Nijkamp, P. and Rietveld, P. 2005. Network competition – the coexistence of hub-and-spoke and point-to-point systems. *Journal of Air Transport Management*, 11(5), 328-334.

Alderighi, M., Cento, A., Nijkamp, P. and Rietveld, P. 2007. Assessment of new hub-and-spoke and point-to-point airline network configurations. *Transport Reviews*, 275, 529-549.

Bowen, J. This volume.

Bowen, J. 2002. Network change, deregulation, and access in the global airline industry. *Economic Geography*, 78, 425-439.

Budd, L. and Hubbard, P. This volume.

Burghouwt, G. and Hakfoort, J. 2001. The evolution of the European aviation network, 1990-1998. *Journal of Air Transport Management*, 7(5), 311-318.

Burghouwt, G., Hakfoort, J. and Ritsema van Eck, J. 2003. The spatial configuration of airline networks in Europe. *Journal of Air Transport Management*, 9(5), 309-323.

Button, K.J., Haynes, K. and Stough, R. 1998. *Flying into the Future. Air Transport Policy in the European Union* (Cheltenham: Edward Elgar).

Denstadli, J. and Gripsrud, M. This volume.

Derudder, B. and Witlox, F. 2008. Physical connection: Airline networks and cities, in 'Connecting Cities: Networks', http://www.metropoliscongress2008.com/default.asp?PageID=123, last accessed 13/03/2009.

Derudder, B., Devriendt, L. and Witlox, F. 2007. An empirical analysis of the position of major former Soviet Union-cities in transnational airline networks. *Eurasian Geography and Economics*, 48(1), 95-110.

Faulconbridge, J., Beaverstock, J. Derudder, B. and Witlox, F. 2009. Corporate ecologies of international business travel: Examples from professional service firms. *European Urban and Regional studies*, forthcoming.

Graham, B. and Goetz, A.R. 2007. Global air transport, in *Transport Geographies – Mobilities, Flows and Spaces*, edited by R. Knowles, J. Shaw and J. Docherty. Oxford: Blackwell.

Hakfoort, J.R., 1999. The deregulation of European air transport: A dream come true? *Tijdschrift voor Economische en Sociale Geografie*, 90(2), 226-233.

Kellermann, A. This volume.

Krätke, S. 2001. Strenghtening the polycentric urban system in Europe: Conclusions from the ESDP. *European Planning Studies*, 9(1), 105-116.

Lassen, C. 2006. Aeromobility and work. *Environment and Planning A*, 38(2), 301-312.

Limtanakool, N., Dijst, M. and Schwanen, T. 2007. A theoretical framework and methodology for characterising national urban systems on the basis of flows of people: Empirical evidence for France and Germany. *Urban Studies*, 44(11), 2123-2145.

Pumain, D. 2006. *Hierarchy in Natural and Social Sciences*. Dordrecht: Springer.

Taylor, P.J., Evans, D. and Pain, K. 2006. Organization of the polycentric metropolis: Corporate structures and networks, in *The Polycentric Metropolis. Learning from Mega-city Regions in Europe*, edited by P. Hall and K. Pain. London: Earthscan, 53-69.

Van Nuffel, N., Saey, P., Derudder, B. Devriendt, L. and Witlox, F. 2009. Measuring hierarchical differentiation: Connectivity and dominance in the European urban network. GaWC Research Bulletin 249, http://www.lboro.ac.uk/gawc/rb/rb249.html, last accessed 03/03/09.

Chapter 4

'Official' and 'Unofficial' Measurements of International Business Travel to and from the United Kingdom: Trends, Patterns and Limitations

Jonathan V. Beaverstock and James Faulconbridge

Introduction

It is now well established that the physical movement of people, as part of their corporate business, is a fundamental process of global working patterns and labour processes, particularly in knowledge-rich, client-focused activities (Frandberg and Vilhelmson 2003, Faulconbridge and Beaverstock 2008, Hislop 2008, Jones 2008, Millar and Salt 2008). The prevalence of business travel in the world economy has become so important for the airline and hotel industry that an entire consultancy sector has mushroomed to provide real-time intelligence for these businesses (for example, Mintel Oxygen, www.mintel.com), as well as for the business traveller (for example www.ctbusinesstravel.co.uk). But, what is of significant interest when studying international business travel, is the dearth of available data, from both the state and private 'unofficial' sources, that charts business travel trends and patterns in the world. In this chapter, we present an analysis of official data collected by the United Kingdom's Statistical Authority on international business visitors in the statistical digest, *Travel Trends*, published by the Office for National Statistics (ONS). We will report several important characteristics of the patterns of overseas residences' business visits to the UK and UK residences' business visits abroad from the late 1970s onwards. We will then supplement these 'official' data of business visit trends by analysing known available 'unofficial' data sources on business travel in order to add depth to the dearth of available data on this form of international labour mobility.

The rest of this chapter is divided into four parts. Following this introduction, we briefly discuss the prevalence and significance of international business travel as an essential facet of transnational work in the global economy, where the requirement of proximity and 'face-to-face' contact remains a crucial organizational strategy of the firm. In parts two and three respectively, we then analyse the geographies of business visitor trends from the ONS's *Travel Trends* and two non-state, private sources, the Corporation of London (2008) and the Barclaycard Business Travel

Survey (Future Foundation 2006). Finally, the chapter will conclude by setting out a research agenda for collecting 'unofficial' data sets on international business travel in the world space economy.

Business Travel as Transnational Work in the Global Space Economy

An analysis of three existing literatures, on the transnational corporation (TNC), migration and mobilities, and management and corporate control, can be helpful to identify the reasons for, and effects of, international business travel in contemporary firms in the global space economy.

Business travel and the transnational corporation

A long line of literatures from Dunning and Norman (1987) to Bartlett and Ghoshal (1998) have described how TNCs have had to manage the difficulties posed by geographically heterogeneous resources, business cultures and regulations that embed subsidiaries' operations outside of the host country. If managed correctly such geographical variations can by turned into competitive advantage, as for example: law firms and retailers have done by opening overseas branches that allow new markets to be tapped (Beaverstock et al. 1999, Wrigley et al. 2005); and, manufacturers have done recently to tap into knowledge-rich labour pools (Henry and Pinch 2000) and circumvent regulatory hurdles that prevent the servicing of emerging consumer markets (see Liu and Dicken (2006) on cars). However, if not managed appropriately, the roll-out of the firm's home-country culture and practices can lead to the alienation of workers, customers and/or regulators (Coe and Yong-Sook 2006, Faulconbridge 2008) and even the failure of subsidiaries (as Wal-Mart's withdrawal from Germany shows, see Christopherson (2007)). At its simplest, international business travel is needed to develop knowledge and awareness of geographically heterogeneous contexts and to develop strategies to exploit resources or strategically adapt so as to ensure variations in culture, regulation or other economic factors do not inhibit the success of a subsidiary. In addition, though, business travel has been shown to have a more fundamental role in the spatial ordering of TNCs activities.

Firms are not only embedded in the places they emerge from and the resources, cultures and regulations of those places they operate in, but are also in sophisticated forms of transnational network relationships that create connections between people and places (Hess 2004). Mirroring the ideas encompassed in Bartlett and Ghoshal's transnational organizational form (1998) and Dunning and Norman's (1983) ownership advantages, studies have suggested that the creation of social and economic space is fundamental for the TNC's success through forms of interconnectivity between subsidiaries. This leads to what Yeung (2005) calls 'organizational space' which is often comprised of project teams (Grabher 2001) and allows new strategies to be devised, knowledge to be produced and competitive advantage created through the synergistic use of the competencies, knowledges and resources of multiple subsidiaries. Examples of the value of such transnational organizational space exist in relation to design and manufacturing (Orlikowski 2002), advertising and law (Jones 2002, Faulconbridge 2006), retail (Wrigley et al. 2005) and business entrepreneurship that cuts across manufacturing and service firms (Yeung 2009).

Business travel has a crucial role in the construction of such 'organizational' space. TNCs have to be assembled as socio-technical systems and an important part of the assemblage process is face-to-face contact facilitated by business travel (see Jones 2005, 2007, this volume). Such travel always exists alongside other virtual forms of communication that help stabilize transnational organizational space when embodied encounter is not possible (see Faulconbridge 2008, Denstadli and Gripsrud, this volume), but management control, innovation and learning and business transactions that occur in transnational organizational space all fundamentally rely on face-to-face meetings. Urry (2003) describes the types of legal and economic compulsions of meetingness associated with such travel by drawing on the ideas of Goffman (1967) to Boden and Molotch (1994) to Storper and Venables (2004) who identify trust, reciprocity and mutual understanding as critical business values and 'resources' that are required for transactions and teamwork and that are most effectively produced through embodied encounter.

Migration and mobility

One of the consequences of the TNCs reliance on business travel for assembling transnational organizational space is both the intensification of trends associated with the emergence of ever-more mobile worlds (Urry 2007) and the creation of a 'class' of mobile elite workers that circulate between world cities (Beaverstock 2006, Sklair 2001). This 'class' is crucial for creating the organizational spaces TNCs need to operate. However, this does not mean rank and file workers do not also travel. Significantly, TNCs are also reliant on business travel by more junior executive involved in the execution of transactions, albeit it travel that is on a less frequent basis than their more senior counterparts. As Millar and Salt (2008) outline, eight different types of mobility can thus be identified, ranging from long-term assignments that require travel punctuated by extended periods of dwelling in an office that if often located away from the employees place of permanent residence, to business travel that involves literally hours spent in another office to attend a meeting or see to the mundanities of completing a transaction. Of course, the rise of the frequent business traveller is not without consequences. The dilemma of how to reduce travel *and* maintain the transnational organizational space that TNCs' need to function is proving hard to resolve. Practically every study of the use of information communication technologies in transnational business work identifies business travel as an essential complementary component in the construction of corporate ecologies, rejecting outright the idea that innovations such as videoconferencing might end the need for travel and face-to-face encounter (see Orlikowski 2002, Faulconbridge 2008, Jones 2007, this volume).

Business travel in management and corporate control

Business travel has multiple roles in the construction of organizational space in TNCs (Jones 2007), but perhaps one of its most significant roles is in the development of organizational control and coherence. As has been widely reported, complex socio-spatial power relations exist between headquarters and subsidiaries in TNCs (Bartlett and Ghoshal 1998, Dicken et al. 2001, Jones 2002, Yeung 2005, Ferner et al. 2006). One of the main difficulties faced by leaders of TNCs is managing at a distance and ensuring that subsidiaries achieve the task set them in a manner that reflects the values and standards of the firm. As a result, business travel has become a key way to manage headquarters-subsidiary relations. Indeed, even in professional service firms such as law where no technical headquarters exists and in theory each branch has autonomy to dictate its own approach to work, it has been shown that business travel acts as a key mechanism by which senior partners and influential players in the firm can subtly manage and control operations in different subsidiaries (see Faulconbridge and Muzio 2008).

Beyond the requirement to manage the headquarter-subsidiary relations, it is also important to note that business travel plays an important operational role in the firm, and between firm and clients/customers/suppliers, which involve both domestic and international travel. Evidence from Hislop's edited (2008) volume, *Mobility and Technology in the Workplace*, Faulconbridge and Beaverstock (2008) and Jones (this volume) show very clearly that business travel can be a fundamental, repetitive (even mundane), everyday working process, for example to: sell products or services; support products or services (for example, computing software); maintain machinery and infrastructure; execute professional training (both inter- and intra firm); provide 'relief' management or specialized functions; and, attend conferences, trade fairs and events. Indeed, in many sectors the role of the transnational 'mobile manager', who functions with all relevant ICT interfaces (PDA, laptop, mobile phone for as associated with the archetypical 'mobile office') remains highly prevalent in many service and high-technological working environments (see Forlano 2008).

Mobile managers travel, train workers and promote the cultures of the firm as part of attempts to inculcate employees into the norms and values of the firm. In this sense, business travel and transnational elites in TNCs have an important political role, not only assembling transnational organizational space to allow collaboration and the synergistic combination of existing and creation of new resources, but also structuring this space around certain social values and norms. Yet there is still important and gaping holes in our knowledge about the subtleties of business travel because of data paucity. We know executives travel, but have little sense of the temporal and spatial patterns and trends of their travel. Knowledge of business travel patterns and trends in terms of, amongst other things, where people travel to and from, how frequently they travel and how long they stay for is needed if we are to better explain the role of travel for management and corporate control. Yet generally we know little about the spatiality of travel and it is, therefore, often impossible to tell how 'directionality' effects outcomes. In the rest of the chapter we, therefore, review the way existing 'official' and 'unofficial' data can help us better understand the nature of business travel in the global economy.

'Official' Data: The United Kingdom's Business Travel Trends

In the UK, official data collected on international travel are derived from the International Passenger Survey (IPS). The IPS started in 1961 and is a year-long face-to-face interview based sample survey undertaken at the UK's main air, sea and tunnel points of entry and exit for international visitors.[1] The survey records information on two types of visitors: overseas residents' who enter the UK; and UK residents' who visit abroad. For each of these two types of visitors, detailed information is collected on 110 variables with important data collected on: the number of visits; total spending of visits (£'s); the duration of visits; mode of travel; country of visit for UK residents; country of residence for overseas resident visitors to the UK; UK region of visit for overseas visitors; purpose of visit; and gender (see *Travel Trends* [ONS 2007], Appendix 1). It is important to note that *Travel Trends* records the number of visits, but not the number of visitors to and from the UK.[2]

---

1   The IPS questions travellers at these main UK points of entry and exit: Air (London Heathrow Terminals 1 to 5 and Transits; Gatwick North and South; Manchester Terminals 1 to 3; Stansted; and Residual airports; Sea (for example, Dover, Portsmouth); Channel Tunnel (London Waterloo – from 2007, London St Pancras International). In 2006, approximately 250,000 visitors were interviewed, representing about 0.3 per cent of all visitors, and the weighting and seasonal adjustment calculations generated estimated figures totalling 32.7 million overseas resident visits to the UK and 69.5 million UK residents making visits abroad.

2   When using IPS data to report trends and patterns in business travel it is important to note that such data do have it limitations and relative weaknesses. As discussed previous, it is derived from a sample survey, which has very low response rates and moreover, is collected from a very limited number of points of departure and entry into the UK. Thus there is a high degree of chance to which the numbers of travellers are either overestimated or underestimated in any one year. Also, and very importantly, given the size of the sample frame (as reported in footnote 1), as the data are sliced by the different cells of information (gender, age, purpose of visit, spend, duration of visit, country of next/last destination, etc.), the reliability of the data as an accurate measure becomes less rigorous as weighted numbers are generated from smaller sampled frames. Beyond the sampling issues, another relative weakness of the data is in the recording of the data itself. The IPS records the main purpose or visit or first destination of next visit or country of arrival. So for example, the activity of 'business tourism' remains unrecorded and whilst the first destination of arrival

Travel Trends reports four categories for the *main* purpose of visit: holiday; business (which includes conference and trade fair visits); visiting friends and relatives (VFR); and miscellaneous. The miscellaneous category records those visits where it is very difficult to determine the travellers' main purpose of visit. For overseas residents' visits to the UK, in 2006 the main purpose of visits for the 32.7 million travellers were divided almost equally between holiday (32 per cent), VRF (28 per cent) and business (29 per cent). But, over the last twenty years, the long-term trend in the purpose of visits have revealed a relative decline in the number of holiday visits (from a 46 per cent share in 1985) and large increases in travellers visiting for business and VFR (see ONS 2007, Table 1.03). In contrast, for the 69.5 million UK resident travellers going abroad in 2006, the most important reason for travel was to have a holiday, which accounted for 65 per cent of all visits (followed by VFRs (17 per cent) and business (13 per cent)). Moreover, an analysis of the longer trends over the over the last 20 years has shown that travel for business has experienced a slight relative fall in the proportionate share of all visits (from 15 per cent in 1985 to 13 per cent in both 2005 and 2006) (ONS 2007, see Table 1.04). In the rest of this part of the chapter, we will briefly present an abridged analysis of these major trends in overseas residents' business visits to the UK and UK residents' business visits to the rest of the world, focusing on: the number of visits; the mode of travel of visits; spending to the UK by overseas residents' and, spending overseas by UK residents'; and the country of residence and UK destination of overseas residents' visiting the UK, and the UK residence and country of visit of UK residents' travelling abroad.

Business travel visits

Since 1977, the numbers of overseas residents' visits to the UK and UK residents' visits abroad for the main purpose of business have both increased by over three-hundred fold (Figure 4.1). In 1977, 2.142 million overseas residents entered the UK for business, a number which had swelled by +321 per cent to 9.019 million by 2006, and during this same period, for UK residents' business visits abroad, the percentage increase was +318 per cent, from 2.154 to 9.102 million (Table 4.1). Rapid increases in business travel for both groups of travellers occurred from the mid-1980s, and from 2001, the annual rate of growth of business visits for both

---

into the UK for an overseas visitor may be recorded as London (via LHR), the actual place of business may involve multiple visits to Reading, Cambridge and Loughborough, UK), which will remain unrecorded. Equally, it may be recorded that the destination of a UK resident for business purposes is the US, but the business activity may occur in one than one city, which again remains unrecorded or in the public domain. Despite many limitations of using the IPS data for analysing business travel trends, it must be noted that its major strength is that is does provide an 'official' measure of business visits and trends to and from the UK which can be used to trace patterns of such mobility alongside other data sets and primary findings.

overseas residents' visiting the UK and UK residents' travelling abroad has been each approximately 5.1 per cent per annum (ONS 2006). Interestingly, the trend lines for both groups of visitors have bucked the global economic cycles with growth recorded in every year since 1977, including the recession of the early 1980s, with the exception of the 2000/2001 period which included the period of the dot.com crash and September 11th attacks in the US, and 2003 (linked to foot and mouth disease in the UK). The most rapid period of five-year growth in business travel for both groups of visitors was during the 1985-1990 period, where the volume of business travel visits increased by +48 per cent for overseas residents' visits to the UK and +50 per cent for UK residents' visits abroad (Table 4.1), but it is interesting to note that from 2003 to 2006, a +29 per cent jump in business travel was recorded for overseas residents' visits to the UK (from 6.967m to 9.019m) which mirrored the period of the expansion of the European Union and a boom in the usage and coverage of the European low cost airline industry (see Mason 2000, Graham and Shaw 2008, Williams and Balaz 2008).

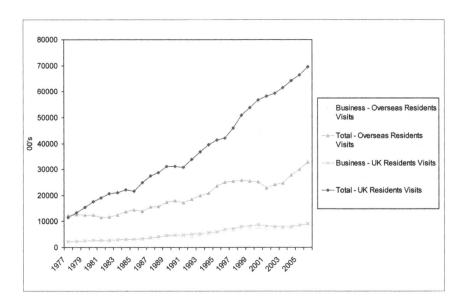

Figure 4.1 Overseas residents' visits to the UK and UK residents' visits abroad, 1977-2006
Source: ONS (1995, 1998, 2003, 2007).

Table 4.1 Business visit trends (000s), 1977-2006

	UK residents' visits abroad		Overseas residents' visits to the UK	
	Visits	% change from previous period	Visits	% change from previous period
1977	2,154	–	2,142	–
1980	2,690	+25	2,567	+20
1985	3,188	+19	3,014	+17
1990	4,769	+50	4,461	+48
1995	6,113	+28	5,763	+29
2000	8,872	+45	7,322	+27
2005	8,556	+4	8,168	+12
2006	9,102	+6	9,019	+10
Growth (77-06)		+318		+321

Source: ONS (1997, 2007).

Men are the dominant faction of business visitors for both overseas residents' visits to the UK and UK residents' travelling abroad (Figure 4.2). Year-on-year since 1996, men have accounted for about an 80 per cent share of business visits for both groups of travellers (ONS 1997 to 2007) and in 2006 the figures stood at an 81 per cent share of overseas residents' visiting the UK (7.274m) and a 79 per cent share of UK residents' going abroad (7.227m) (ONS 2007). In terms of growth, for both groups of visitors, the numbers of female business visits are growing relatively faster than their male counterparts. Between 1996 and 2006, the number of female business visits grew by +91 per cent for overseas residents' visiting the UK (compared to +40 per cent for men), from 0.955m to 1.745m, and +43 per cent for female UK residents' leaving the UK (compared to +30 per cent for men), from 1.307m to 1.875m (Figure 4.2, ONS 1997 to 2007).

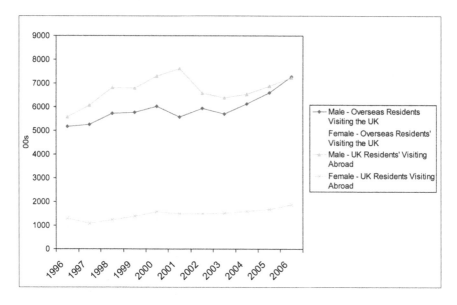

Figure 4.2 Overseas residents' visits to the UK and UK residents' visits abroad by gender, 1996-2006

Source: ONS (1998, 2001, 2004, 2007).

Mode of travel for business visits

Contrary to popular belief, business travel visits are not solely undertaken by air, as visitors also enter and leave the UK by sea and channel tunnel (Eurostar rail service to mainland Europe). But, air travel has always been the most important mode of transport for business travel to and from the UK for both groups of visitors (Figures 4.3 and 4.4, Table 4.2).[3] In 2006, air accounted for 73 per cent of the share of all business travel visits to the UK from residents overseas, but this proportion had reduced from 80 per cent ten years earlier (due primarily from Eurostar channel tunnel competition) (Table 4.2). During this same time period, from 1996 to 2006, business visits to the UK by air from overseas residents increased by +34 per cent from 4.896 million to 6.571 million, but a much higher increase was experienced by channel tunnel and the use of Eurostar of the magnitude of +105 per cent, from 0.481 million to 0.984 million. In contrast, air remains the most important mode of travel for UK residents visiting abroad for business purposes. In 1996, air accounted for 70 per cent of the share of all UK residents' business visits abroad, which had increased to 82 per cent ten years later. Indeed, whilst the number of

---

3   As the Channel Tunnel became fully operational from the mid-1990s, this part of the data analysis will report the main trends in air, sea and rail modes of business travel over a ten year period from 1996.

travellers using air as the mode of travel had increased by +46 per cent from 5.552 million to 7.499 million between 1996 and 2006, during the same period business travel using Eurostar channel tunnel had only grown by +10 per cent, from 0.666 million to 0.890 million, but it is important to note that this is directed specifically in the Paris-Brussels corridor and not European wide as reflected in the air data. It is most also be noted that the European low cost airline industry has had a significant effect on travel in the region (Williams and Balaz 2008).

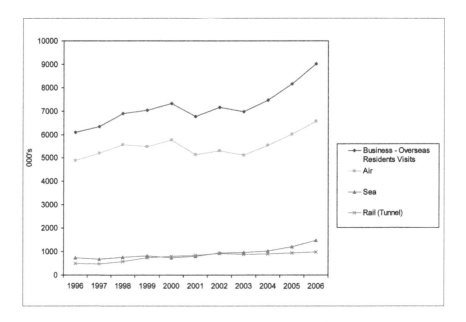

Figure 4.3 Overseas residents' business visits to the UK by mode of travel, 1996-2006

Source: ONS (2001, 2004, 2007).

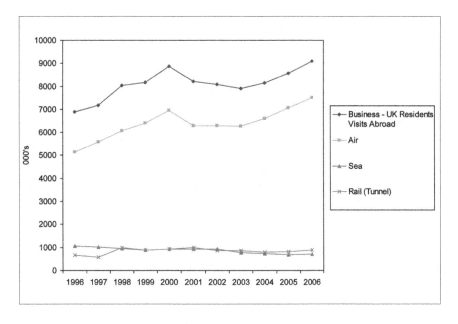

Figure 4.4 UK residents' business visits abroad by mode of travel, 1996-2006
Source: ONS (2001, 2004, 2007).

**Table 4.2 Overseas residents' and UK residents' business visits,
by mode of travel, 1996-2006 (000s)**

Overseas residents' business visits to the UK

	1996	1998	2000	2002	2004	2006
Air	4,896	5,555	5,776	5,297	5,536	6,571
Sea	745	756	741	947	1,032	1,464
Tunnel	481	571	804	914	902	984
Total	6,095	6,882	7,322	7,158	7,470	9,019

UK residents' business visits abroad

	1996	1998	2000	2002	2004	2006
Air	5,152	6,077	6,946	6,281	6,604	7,499
Sea	1,061	955	933	926	732	712
Tunnel	666	1,000	933	866	804	890
Total	6,879	8,033	8,872	8,073	8,140	9,102

Source: ONS (2001, 2004, 2007).

Spending (£ millions) and length of visits

Travel Trends data for all visits indicated that 2006 experienced record amounts of money being spend on visits to the UK and abroad by both groups of visitors, topping £16 and £34.4 billions respectively (Table 4.3). Spending by overseas residents to the UK for business purposes has increased by +268 per cent since 1985, from £1.293 to £4.753 billions, and it share of all spending has increased from 24 per cent in 1985 to 30 per cent in 2006. Moreover, when the data are analysed for average spending per day for overseas residents' in the UK, more spending is made per business day than for holidays and VFRs, which in 2006 was £122, £67 and £35 respectively, and the highest spend per day for business, comes from overseas residents who are from North America (£202), followed by Europe (EU25) (£109) (ONS 2007, Table 2.06). In 2006, the highest average money spent per day on a business visit to the UK was from those residents of Tunisia (£228), Iceland (£227), Cyprus (£211), Norway (£210) and the USA (£209) (ONS 2007, Table 4.05). Not surprisingly, the most money spent on business travel by overseas residents was those who visited London, which accounted for £2.6 billion in 2006, which was over half of all business visit spending (55 per cent) in 2006 (ONS 2007, Table 2.06).

Whist the total share of spending on business travel visits has declined as a proportion of all spending for UK residents' who travel abroad (from 22 per cent in 1985 to 15 per cent in 2006), spending by UK residents' abroad has increased by +371 per cent over the period, from just over £1 billion to about £5 billion (Table 4.3). Again, as with overseas residents' visiting the UK, when the data are analysed for average spending per day, more spending is made by UK residents abroad on business visits (£108), followed by holiday (£52) and VFRs (£24), with the highest daily spend per to North America (£124) and Europe (EU25) (£113) (ONS 2007, Table 3.06). In 2006, the most expensive average spend per day for a business visit for UK residents' visiting abroad were to Hong Kong (£167), Luxembourg (£159), Denmark (£148), Finland (£141), and the Czech Republic (£138).

Turning to the duration of stay of business visits for both groups of travellers (as measured in nights away), those overseas residents' who travel from Other Countries to the UK and those UK residents' who travel to Other Countries have consistently been away from their place of resident for the most nights during the 2000s (Figures 4.5 and 4.6), where distance travelled is an important discriminator for the length of stay. In 2006, for overseas residents' visits to the UK for business purposes, those who stayed in the UK for the longest periods of time came from places where business travel might have been linked closely to VFRs, for example, Jamaica (46 nights), India (25 nights), Thailand (14 nights), Other Africa (including West Africa – 14 nights) and Pakistan (13 nights). The length of stay away from places like Australia and New Zealand (9 nights), Hong Kong (6 nights), Japan (6 nights), the USA (5 nights) were relatively short given there distance from the UK, and in Europe the relatively longer visits (for more than 4 nights) came from eastern European destinations (ONS 2007, Table 4.05). In 2006, on the whole, the duration of visits of UK residents' around the world were more than the stay of overseas residents' to the UK, respectively, 5.2 nights compared to 4.3 nights (see ONS 2007, Tables 2.05 and 3.05). The longest length of stay of 29 and 23 nights away for business purposes were recorded for Barbados and Israel (perhaps both also associated with VFRs and, or business tourism), but in general, the length of stay away from the UK matched the distance travelled (New Zealand 20 days; Thailand 18; Hong Kong 16; Australia 14; the Middle East 12 (excluding UAE); US 8). In Europe, whilst the average length of stay away from the UK was 3.5 nights, UK business visitors to Belgium only stayed two nights in 2006, the lowest recorded for all destinations (ONS 2007, Table 5.05).[4]

Table 4.3 Business visits by spending (£m), 1985-2006

Overseas residents' business visits and spending in the UK				
Year	Visits	Spending	% of total spend	Total spend
1985	3,014	1,293	24	5,442
1990	4,461	2,174	28	7,748
1995	5,763	3,219	27	11,763
2000	7,322	4,048	32	12,805
2005	8,168	4,055	28	14,248
2006	9,019	4,753	30	16,002

UK residents' business visits and spending abroad				
Year	Visits	Spending	% of total spend	Total spend
1985	3,188	1,075	22	4,781
1990	4,769	1,836	19	9,886
1995	6,113	2,974	19	15,386
2000	8,872	4,732	20	24,251
2005	8,556	4,611	14	32,154
2006	9,102	5,067	15	34,411

Source: ONS (1997, 2000, 2003, 2007).

---

4   From this date, it is impossible to determine a relationship between duration of visit and function or purpose of business travel, especially as travelling longer distances, for example East or West between continents, builds in extra time to allow for the inconveniences of jet-lag and gaining/losing days when crossing significant time-zones, and also may involve VFRs and, or business tourism (see Kellerman this volume). Indeed, case study evidence from many financial and professional service firms indicates that the purpose of business travel from London to Frankfurt (which might involve an overnight stay) or from London to Hong Kong or Singapore (which may be several days) may actually be the same, for example to visit clients in situ, attend meetings with work colleagues in the firm's international office or for training purposes (see Beaverstock 2006, Faulconbridge and Beaverstock 2008).

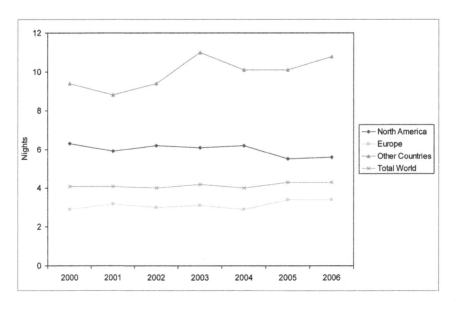

Figure 4.5 Average length of stay for overseas residents' business visits in the UK by region of residence, 2000-2006

Source: ONS (2001, 2002, 2003, 2004, 2005, 2006, 2007).

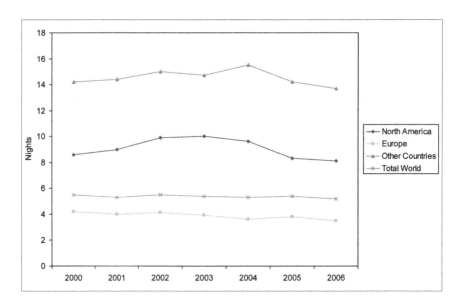

Figure 4.6 Average length of stay abroad for UK residents' business visits by region of visit, 2000-2006

Source: ONS (2001, 2002, 2003, 2004, 2005, 2006, 2007).

The geography of business travel visits:
Overseas residents' visits to the UK and UK residents' business visits abroad

An analysis of business travel visits for both groups of visitors from 1993 to 2006 reveals three key trends (Table 4.4). First, Europe (EU15) is the most important regional destination and region of residence for business visits as a proportion of all business visits for both overseas and UK residents. Over this period, Europe (EU15) has been the source of an average of 66 per cent of the total share of overseas residents' business visits to the UK, compared to an average of 72 per cent for UK residents' business visits to Europe. In 2006, Europe (EU25-EU15 and Other Europe) accounted for 72 per cent of all overseas business visits to the UK and a 78 per cent share of all UK residents' business visits abroad.

Table 4.4 Number of business visits by destination and region of residence (000s), 1993-2006

Overseas residents' business visits to the UK by region of residence

	1993	1995	1997	1999	2001	2003	2005	2006	Growth
North America	663	731	809	935	847	803	898	983	+48%
Europe (EU15)	3,035	3,755	4,240	4,631	4,486	4,686	5,038	5,430	+79%
Other Europe	428	521	579	696	712	814	1,426	1,048	+145%
Other Countries	582	757	719	782	734	664	806	871	+50%
Total World	**4,706**	**5,763**	**6,347**	**7,044**	**6,778**	**6,967**	**8,168**	**9,019**	**+92%**

UK residents' business visits by region of visit

	1993	1995	1997	1999	2001	2003	2005	2006	Growth
North America	479	573	646	810	834	720	855	921	+92%
Europe (EU15)	3,893	4,489	5,226	5,871	5,979	5,720	5,839	5,968	+53%
Other Europe	522	534	635	787	251	260	318	397	-24%
Other Countries	403	517	659	693	655	683	919	1,083	+169%
Total World	**5,297**	**6,113**	**7,166**	**8,161**	**8,220**	**7,892**	**8,556**	**9,102**	**+70%**

Source: ONS (1998, 2007).

Second, there has been an increase in all business visits to and from the U.K. for overseas and UK residents' respectively, with sharp increases in Other Europe for overseas residents' business visits to the UK (+145 per cent) and UK residents' business visits to Other Countries (+169 per cent) (Table 4.4) (ONS 2007). A fine grain analysis of the geography of business travel visits for 1995 and 2006, shows that France, Germany, the USA, EIRE and the Netherlands dominate the highest proportional share of region of residence and country of visit for overseas residents' visits to the UK (Table 4.5) and UK residents' visits abroad, respectively (Table 4.6). In contrast, an analysis of the highest percentage growth rates in the country of residence for overseas business visits to the UK and country of destination for UK residents' abroad since the opening of the EU in 2003 (comparing ONS data from 2004 to 2006), indicates the importance of the Accession States like Poland and emerging markets like Mexico, Other China (excluding Hong Kong) and India (ONS 2005, 2007) (Figures 4.7 and 4.8).

Table 4.5 Number of overseas residents' business visits to the UK by the top ten countries of residence (000s), 1995 and 2006

Residence (business visits, % of total business visits)	
1995	**2006**
France (817, 14%)	Germany (1,160, 13%)
USA (693, 12%)	France (1,040, 12%)
Germany (652, 11%)	USA (880, 10%)
EIRE (590, 10%)	Netherlands (656, 7%)
Netherlands (447, 8%)	EIRE (637, 7%)
Belgium (317, 5%)	Poland (500, 6%)
Italy (272, 5%)	Spain (444, 5%)
Eastern Europe (196, 3%)	Italy (429, 5%)
Spain (187, 3%)	Belgium (365, 4%)
Switzerland (146, 2%)	Switzerland (247, 3%)
Total World (5,895)	**Total World (9,019)**

Source: ONS (1996, 2007).

**Table 4.6 Number of UK residents' business visits by country of visit (000s),
1995 and 2006**

Country (business visits, % of visits)	
1995	**2006**
France (1,115, 18%)	France (1,316, 14%)
Germany (898, 14%)	Germany (1,015, 11%)
EIRE (603, 10%)	USA (842, 9%)
USA (552, 9%)	EIRE (799, 9%)
Netherlands (486, 8%)	Netherlands (736, 8%)
Belgium (426, 7%)	Belgium (521, 6%)
Italy (299, 5%)	Spain (479, 5%)
Spain (262, 4%)	Italy (405, 4%)
E. Europe (208, 3%)	Switzerland (341, 4%)
Switzerland (182, 3%)	Denmark (170, 2%)
Total World (6,113, 100%)	**Total World (9,102, 100%)**

Source: ONS (1996, 2007).

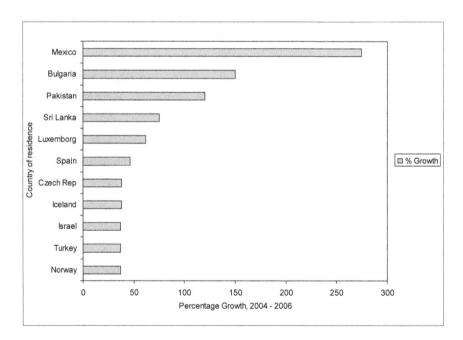

**Figure 4.7 Percentage growth in overseas residents' business visits to the
UK by country of residence, 2004-2006**
Source: ONS (2005, 2007).

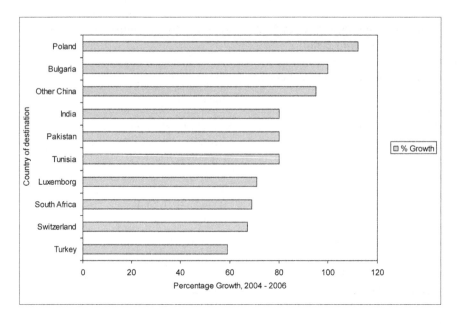

Figure 4.8 Percentage growth in UK residents' business visits abroad, 2004-2006
Source: ONS (2005, 2007).

Third, an analysis of the first destination country and area of visit for overseas residents' business visits to the UK shows the importance of England, and London especially, as a destination for visits to the UK (Table 4.7). For both 1995 and 2006, London received the highest share of overseas residents' business visits to the UK which accounted for 43 per cent and 41 per cent of all business visits, respectively. In 1995 and 2005, four regional destinations, London, the West Midlands, Manchester and Berkshire accounted for over 50 per cent of all overseas residents' business visits to the UK (Table 4.7).

As with other work on UK official migration and mobility statistics (Findlay and Li 1999), too many assumptions are often needed to interpret its geography and *functionality*. Consequently, whilst data providing a general overview of the major patterns and trends in business travel visits to and from the UK are helpful, we suggest that a more nuanced and sophisticated understanding is likely to emerge from analyses of 'unofficial' business travel data. We exemplify this argument by drawing upon two important unofficial data sources: the Corporation of London's survey of business travel in the City of London; and the Barclaycard Business Travel Survey.

**Table 4.7 Overseas residents' business visits to the UK by country and by
top ten areas of visit (000s), 1995 and 2006**

Country of visit	Visits (% of all visits)		Growth (%)
	1995	2006	
England	3,753 (65%)	7,188 (80%)	+92%
Scotland	261 (5%)	415 (5%)	+59%
Wales	94 (2%)	226 (3%)	+140%
Other	1,165 (18%)	1,190 (13%)	+2%

Area of business visits (visits, % share of all visits)

	1995		2006
London	2,541 (43%)	London	3,659 (41%)
West Midlands	296 (5%)	West Midlands	529 (6%)
Manchester	194 (3%)	Manchester	420 (5%)
Berkshire	152 (3%)	Berkshire	232 (3%)
Surrey	142 (2%)	Merseyside	195 (2%)
Cambridgeshire	124 (2%)	West Yorkshire	191 (2%)
Hampshire	116 (2%)	Surrey	181 (2%)
Kent	110 (2%)	Oxfordshire	172 (2%)
Lothian	109 (2%)	Kent	163 (2%)
Strathclyde	106 (2%)	Hampshire	145 (2%)

Source: ONS (1996, 2007).

'Unofficial' Business Travel Data:
The Corporation of London and Barclaycard Business Travel Surveys

Many private organizations, usually consultancies, undertake primary data
collection on business travel for an array of industries whose existence is linked
closely to the spending and multiplier-effects of business travel in the global
economy. Two highly-informative analyses of business travel have been undertaken
by York Aviation, using Civil Aviation Authority (CAA) business passenger data,
for the Corporation of London (the Local Government Authority for the City of
London) and the Future Foundation for Barclaycard.

Business travel and the City of London

The Corporation of London's (2008) latest report on *Aviation Services and the
City*, uses CAA Departing Passenger Data for 2003 and 2006 to investigate the
use of air services for UK and foreign business class travel (single journeys) by
firms based in the City of London, covering five airports (London City, Heathrow,

Gatwick, Luton and Stansted). Several key trends can be identified from these data. First, with respect to the number of business passengers, in 2006 there were an estimated 1.268 million UK and foreign passengers travelling to or from their City office engaged in business, which was a +1 per cent increase from 1.262 in 2000. During this same period, an estimated 8.866 million UK and foreign business passengers entered or left the CLBD, a +6 per cent increase from 8.349 million in 2000. If departures from the passengers' home residence are included in these data (rather than the place of work as stated above), it has been estimated that the 'true' demand for UK and foreign business passenger air travel to and from the City was 2.658 million passengers in 2006, compared to 2.011 million in 2000 (+32 per cent). If these places of home departures are included in the CLBD figures, then 13.75 million international business passengers entered or left the region in 2006, compared to 11.70 million in 2000 (+18 per cent) (Corporation of London 2008, see Tables 10, 11 and 12).

Second, in terms of the main industrial activities of the UK and foreign business passengers coming into and from the City, by far the largest segment of passengers were employed in banking and business services, which accounted for 72 per cent of all total responding passengers (751,972), followed those employed in Government and Other Services (8 per cent of the total share, 79,841) (Corporation of London 2008, see Table 16).

Third, and of great importance, the CAA Survey used in the Corporation of London's (2008) report outlines the main purpose of an individual passenger's business travel to and from the City of London, by country of residence, either UK, EU or Other (the rest of the world) (Table 4.8). By far, the two most important reasons for engaging in business travel from all countries of residence were: attending international company business (which represented 39 per cent of the total number of passengers); and for meetings with customers/others external to the business (representing 38 per cent of the total share). Moreover, the Corporation of London's (2008) report suggests that there has been little change in these reasons for the demand of business travel from 2000 and 2003. Fourth, an analysis of the points of departure to and entry from the City of London and CLBD indicates the significance of travel to and from the EU (accounting for 50 per cent and 45 per cent of City and CLBD business traffic respectively), followed by internal, domestic travel (23 per cent for the City and 18 per cent for CLBD) (Table 4.9), where the top destinations for City of London business passengers were Edinburgh (15 per cent), Dublin (11 per cent), Amsterdam (9 per cent), Frankfurt (9 per cent) and New York, JFK (8 per cent) (Table 4.10) (Corporation of London 2008).

Table 4.8 Detailed purpose of business travel, 2006

Purpose	UK	EU	Other	Total	% of total
Attending internal company business	199,236	162,944	144,473	506,652	39
Meetings with customer/ others external to the company	206,689	184,528	99,445	490,662	38
Conference/Congress	38,572	49,037	33,555	121,164	9
Trade fair/Exhibition	5,782	4,319	2,532	12,682	1
Contract Home Leave	4,773	5,784	124	10,682	1
Overseas Employment – less than 12 months	4,504	5,219	0	9,723	1
Studies paid by employer – formal academic course	304	1,445	3,712	5,461	<1
Studies paid by employer – other course	0	1,590	2,084	3,674	<1
Airline Staff	1,187	320	58	1,565	<1
Sub-total of detailed responses	461,046	415,186	285,983	1,162,215	90
Business (no detail)	48,584	26,908	48,703	124,194	10
Total	**509,630**	**442,094**	**334,686**	**1,286,410**	**100**

Source: CAA Departing Passenger Survey 2006 quoted in the Corporation of London (2008, Table 17).

Table 4.9 City of London and CLBD business passenger origins/destinations, 2006

	City	% of City	CLBD	% of CLBD
Domestic	291,381	23	1,624,567	18
European Union	638,878	50	4,102,402	46
North America	143,508	11	1,246,226	14
Other W. Europe	108,487	8	644,235	7
Asia & Australasia	36,244	3	428,858	5
Eastern Europe	29,053	2	380,100	4
Middle East/N.Africa	20,845	2	238,175	3
Other Africa	13,365	1	149,710	2
Caribbean/Latin America	4,650	<1	46,478	1
Total	**1,286,410**	**100**	**8,860,751**	**100**

Source: Corporation of London (2008, adapted from Tables 18 and 19).

Table 4.10 Top 20 destinations for City of London business passengers, 2006

Destination	Passengers	% of total passengers
Edinburgh	118,796	15
Dublin	86,177	11
Amsterdam	77,135	9
Frankfurt	69,914	9
New York JFK	69,470	8
Glasgow	57,377	7
Zurich	54,067	7
Milan Linate	34,123	4
Munich	30,678	4
Manchester	24,702	3
Dusseldorf	23,445	3
Copenhagen	23,363	3
Rotterdam	23,090	3
Geneva	22,123	3
New York EWK	21,003	3
Belfast	19,018	2
Stockholm Arlanda	18,026	2
Paris Orly	15,743	2
Brussels	14,866	2
Milan Malpensa	14,694	2
Total	**817,808**	**100**
% of total travel	**63.6**	
Grand total	**1,286,410**	

Source: CAA Departing Passenger Survey 2006 cited in the The Corporation of London (2008, adapted from Table 24).

The Barclaycard Business Travel Survey 2005/06

The Barclaycard Business Travel Survey, undertaken by The Future Foundation (2006), was derived from a survey of 2,500 Barclaycard Business commercial cardholders (for example, CEOs, Directors, sole traders) in order to track the current state of the business travel industry and predict what the industry might experience in 2015. The report highlights several key findings for 2005/06:

i.   the typical male business traveller, aged between 41 and 65, is married with children, in a managerial position, travelling on business 2.5 days per week, and covering on average 662 miles and being away from home 4.3 nights per month;

ii.   the typical female business traveller is aged between 31 and 40, married, in a managerial position, will travel for 2.2 days per week, covering an average of 335 miles and being away 3.8 nights per month;

iii.   45 per cent of business travellers said that they travelled more for business in 2005/06 than 2004/05, with 51 per cent of the sample reporting that this was due to business expansion overseas (33 per cent) and in the UK (18 per cent);

iv.   distance travelled for business travel per month had decreased from 642 miles in 2004/05 to 608.5 in 2005/06, and the number of days spent travelling per week had fallen slightly to 2.4 (from 2.5), and a quarter of the sample had suggested that they were travelling less on business travel because of the substitution effect of technology (25 per cent);

v.   37 per cent of the business travellers preferred to travel by car, followed by rail (32 per cent) and air (29 per cent);

vi.   for air travel, 43 per cent of travel for business was undertaken in Standard/ Economy, with only 17 per cent in Business Class and 30 per cent using a low-cost provider (for example Easyjet, BMI Baby), and those who did fly for business purposes were much more likely to use business class for long (33 per cent) rather than short-haul flights (10 per cent);

vii.   on average, business travellers spent £99.60 (outside London) or £115.70 (in London) on a hotel in 2005/06, with 58 per cent of the sample using a budget hotel to save costs

viii.   the most important technologies used by business travellers during their journey were (with multiple-answers): laptops and mobile phones (66 per cent); and facilities to enable remote access to email (40 per cent).

Looking towards 2015, the report predicts that:

i.   the continual requirement to engage in face-to-face contact will mean that business travel will increase by 17 per cent, with travellers clocking up an average of 712 miles per month as the increase is travel is driven by continued overseas expansion of business;

ii.   business travel using air is set to increase for an individual by 12 per cent to an average of 8.5 flights per year, with distance travelled getting much longer, fuelling the requirement for more long-haul flights;

iii.   rail travel will be reduced by at least 10 per cent as people substitute travelling short journeys for new technologies.

The report concludes by suggesting that,

while technology is encouraging remote and virtual interactions, face-to-face contact will still continue to be important in 2015. It is believed that business across international borders incurs issues such as cultural or language barriers and incompatible time zones all of which are better overcome with face-to-face

contact. There is a sense that remote communication – even with visual presence
– cannot replace face-to-face contact. (Future Foundation 2006: 20)

In tandem, these two 'unofficial' reports, derived from the airline industry and
business travellers themselves, shows clearly that the process of business travel
is, and will remain, a fundamental working pattern in contemporary society as
the requirement to physically travel to engage in business with customers and
clients or for intra-company business, will not be diminished by improvements
in ICT and other communication technologies. Moreover, the future implications
of an increased frequency and duration of business travel as firms continue to
expand abroad, as reported in the Barclaycard Survey, are quite stark from an
environmental perspective.

Conclusions

'Official' and 'unofficial' data on business travel provide, then, a number of
important insights into the volumes, origins, destinations and duration of business
travel as well as some insights into the identity of travellers and their motivations
for travel. In many ways, then, it helps confirm the ideas in existing literatures
about: (1) the necessity of business travel and its growing importance over the
past 20 years in TNCs; (2) the managerial function of many business travel trips;
and (3) the major challenges associated with reducing volumes of business travel.
Yet these data do not help us develop new answers to key questions such as how
business travel can be used more effectively alongside virtual communication, or
how travel can effect relationships between subsidiaries in TNCs. Indeed, existing
data do not even reveal a full picture of who is travelling and the major trends in
origin/destination of travel.

It would seem, therefore, that a two-fold challenge exists. First, to develop
more comprehensive quantitative databases of the geographies of business travel.
The will inevitably require firm-level studies that can be used to extrapolate
broader trends at industry-levels. Second, in-depth qualitative studies are needed
that offer greater insight into how the purpose of travel, who travels to/from
where, how often they travel, how long they travel for and how travel is used
alongside virtual communication all effect the success and outcomes of business
travel. Only with the development of such work that focuses squarely on business
travel and all of its uses are we likely to get a more detailed understanding of
how mobility now pervades business life. Similarly such work would allow both
more sophisticated academic theoretical explanations of business travel and policy
recommendations about ways to support but also encourage the management and
reduction of travel. We would argue that any future theoretical explanation of
business travel must engage in a number of substantive issues, like for example
the need to understand:

- the definition, role, function and purpose of business travel within the organization and between the organization and its clients, customers and suppliers, which may change depending on different sectors and firm cultures;
- the role that ICT has in reducing or perpetuating the requirement to physically travel for business purposes;
- the inter-relationships between business travel and business tourism;
- the concept of the 'mobile worker', who engages in both repetitive and more specialized business activities;
- how age, gender, race and nationality reproduces different practices and forms of business travel;
- the major differences and practices of business travel in the private and public sectors of economy;
- the physical, psychological and personal effects that occasional and constant business travel has on the individual and their social lives and work-life balance;
- the impacts that business travel has on infrastructure capacity and the environment.

It seems, then, that there is much theoretical an empirical research work still complete on the topic of business travel.

References

Bartlett, C. and Ghoshal, S. 1998. *Managing Across Borders: The Transnational Solution.* London: Random House.

Beaverstock, J.V. 2006. World city networks from below: International mobility and inter-city relations in the global investment banking industry, in *Cities in Globalization: Practices, Policies, Theories*, edited by P.J. Taylor, B. Derudder, P. Saey and F. Witlox. London: Routledge, 52-71.

Beaverstock, J.V., Smith, R. and Taylor, P.J. 1999. The long arm of the law: London's law firms in a globalising world economy. *Environment and Planning A*, 13(10), 1857-1876.

Boden, D. and Molotch, H. 1994. The compulsion of proximity, in *NowHere. Space, Time and Modernity*, edited by R. Friedland and D. Boden. Berkeley: University of California Press, 257-286.

Christopherson, S. 2007. Barriers to 'US style' lean retailing: The case of Wal-Mart's failure in Germany. *Journal of Economic Geography*, 7(4), 451-469.

Coe, N. and Yong-Sook, L. 2006. The strategic localization of transnational retailers: The case of Samsung-Tesco in South Korea. *Economic Geography*, 82(1), 61-88.

Corporation of London 2008. *Aviation Services and the City*. London: Corporation of London, Guildhall.

Denstadli, J. and Gripsrud, M. This volume.

Dicken, P., Kelly, P.F., Olds, K. and Yeung, H.W.-C. 2001. Chains and network, territories and scales: Towards a relational framework for analysing the global economy. *Global Networks*, 1(2), 89-112.

Dunning, J. and Norman, G. 1983. Theory of multinational enterprise. *Environment and Planning A*, 15(5), 675-692.

Faulconbridge, J.R. 2006. Stretching tacit knowledge beyond a local fix? Global spaces of learning in advertising professional service firms. *Journal of Economic Geography*, 6(4), 517-540.

Faulconbridge, J.R. 2008. Managing the transnational law firm: A relational analysis of professional systems, embedded actors and time-space sensitive governance. *Economic Geography*, 84(2), 185-210.

Faulconbridge, J.R. and Beaverstock, J.V. 2008. Geographies of international business travel in the professional service economy, in *Mobility, Technology and the Workplace*, edited by D. Hislop. London: Routledge, 99-121.

Faulconbridge, J.R. and Muzio, D. 2008. Organizational professionalism in globalizing law firms. *Work, Employment and Society*, 22(1), 7-25.

Ferner, A., Quintanilla, J. and Sanchez-Runde, C. 2006. Introduction: Multinationals and the multilevel politics of cross-national diffusion, in *Multinationals, Institutions and the Construction of Transnational Practices. Convergence and Diversity in the Global Economy*, edited by A. Ferner, J. Quintanilla and C. Sanchez-Runde. Basingstoke: Palgrave Macmillan, 1-24.

Findlay, A.M. and Li, F.L.N. 1999. Methodological issues in researching migration. *The Professional Geographer*, 51(1), 50-59.

Forlano, L. 2008. Working on the move, in *Mobility and Technology in the Workplace*, edited by D. Hislop. London: Routledge, 28-42.

Frandberg, L. and Vilhelmson, B. 2003. Personal mobility: A corporeal dimension of transnationalisation. *Environment and Planning A*, 35(9), 1565-1587.

Future Foundation 2006. *The Barclaycard Business Travel Survey 2005/06*, http://www.barclaycardbusiness.co.uk/information_zone/travel, last accessed 29/09/08.

Graham, B. and Shaw, J. 2008. Low-cost airlines in Europe: Reconciling liberalization and sustainability. *Geoforum*, 39(3), 1439-1451.

Goffman, E. 1967. *Interaction Ritual: Essays on Face to Face Behaviour*. New York: Doubleday and Company.

Grabher, G. 2001. Ecologies of creativity: The village, the group and the heterarchic organisation of the British advertising industry. *Environment and Planning A*, 33(2), 351-374.

Henry, N. and Pinch, S. 2000. Spatialising knowledge: Placing the knowledge community of Motor Sport Valley. *Geoforum*, 31(2), 191-208.

Hess, M. 2004. Spatial relationships? Towards a reconceptualization of embeddedness. *Progress in Human Geography*, 28(2), 165-186.

Hislop, D. 2008. *Mobility, Technology and the Workplace*. London: Routledge.

Jones, A. 2002. The global city misconceived: The myth of 'global management' in transnational service firms. *Geoforum*, 33(3), 335-350.

Jones, A. 2005. Truly global corporations? Theorizing organizational globalisation in advanced business-services. *Journal of Economic Geography*, 5(2), 177-200.

Jones, A. 2007. More than 'managing across borders?' The complex role of face-to-face interaction in globalizing law firms. *Journal of Economic Geography*, 7(3), 223-246.

Jones, A. 2008. Beyond embeddedness: Economic practices and the invisible dimensions of transnational business activity. *Progress in Human Geography*, 32(1), 71-88.

Jones, A. This volume.

Kellerman, A. This volume.

Liu, W. and Dicken, P. 2006. Transnational corporations and 'obligated embeddedness': Foreign direct investment in China's automobile industry. *Environment and Planning A*, 38(7), 1229-1247.

Mason, K.J. 2000. The propensity of business travellers to use low-cost airlines *Journal of Transport Geography*, 8(1), 107-119.

Millar, J. and Salt, J. 2008. Portfolios of mobility: The movement of expertise in transnational corporations in two sectors-aerospace and extractive industries. *Global Networks*, 8(1), 25-50.

Office for National Statistics 2007. *Travel Trends 2006.* HMSO, London.

Office for National Statistics 2006. *Travel Trends 2005.* HMSO, London.

Office for National Statistics 2005. *Travel Trends 2004.* HMSO, London.

Office for National Statistics 2004. *Travel Trends 2003.* HMSO, London.

Office for National Statistics 2003. *Travel Trends 2002.* HMSO, London.

Office for National Statistics 2002. *Travel Trends 2001.* HMSO, London.

Office for National Statistics 2001. *Travel Trends 2000.* HMSO, London.

Office for National Statistics 2000. *Travel Trends 1999.* HMSO, London.

Office for National Statistics 1999. *Travel Trends 1998.* HMSO, London.

Office for National Statistics 1998. *Travel Trends 1997.* HMSO, London.

Office for National Statistics 1997. *Travel Trends 1996.* HMSO, London.

Office for National Statistics 1996. *Travel Trends 1995.* HMSO, London.

Orlikowski, W. 2002. Knowing in practice: Enacting a collective capability in distributed organizing. *Organization Science*, 13(3), 249-273.

Sklair, L. 2001. *The Transnational Capitalist Class.* Oxford: Blackwell.

Storper, M. and Venables, A.J. 2004. Buzz: face-to-face contact and the urban economy. *Journal of Economic Geography*, 4(4), 351-370.

Urry, J. 2003. Social networks, travel and talk. *British Journal of Sociology*, 54(2), 155-175.

Urry, J. 2007. *Mobilities.* Cambridge: Polity.

Williams, A.M. and Balaz, V. 2008 Low-cost carriers, economies of flow and regional externalities. *Regional Studies*, forthcoming.

Wrigley, N., Coe, N. and Currah, A. 2005. Globalizing retail: Conceptualizing the distribution-based transnational corporation (TNC). *Progress in Human Geography*, 29(4), 437-457.

Yeung, H.W.-C. 2005. Rethinking relational economic geography. *Transactions of the Institute of British Geographers NS*, 30(1), 37-51.

Yeung, H.W.-C. 2009. Transnationalizing entrepreneurship: A critical agenda for economic geography. *Progress in Human Geography*, forthcoming.

Chapter 5

The 'Bizjet Set': Business Aviation and the Social Geographies of Private Flight

Lucy Budd and Phil Hubbard

Introduction

It has become something of a cliché – in geography textbooks, at least – to speak of a 'shrinking' world in which communication advances and improvements in enabling technologies are eroding the frictional effects of distance. The sheer increase in passenger numbers and freight movement by air is often presented as the key evidence for this, being indicative of the increasingly routine and frequent nature of flying. The development of new airports, the construction of additional runways, and the provision of new air routes are also grist to the mill for those who identify aeromobility as a key indicator of our 'global times'. More nuanced accounts, however, look beneath the surface of such statistics to draw a rather different conclusion: air travel may be becoming more frequent for some, but this not the case for the vast majority of citizens. As Cresswell (2006) makes clear, airports are not only spaces of the transnational business elites whose lifestyles can be described as truly global, but also the space of vacationers, nervous first-time flyers, immigrants, drug smugglers, and a multitude of cleaners, shop assistants, and maintenance staff, many of whom remain resolutely rooted in national-spaces, lacking either the means or inclination to fly.

Accordingly, we begin our chapter from the standpoint that although the world may be becoming smaller for some this is the exception rather than the norm. Alongside speed, there is slowness; alongside the frequent flyer, there are millions – possibly billions – who are unable to access air travel and benefit from the expansion of air services. An awareness of the multiple spaces, mobilities, and power geometries of air travel leads us to our discussion of private business aviation – arguably the most obvious expression of a kinetic aeromobile elite who travel in an exclusive world of VIP suites and private aircraft, far removed from the hassles and delays associated with major passenger airports. Yet even among the most frequent flyers – transnational businessmen, politicians, sports stars, and members of the putative 'creative class' – there is a staggering variety of ways of flying – from full-service business class (see Bowen, this volume) to a low(er) cost seat on a 'no-frills' airline or a private aircraft specially chartered for the occasion. Consequently, there is a huge difference between the experience of a business traveller on a frequent-flyer programme who passes seamlessly from a dedicated lounge into their business class seat and budget traveller who is forced to walk to the most remote gate at the airport before jostling for an unallocated seat. At the higher end of the market, and in stark contrast to the 'wretched test of endurance' of economy and low-cost travel – 'typified by delays, crowds, the flatulence of your fellow passengers and the cold, hard stares of cabin crew' (Duerden 2006: 24) – business and first class travel offers passengers enhanced standards of comfort, service, and mobility. For the truly super-rich, however, a private jet is the preferred vehicle of aeromobility. For them, a private jet is a tool that offers unfettered access to global mobility; a means through which to bypass established networks of air routes, create bespoke geographies of personal movement and convenience, and demonstrate their wealth and influence (Hutton 2008).

As we outline in this chapter, the decision of how to fly is based on a number of interlocking factors, including, but not limited to, convenience, price, and comfort. We contend that each of these possibilities has a socio-cultural significance that goes well beyond the simple facts of travelling from A to B, encompassing ideas of personal status, corporate achievement, and prestige. By focusing on the changing nature and the unique space-times of private aviation, this chapter prises open debates on business air travel to explore the increasingly important role of private aviation as a means of travel and show how the sector is transforming the mobilities of a small but significant (and growing) number of travellers. Sidestepping crucial but perhaps irresolvable questions about whether business flights are necessary or indeed useful in an era of global e-communication, we instead explore the reasons for the growth of the 'bizjet' market, focusing particularly on the supply and demand for private flying before moving on to document the possible implications of private flight for the 'global space of flows'. Before describing the emerging geographies of private flight, however, we begin by arguing that studies of business air travel in particular, and movement in general, benefit from a perspective that highlights the material, affective and embodied nature of mobility (Urry and Sheller 2006), and is duly cognisant of the difference between different forms of air travel, given that the 'world of transit doesn't operate at the same velocity, or in the same mode, in every place' (Fuller 2003: 3).

Embodying Air Travel

> Transportation is more than just the provision of infrastructure, facilities, networks, or investment; it is inextricably intertwined with how humans interact through policies, ideologies, and societies across time and space. (Keeling 2007: 217)

While research into the different facets of air transport has reached new heights of analytical sophistication in recent years, the social and cultural dimensions of air travel remain under-researched and theorized. Indeed, many analyses of flying arguably fall into the same trap as other attempts at mapping global flows of people – they forget that each line on a map actually represents a group of living, breathing human subjects, each of whom has their own experience of flying and relates to the plane's hardware and software in different ways (Dodge and Kitchin 2004). Adey et al. (2007) thus advocate a new social geography of flight that does more than simply reduce flying to a skein of lines on a map or tables of statistics. Yet for many transport economists and transport geographers, this human diversity and richness is lost, and in a world in which millions use the airline network every day, research on average load factors and service frequencies gains more attention than detailed ethnographic studies of *real* passengers. As Adey (2008) contends, discourses and models that merely describe passengers in terms of aggregate units, or 'PAX', can only provide an indication of what real passengers look like, think or feel.

Drawing on the work of Thrift (2004), Merriman (2004) and others, we argue for an embodied perspective that recognizes that passengers move through, inhabit and transform the spaces of air travel in distinctive embodied ways. The fact that passengers spend the vast majority of their journeys in a sedentary state, strapped into their seat, plugged into the in-flight entertainment system, or perhaps working on their laptop, does not mean that the body in flight is passive. To the contrary, it has to actively work to 'get comfortable' (Bissell 2008), and some bodies have to work harder than others to achieve this depending on their height, physical fitness, the dimensions of the seat, and the leg room that is available. For the very young, the elderly, and those in poor health, the re-circulated, dehumidified, and pressurised air in the aircraft cabin can cause a range of bodily discomforts and health effects, including dizziness, headaches, and nausea. Ebbing and flowing through these states of (dis)comfort, the body also experiences other sensations in flight: the smells and tastes of airline food, the captivating views from the windows, the occasional judder as the plane hits turbulence, the sounds of call bells, engines, in-flight entertainment systems, other passengers' conversations, as well as their perfume, aftershave and body odour. The in-flight body is also affected by the availability of light and fresh air, and the aircraft's air conditioning and lighting systems may be used to promote periods of sleep or activity among its passengers.

In short, passengers are constantly moving and being moved in various ways, with the experience of one flight potentially being very different to another. Embodying the flight in this way thus alerts us to these corporal dimensions and forces us to remember that human beings are of different shapes and sizes, with different cultural dispositions, backgrounds and resources. It also reminds us that human beings are expressive, and this expressiveness is not something that needs to be stripped out of any study of air travel prior to commencing analysis (see Latham and McCormack 2004). Flying, after all, involves particular kinds of social interaction, as passengers engage with one another, the cabin crew, and the aircraft itself. These relations are enmeshed in gendered, aged, sexed, racialized, and nationalized processes of inclusion and exclusion, creating different subjectivities of what it means to be a passenger or a 'flier'. This means that merely conceptualising 'aeromobility' as the super-structure of advanced global capitalism, reducing it to a space of flows, does not allow for the sheer diversity of ways of flying or occupying airspace.

Our argument for 'fleshing' out analyses of air travel is one that draws on related arguments being made by scholars inspired by the putative 'mobilities turn' in the social sciences. Most associated with the work of the sociologist John Urry, this is evident in a new approach or paradigm in transport studies that does not assume that the world is speeding up for all but takes seriously the concomitant suggestion that new forms of transport also create immobilities and exclusions. As Urry (2001, 2007) points out, both upward and downward mobilities may be associated with the same technologies, and multiple forms of social life may be co-present in the same spaces of transportation. Different people, in short, are networked in different ways, with the new mobilities paradigm concerned with elucidating the different ways that people 'dwell' in places that are 'on the move'. As he notes, studying mobility means thinking about the individual, lumpy, embodied, fragile and 'embaggaged' experience of travel, rather than transforming passengers into an aggregate mass of statistics (c.f. Button and Vega 2008).

But while our key launching pad is the literature on mobility, our focus on the corporal geographies of flying is also inspired by ongoing work in the social sciences on the *affective*. Whilst difficult to characterize, such work takes seriously the notion that there is a constant push and pull of affect between the body and its surroundings (Thrift 2004). This is somewhat different to the notion of emotion – experiences that are often seen to emerge from *within* – as it stresses that the setting in which emotions arise is more than contextual (i.e. settings have the capacity to affect). Informed by phenomenological ideas about being-in-the-world, work on affect nonetheless grapples with the question as to how we can register the affective dimension, which often appears beyond representation:

> The emphasis is on practices that cannot adequately be spoken of, that words cannot capture, that texts cannot convey – on forms of experience and movement that are not only or never cognitive. Instead of theoretically representing the world, "non-representational theory" is concerned with the ways in which subjects know the world without knowing it, the "inarticulate understanding" or "practical intelligibility" of an "unformulated practical grasp of the world". (Nash 2000: 655)

The privileging of 'ordinary' people's knowledge is crucial here, with the politics of non-representational theory stressing the importance of 'appreciating, and valorising, the skills and knowledges' of embodied beings that 'have been so consistently devalorised by contemplative forms of life, thus underlining that their stake in the world is just as great as the stake of those who are paid to comment upon it' (Thrift 2004: 46). Or, as Laurier (2001) has put it, it is about valuing people's everyday competencies rather than the world-views of theory-driven, professional researchers.

In relation to business air travel, we are making the case for moving beyond simple quantitative analysis, or even consideration of the perceptive or aesthetic dimensions of travel, by insisting on the need to think about the feelings, motions and emotions associated with particular ways and forms of flying: the more than human, more than textual worlds of aeromobility, no less. Such an agenda forces us to dispense with rational economic analysis of why people fly from A to B in a certain way to consider questions of what the experiences of flying are, taking in not just the speed or cost of travel, but also multisensory issues of comfort, conviviality and convenience. As we shall show, it is only through consideration of such factors that an adequate explanation for the rising importance of private air travel is possible.

Practised Aeromobilities: The Growth of Business Air Travel

Geographers have traditionally described the spatial patterns of air transport as a network, with flows of air traffic linking airports that stand as gateways to global city-regions (see O'Kelly 1998, Smith and Timberlake 2002). Castells (1996) argues that this space of flows creates a hierarchy of hubs that can be arranged according to their relative importance and which can accordingly be used to identify cities' centrality in global urban networks. While some researchers have hence examined the geographies of the world city network through flows of passenger and freight traffic between major hubs (Witlox et al. 2004, Zook and Brunn 2006), there has been no comparable study of the geographies of global business aviation, despite a history that stretches back to the early 1920s when large corporations including Standard Oil, Texaco, and Shell began using decommissioned military aircraft to shuttle senior executives between offices and production sites (Sheehan 2003). This lacuna is due, in part, to the ad-hoc nature of the sector and the lack of data on air traffic movements, but also discourses of commercial confidentiality that preclude empirical analysis of the airline industry's most prestigious sectors. Indeed, many members of the super rich go to extraordinary lengths to retain their privacy (see Hutton 2008), including, in the context of business aviation, flying in unmarked aircraft and using smaller airports that are well away from the gaze of the paparazzi and the public at large.

What is clear, however, is that the increasingly de-regulated and competitive global air transport market has resulted in considerable fragmentation of the airline product and the emergence of new forms of aeromobility (Budd and Graham 2009). It is no longer merely enough to operate a safe and punctual air service: airlines have to compete for custom by offering the lowest fares, the widest seats, the best in-flight cuisine, and the most generous frequent flyer perks. In an increasingly cut-throat market, dominated by high fuel costs and low margins, carriers are desperate to attract and retain the custom of lucrative business travellers with promises of ever more attentive and thoughtful service and enhanced levels of in-flight comfort (IATA 2007). Consequently, limousine transfers, complementary spa treatments, lie-flat beds, fluffy bath robes, amenity kits containing designer cosmetics, and on-demand meal services are the norm for most first and business class customers.

Crucially, it is within this context of deregulation and fragmentation that business aviation has expanded its scope and range. Broadly defined, we take business aviation to represent that sector of the aviation industry which 'concerns the operation or use of aircraft by companies for the carriage of passengers or goods as an aid to the conduct of their business, flown for purposes generally considered not for private hire and piloted by individuals having ... a valid commercial pilot licence with an instrument rating' (IBAC 2008). This definition excludes business or first class travel on conventional airlines, but includes the use of aircraft that are flown by a third party commercial operator on behalf of a private client, as well as the non-commercial use of aircraft that are flown on business purposes by company employees and owner-operated business aviation.

Today, business aircraft from all three categories are an increasingly common sight at airports around the world. The world's business aviation fleet currently exceeds 26,700 airframes, and the market represents one of the fastest-growing sectors of the aviation industry. Despite being the near-exclusive preserve of the United States (and, to a lesser extent, Europe) for many years, business aviation is rapidly spreading into other global markets, most notably in India, Russia, China, Brazil, and the Middle East (Sarsfield 2006, Perrett 2007, Ingleton 2008). Given the flexibility and high level of service offered by many traditional airlines, the question remains as to why so many business travellers, particularly from price-sensitive small- and medium-sized enterprises, are using private aircraft. Here, two factors – convenience and comfort – appear to intersect with cost in significant and sometimes contradictory ways. Indeed, cheaper forms of flying may ultimately be judged poor value for money if they are time consuming, provide few opportunities for 'productive' work en-route, and leave the worker-traveller too exhausted and stressed to work effectively. Unsurprisingly, convenience/flexibility and increased productivity have been cited as the principal benefits of business aviation (Ingleton 2008). However, we contend that these factors are not the only drivers of demand and issues of personal comfort, safety, and security can be just as important. In this way, we place understandings of the body at the forefront of our analysis.

Convenience, flexibility and productivity

In an era where instantaneous email communication, telephony and video-conferencing technologies provide multiple opportunities for long distance communication, the role of business travel is often questioned (see Denstadli and Gripsrud, this volume). However, many commentators have noted that the emergence of a truly global economy requires new forms of team-working, consultancy and secondment where face-to-face interaction ('facework') is vital. The decisive shift from internationalism to transnationalism is thus registered in the proliferation of business workers – cosmopolitan 'fast subjects' – who dwell in Castells' space of flows, to-ing and fro-ing between the hubs and spokes of the global economy. While conventional airlines draw the world's major cities closer together in a web of interconnecting air routes, economics dictates that only profitable routes with healthy levels of passenger demand are operated and while the most popular routes, such as Madrid to Barcelona, are served with upward of 50 return flights a day, others, such as Norwich to Guernsey or Bristol to Turin, may receive as little as one return service a week. The scheduled aviation network, built around a number of key hubs, thus often requires passengers to route through intermediate airports, adding to the total journey time and distance flown. Need to fly from central London to Madrid? The airline schedules dictate that you leave from London/Heathrow and alight at Madrid/Barajas, both many miles away from the city centre, at times that suit the airlines, not the passenger. Fly on a private aircraft, however, and you can take off from smaller, less congested airfields like London/Biggin Hill or Northolt, at a time to suit you, and land at Torrejon airport away from the bustle of Madrid's main airport. By maximizing direct point-to-point services, business aviation eliminates the delays associated with transferring between flights, and serves shorter routes over which scheduled traffic, with its longer check-in times and fixed timetables, cannot practicably serve (Marsh and Hammouda 2008).

One of the most significant repercussions of the growth of the business aviation sector is therefore likely to be a selective elaboration and expansion of the networked geographies of global flight. Studies in Europe have already shown that the business aviation network is more diffuse than that of the scheduled airline sector. Indeed, in 2007 business aircraft linked in excess of 100,000 European city pairs, over three times as many as the scheduled market (Marsh and Hammouda 2008). Like low-cost carriers, business aircraft operators generally eschew the cost, delays, and congestion of major airports by flying to smaller facilities. Unlike their low-cost counterparts, however, the smaller size of business aircraft enable business operators to access a wider range of airports that may not have the infrastructure or passenger handling capabilities to support large passenger aircraft. The use of these so-called 'reliever' airports has already had significant implications for some of the larger sites. London/Farnborough and London/Biggin Hill, for example, have developed into major year-round business aviation centres with dedicated executive passenger terminals and maintenance facilities, while other airports see a huge influx of traffic once or twice a year during major sporting fixtures or cultural events (Marsh 2006). Significantly, while the majority of the top 20 busiest business airports in Europe are located in or near major world cities and business centres, at least three (Cannes, Palma de Mallorca and Nice) are popular destinations for the so-called 'jet for leisure' segment of the business aviation market (Figure 5.1).

Figure 5.1 The top 20 business aviation airports in Europe, 2007

In addition to being able to access airports and airfields that are closer to the intended destination, business aircraft can be chartered at a few hours' notice and booked to depart at a time that suits the user. Thanks to the lack of other scheduled flights, passengers can arrive at the airport as little as ten minutes before take off as the lack of queues means security and immigration formalities can be conducted in a matter of seconds. At some airports, customers can even drive up to the door of the aircraft, making the process, according to one operator, 'as easy as going to a taxi rank and hailing a cab' (Blink 2008). Arrival is designed to be similarly rapid, with limousines and helicopters waiting to whisk passengers directly to their meeting.

By freeing users from the constraints of airline schedules, minimum check-in times, and security queues, business aviation is marketed as a solution to the temporal profligacy of other forms of aeromobility that compel passengers to spend hours waiting in airports. 'Whether you need to fly to Birmingham, Brussels or Barcelona, Airtime Charters will *take you from your nearest airport* with average check in times of just 15 minutes, *you'll not be hanging around*. Upon arrival, you'll find your means of onward travel waiting for you, at some airports coming to your aircraft side, enabling *a seamless transfer to your destination* ... where you'll be ready for business' (Airtime Charters 2007, our emphasis). By circumnavigating many of the inefficiencies associated with regular air travel, business aircraft can be conceptualized as time or productivity multipliers that enable users to do more things, with more people, more efficiently than was previously possible: 'Pack more cities into a day. Avoid the traffic and the crowds. Fly in and out of airports that are close to your meetings. Work with your team on the flight. Be home in time to kiss the kids goodnight' (NetJets 2008).

Passenger surveys have confirmed that company employees feel they are significantly more productive aboard business aircraft than they would have been on conventional airlines or even in their own office. 'Productive collaboration' between staff reportedly occurs eight times more frequently than when those same staff were on a scheduled airline, and company employees are reported to be less likely to be resting or reading non-work related materials during a flight (NBAA 2004). Because of this, operators claim that business aircraft are good for a company's bottom-line, and cite evidence that suggests that companies that use business aircraft consistently outperform non-operators on many key performance indicators, including cumulative returns, and that CEOs believe business aircraft help them identify and execute strategic opportunities for new relationships and alliances by enabling them to increase contact with clients and develop new markets (NBAA 2004).

In addition to recognizing that the demand for convenience and flexibility drives business aviation growth, it is important to note that new developments, principally the emergence of new aircraft leasing and ownership arrangements, are enabling more people to access private aircraft by making them more affordable and accessible. The price of business aircraft (around six million pounds for a Learjet 45, £15m for a larger Dassault Falcon 2000EX, and £43m for a Boeing Business Jet) means they are too expensive for most people to purchase (Walsh 2006). In the light of this, new business models are offering potential customers a range of cheaper ways of getting airborne. For example, fractional jet ownership schemes are the equivalent of 'aerial timeshares'. The fractional operator finances the purchase of an aircraft and then recoups their capital by selling flight time to third parties. These schemes allow companies or individuals to access an aircraft for a certain number of hours a year at a fraction of the cost of purchasing the aircraft outright (Walsh 2006).

The price of fractional governorship varies according to the size, popularity of the aircraft, and the number of hours that are required. Clients typically buy a share in an aircraft in 25-hour blocks (or multiples thereof) which range from around £80,000 for 25 hours on a seven-seat Citation Bravo to £800,000 for 50 hours in a 10-seat Dassault Falcon 2000EX (Walsh 2005). Additional charges for fuel, maintenance, ATC charges, pilots, insurance, and selected add-ons such as catering are also levied (Maslen 2004). Despite these additional charges, fractional operators stress that the price difference between hiring a private aircraft and travelling first or business class on a conventional airline is not excessive (Crainer and Dearlove

2001). By offering a range of aircraft types, fractional ownership providers can offer bespoke travel solutions for a wide range of business requirements, from short-haul domestic flights to long-haul transoceanic services. Once an account is opened and a 'flight card' purchased, flights can be booked with as little as 10 hours notice and aircraft are available, in theory, 24 hours a day, 365 days a year. Yet the costs of such arrangements are, for most individuals, prohibitive, underlying that mobility is a resource to which not everyone has an equal relation: far from being a democratisation of flying, private air travel rewrites the global space of flows in the interests of a mobile elite who enjoy a particular embodied relationship with the spaces of flight (see Urry and Sheller 2006: 211).

Comfort and class

As has been implied above, the growth of business aviation can be explained as a by-product of global processes that have conspired to make *time* the most precious of all commodities, too important to waste in traffic jams or at airports (Done 2007, Rothkopf 2008). Yet alongside convenience there is comfort. For Bissell (2008), comfort is an integral aspect of the corporeal experience, yet it is something that remains poorly defined and often overlooked in academic study (but see Hubbard 2003). In contrast to the idea that comfort is innate in particular forms of locomotion, or that particular visual ensembles provoke feeling of comfort, Bissell hypothesizes comfort as a specific affective resonance that circulates between a body and the objects it encounters (whether a seat, a plane, or an airport lounge). Comfort is something that, as he argues, develops from a number of other sensibilities, such as solitude, stillness, relaxation and beauty and is a response to a variety of tactile, visual and audio stimuli – including the marketing rhetoric which promises that those travelling in a particular manner will have a pleasant bodily experience. Despite the promises of those who market air travel, comfort is something that passengers strive for, but often rarely achieve, with the body forced to negotiate proximate objects in a variety of ways as it strives to avoid discomfort and pain.

In recent years, airports and commercial air travel have become associated with a range of increasingly unpleasant physical and psychological inconveniences including, but not limited to: uncomfortable seats; inedible food; intrusive security checks; air rage; confusing hand baggage restrictions; claustrophobia; lost luggage; boredom; health concerns (particularly relating to deep vein thrombosis and contaminated cabin air); delays; cancellations; and general feelings of anxiety exacerbated by a loss of control. As the architectural critic Stephen Bayley recently noted:

> Within a generation, what was once a romantic, privileged adventure has turned into a humiliating ordeal ... no other experience in contemporary life requires an individual to forgo his [sic] independence and endure such joyless, harrowing

regimentation as travelling by plane ... what a horrible, inhuman, artless culture
air travel has become. (Bayley 2008: 29)

While some have claimed that the progressive deregulation of global airline
markets has enabled more people to travel to more places, more often, critics
contend that the drive to lower fares and increase passenger numbers has in fact
removed the last vestiges of comfort that were once associated with air travel and
made travelling by air an increasingly gruelling experience (Steel 2007, Usborne
2008).

One of the main targets of this criticism are the low-cost or 'no-frills' carriers
who, unlike their full service counterparts, make few (if any) concessions to
passenger comfort or service – seating densities are higher than other carriers,
there are no business class seats, and if you want a cup of tea or coffee you have to
pay for it (Calder 2002). These new ways of flying operate in stark contrast to the
imagined opulence of the air travel experience of old when passengers 'dressed
up' for flights and were served afternoon tea on bone china tableware by liveried
stewards. However, as long ago as the late 1940s, commentators were suggesting
that the only way for airlines to make any money was to ditch these elements of
luxury and concentrate instead on providing a safe and reliable air service. 'The
sooner air transport grows out of the salmon and champagne era and gets down to
kipper and tea traffic', wrote a contributor to the *Aeroplane* magazine in December
1949, 'the sooner it will be able to justify its existence ... it is perfectly possible to
be decent without providing powder-rooms, cocktail bars, promenade decks and
all the rest' for a benefit of a few wealthy passengers (cited in Hudson and Pettifer
1979: 131).

Now, it would seem, the experience of mass aeromobility has swung the
pendulum to the other extreme. In 2007, a respondent to a UK House of Commons
survey into passenger experiences of air travel wrote passionately about the
profoundly unpleasant experience of flying on 'Chavair', a collective term he had
devised to describe low-cost airlines that, he believed, were predominately used
by the lower middle classes, football supporters, stag and hen parties, second-
home owners, and 'self employed Costa Tax Dodge chavs'. He remarked that
their conduct is 'often very unpleasant, a good proportion of people shout the
length of the cabin, walk around with drinks, use foul language and are generally
awful ... Everything is charged for and the passengers are given no service' (cited
in House of Commons Transport Committee Report 2007: 38). Not withstanding
the prejudices of class which underpin this analysis, the idea air travel subjects
the passenger with a series of uncomfortable encounters with others is illustrative
of the multiple modalities of air travel and the fact that the journey between two
points can be too-full of life for some, and not the smooth, seamless journey often
advertised and anticipated.

Another factor that has made air travel less comfortable for many has been the
introduction of new security procedures at airports. Following the 9/11 attacks,
the failed attempt by the 'shoe bomber' Richard Reid to detonate an explosive

device that was concealed in his shoe on an aircraft, and the alleged plot to blow up seven transatlantic airlines heading for North America from London in August 2006, new security procedures have been introduced which have directly led to passengers' experiences of conventional air travel declining significantly. On the morning of 10 August 2006, British police acted to stop a suspected plot to blow up transatlantic flights leaving London/Heathrow, possibly using liquid explosives contained in hand luggage. Immediate restrictions on hand luggage were introduced, and passengers were only allowed to carry essential documentation and medical supplies into the cabin. Though the blanket ban on liquids has since ended, at the time of writing, passengers are still only permitted to carry small quantities (under 100ml) of liquid in their hand luggage.

As a result of these restrictions, passengers found themselves subject to increasingly intrusive surveillance and the time taken to pass through security checkpoints doubled. In the UK, the Airport Operator's Association admitted that: '[t]he combination of long queues, substantial disrobing and complicated security leaves the passenger with an experience of having been through an intrusive and degrading process (cited in House of Commons Transport Committee Report 2007: 29). Female travellers, in particular, complained that they were subject to intrusive and embarrassing body security searches that left them feeling violated and humiliated, while those travelling with small children reported they were targeted by officious security staff (*Sunday Times* 2008, Williams 2008). In recognition that conventional air travel may all too often represent a 'distressing proposition' regardless of how much passengers pay for their seat, business aircraft operators market their services on 'quality of life' grounds, suggesting that flying by private jet 'offers fast relief from the aches and pains associated with commercial air travel' (Netjets 2008). In addition to offering more comfortable seats, fine dining, and personalised service, some business aircraft operators also now mention that their staff will be approachable, polite and courteous and treat their customers with respect, something that conventional airlines do not always manage as new models of in-flight service come to dominate.

As well as serving their traditional core market of high-ranking corporate flyers, aircraft manufacturers and business aircraft operators are also now targeting wealthy individuals for whom a private jet is not only a vehicle of personal mobility, but also a lifestyle choice. Harking back to the early days of passenger flight when flying was adventurous, exciting, fashionable, and fun, the acquisition of a private jet is being promoted as a way to reclaim some of the glamour of flight which has been lost in an age of deregulation and mass aeromobility. For high net worth individuals, the acquisition of a private jet is promoted as the next logical purchase for people who already count luxury yachts, valuable art collections, a string of vintage sports cars, and a number of pedigree racehorses among their possessions (Beaverstock et al. 2004). As with most cars, buyers can customise the exterior paintwork and interior fittings of their aircraft using designs devised by some of the world's leading luxury brands, including BMW and Versace. Learjet accordingly claim their private jets are the 'sports cars of the skies', a 'perfect blend' of performance, technology, and style that are flown 'by overachievers and leaders the world over' (Learjet 2008). In a sector where convenience is taken as a given, industry commentators have noted a shift in customer requirements from corporate to 'lifestyle' considerations (Warwick 2006):

> The Bombardier Learjet 60XR comes elegantly appointed ... The spacious stand-up cabin is completed with precious wood veneers, rich, supple leathers and the finest fabrics ... [and] the galley's gourmet capabilities elevate the experience to the exquisite. (Learjet 2008)

A recurring theme in the marketing literature is that these aircraft naturally complement the high-flying lifestyles of the rich and famous and will meet the needs of even the most discerning customers.

> Soaring high above congested flight lanes and unstable weather, in and out of the world's most challenging airfields, the Bombardier Learjet ... the jetset original, exude an irresistible vital force ... Unmistakable beauties, Learjet aircraft are the ultimate runway models, famed for their ramp appeal and admired for their constant evolution in design and performance. (Learjet 2008)

For those who demand an even more luxurious aircraft or wish to engage in aeronautical 'one-upmanship', larger 'VVIP' aircraft, including the Airbus A319CJ Corporate Jet and the Boeing Business Jet (based on the B737) are available (Done 2007). In 2007, Airbus revealed it had received an order for an executive A380 'super jumbo' from a Middle Eastern head of state. Featuring a hot tub, Bedouin-style tented lounge, a games room, and en-suite master bedroom, the £225m A380VVIP will reportedly be the largest and most expensive private jet in the sky (Bale 2007).

Underlining that the ways someone travels – their mobility – is never reducable to their motility (i.e. the ability of a person to move socially and spatially), such takes on the geographies of private aviation highlight the ways in which question of status and comfort entwine. As positional and prestige goods, private aircraft carry with them iconic weight and status. Yet unlike some other positional goods, their value is not just symbolic as they are still essentially an enabling technology that allows for a particular form of mobility that embodies speed and comfort. It is of course difficult – if not impossible – to articulate the difference between private flying and conventional forms of flying in terms of their felt and sensed experiences unless one completes ethnographic or ethnomethodological research focused on the embodied practices of flying (perhaps following the model provided by Laurier (2001) in his work on travelling salespeople). Yet even in the absence of such detailed non-representational work it becomes clear that the demand and supply of private business travel is hard to comprehend unless one pushes existing analyses beyond the economic realm into one where the economy is always and already thoroughly encultured and embodied.

Challenges of Growth: Contesting Personal Aeromobilities

Given the seemingly increasing desire for speed and comfort among a kinetic elite, the rise in private aviation is explicable yet in some senses unpredicted, unregulated and unmanageable. Indeed, although business aviation only represents a small proportion of total air traffic, the predicted increase in flights is likely to have serious socio-environmental and operational implications (Learmount 2008). In Europe alone, the volume of business aviation traffic is growing at over twice the rate of all other air traffic (Marsh and Hammouda 2008). The number of business aviation flights in European airspace reached almost 750,000 in 2007 (up 10 per cent on 2006 figures), and during that year the sector as a whole contributed nearly €20bn to the European economy (Sarsfield 2008).

Some business airports, including London's heliport at Battersea, have had to introduce slot restrictions to regulate and limit the flow of traffic, while others have submitted planning applications to expand their facilities. Unsurprisingly, most expansion plans have been met with vociferous local opposition with local residents opposing any development and the inevitable increase in flights, noise, and pollution, it would cause. Already, communities living near the UK's major business aviation airports and heliports have complained about the noise and pollution business aircraft produce and are opposing plans for expansion, while residents in St Tropez on the French Riviera are calling for restrictions on the number of helicopter flights that are allowed to buzz overhead (Pulford 2004, Davies 2008).

In addition to local noise issues, concern about the global environmental effect of aircraft pollution has risen in recent years, and a range of policy measures, from emissions trading schemes to taxes on aviation fuel, have been proposed as a means of reducing pollution. According to some reports, commercial aviation represents the fastest-growing source of CO_2 emissions of any industrial sector and 'frivolous' or 'binge' flying has become the *bête-noire* of the environmental movement (Pulford 2004, Monbiot 2006). At the time of writing, small business aircraft (those under 5,700kg), will be exempt from the European Emissions Trading Scheme, a programme that is designed to make air operators pay for the environmental pollution they cause (Webster and Watson 2006) and this may have the unintended consequence of making private flight a more attractive financial proposition than first or business class travel on conventional airlines.

In recent years, members of the transnational class have been under attack for their ecologically unsustainable practices of travel and tourism (Veevers 2007, Osley 2008). Though the evidence is largely anecdotal, it would appear that many users of business jets are largely unconvinced about the environmental implications of their personal mobility: 'the engines [on my private aircraft] are more fuel efficient than on big airliners. I don't think they are as environmentally damaging' (cited in Brown 2006: 18). Moreover, it has been suggested that business aircraft have become part of the 'corporate capture' of sustainability discourses in which private flying becomes 'sustainable travel', with many companies viewing private flying as more time-efficient and therefore less wasteful than scheduled airlines (McVeigh 2008).

In addition to these socio-environmental concerns, the growth of business aviation is presenting a number of operational and safety challenges. Business aircraft are often slower than commercial aircraft, cut across major traffic flows, cruise at higher altitudes, and require enhanced air traffic control separation that 'wastes' valuable airspace (Clark 2006). Concern has also been raised about the levels of training, supervision, and insurance of new pilots, as well as the wisdom of allowing business aircraft to share airspace with commercial flights (Matthews 2008). In September 2006, an Embraer Legacy business jet and a Gol airlines Boeing 737 collided over the Amazonian rainforest killing all 154 people on the commercial airliner, while in 2008 a Cessna Citation business jet crashed into a house near London's Biggin Hill airfield killing all the occupants (Barney 2008, Webster 2008). These, and other tragic incidents, have been cited as evidence of the danger of escalating volumes of business traffic.

In this light, the recent entry into service of a new category of Very Light Jets (VLJs) may well exacerbate such problems. The unique operating performance of VLJs (which includes their speed and their ability to operate from airports with short runways and limited ground handling facilities) will mean that business travellers can access an even wider range of airports. The manufacturers of new VLJ models, such as the Cessna Mustang and the Eclipse 500, claim they will be much cheaper to purchase and operate than existing aircraft and over 2500 VLJs have been ordered to date, many by new start-up air taxi companies (Bowes 2006, O'Connell 2008, Sarsfield 2008). While proponents claim VLJs will herald a new era of increasingly affordable and accessible private air travel that will enable another layer of people to use private jets (Bowes 2006, Woods 2006), critics fear VLJs will 'clutter the skies, attract dangerous owner-fliers and degrade the swank-value of private flight' (Brown 2006: 18).

Conclusion

Air travel has been seen as a major enabler – and beneficiary – of the demand for international business travel. However, there is little question that the rapid growth in passenger numbers during the late twentieth century and the new techniques of passenger screening that have been introduced to combat terrorist threats have caused conventional air travel to become an increasingly overcrowded, stressful and unpleasant experience. The architectural and procedural shortcomings of certain passenger airports have been the subject of much debate, and airline executives, business leaders, and government officials have cautioned that many major airports are no longer 'fit for purpose' and may actively be discouraging passengers from travelling (Calder 2007, Milmo and Hickman 2007). In this chapter we have suggested that those business travellers that can afford to are increasingly choosing to by-pass lengthy security and immigration queues and avoid congested hubs by chartering or buying their own aircraft and flying between smaller, less crowded airports (Clark 2006), marking out their own social status in the process as part of an exclusive kinetic elite that does not want to or have to travel with the masses. To meet this burgeoning demand for comfortable and convenient privatized travel, a range of new ownership, and chartering solutions are emerging, effectively bringing many small, previously under-used airfields into the global space of business flows.

Accordingly, we have attempted to show that whereas business aircraft used to be seen as symbol of success, now they are increasingly considered *a path to* success in the business world. Within a fragmenting airline industry, private air travel has accordingly emerged as a significant sector whose growth is a result of a complex and interlocking series of supply and demand factors that combine to make flying by private aircraft, for those who can afford it, a financially viable, convenient and comfortable alternative to premium-class airline travel. Tacking between the scales of the body and the global, this chapter has hence offered explanations for the rise of private business air travel. However, many questions remain about the spatial imprints of business aviation and its long-term implications for patterns and practices of business travel. Additionally, the ways in which private aviation shields flyers from the need to deal with social Others – effectively creating secessionary spaces of mobility – requires further investigation given this mirrors wider tendencies for the elites to try to escape the 'gravity' of democratic social relationships and public space (Atkinson and Flint 2004). Uncovering further details of the global flows of private aviation will no doubt prove difficult, but without consideration of this sector, our understanding of global aeromobilities will remain emaciated indeed.

References

Adey, P. 2008. Airports, mobility, and the calculative architecture of affective control. *Geoforum*, 39(1), 438-451.

Adey, P., Budd, L. and Hubbard, P. 2007. Flying lessons: Exploring the social and cultural geographies of global air travel. *Progress in Human Geography*, 31(6), 773-791.

Airtime Charters 2007. Corporate website, last accessed 03/07/2007.

Atkinson, R.G. and Flint, J.F. 2004. Fortress UK? Gated communities, the spatial revolt of the elites and time–space trajectories of segregation. *Housing Studies*, 19(6), 875-892.

Bale, J. 2007. The flying palace that's fit for a king who has no qualms about his carbon footprint. *The Times*, 30/03/2007, 29.

Barney, K. 2008. Five die in massive fireball as private jet plunges into housing estate. *The Independent*, 31/03/2008, 29.

Bayley, S. 2008. Want to rediscover the joy of travel? Take the train … *The Observer*, 13/04/2008, 29.

Beaverstock, J.V., Hubbard, P. and Short, J.R. 2004. Getting away with it? Exposing the geographies of the super-rich. *Geoforum*, 35, 401-407.

Bissell, D. 2008. Comfortable bodies: Sedentary affects. *Environment and Planning A*, 40(7), 1697-1712.

Blink 2008. Corporate website, last accessed 20/07/2008.

Bowen, J.T. This volume.

Bowes, G. 2006. The birth of the mini jet. *The Observer Escape*, 03/09/2006, 4.

Brown, H. 2006. The height of indulgence. *The Independent*, 01/07/2006, 18-19.

Budd, L., and Graham, B.J. 2009. Unintended trajectories: Liberalization and the geographies of private business flight. *Journal of Transport Geography*, 17, 285-292.

Button, K. and Vega, H. 2008. The effects of air transport on the movement of labour. *Geojournal*, 71(1), 67-81.

Calder, S. 2002. *No Frills: The Truth Behind the Low-cost Revolution in the Skies.* London: Virgin Books.

Calder, S. 2007. Is it all a conspiracy? Why Heathrow is so awful. *The Independent Traveller*, 29/09/2007, 3.

Castells, M. 1996. *The Rise of the Network Society.* Oxford: Blackwell.

Clark, A. 2006. Business travellers switch to private jets. *The Guardian*, 05/05/2006, 26.

Crainer, S. and Dearlove, D. 2001. *The Financial Times Guide to Business Travel.* London: Prentice Hall.

Cresswell, T. 2006. *On the move.* London: Routledge.

Davies, L. 2008. Trés fatigues! St Tropez locals declare war on 'helicopter hell' of rich and famous. *The Guardian*, 28/07/2008, 15.

Denstadli, J.M. and Gripsrud, M. This volume.

Dodge, M. and Kitchin R. 2004. Flying through code/space: The real virtuality of air travel. *Environment and Planning A*, 36(2), 195-211.

Done, K. 2007. Demand for business jets increases to record level. *Financial Times*, 13/02/2007, 25.

Duerden, N. 2006. It's the only way to fly. *The Independent on Sunday Magazine*, 15/01/2006, 22-25.

Fuller, G. 2003. Life in Transit: Between airport and camp. *Borderlands e-journal*, 2(1), www.borderlandsejournal.adelaide.edu, last accessed 30/01/2004.

House of Commons Transport Committee 2007. *Passengers' Experiences of Air Travel Eight Report of Sessions 2006-2007*, Vol. 1, HC435-1, 18/07/2007.

Hubbard, P. 2003. A good night out? Multiplex cinemas as sites of embodied leisure. *Leisure Studies*, 22, 255-272.

Hudson, K. and Pettifier, J. 1979. *Diamonds in the Sky: A Social History of Air Travel.* London: The Bodley Head.

Hutton, W. 2008. Feeble government lets the superclass soar over the rest of us. *The Observer*, 04/05/2008.

Ingleton, P. R. 2008. The scope and impact of business aviation. *International Civil Aviation Organization Journal*, 63(2), 33-35.

International Air Transport Association 2007. *Corporate Air Travel Survey 2007 Report.* Montreal: IATA.

International Business Aviation Council (IBAC) 2008. Corporate website, last accessed 10/08/2008.

Keeling, D.J. 2007. Transportation geography: New directions on well worn trails. *Progress in Human Geography*, 31(2), 217-225.

Latham, A. and McCormack, D. 2004. Moving cities: Rethinking the materialities of urban geographies. *Progress in Human Geography*, 28, 701-724.

Laurier, E. 2001. Why people say where they are during mobile phone calls. *Environment and Planning D: Society & Space*, 19, 485-504.

LearJet. 2008. Corporate website, www.learjet.com, last accessed 11/05/2008.

Learmount, D. 2008. Traffic alert. *Flight International*, 173(5138), 13-19 May, 52-54.

Marsh, D. 2006. *Getting to the Point: Business Aviation in Europe.* Eurocontrol: Trends in Air Traffic Volume 1. Brussels, Eurocontrol.

Marsh, D. and Hammouda, K. 2008. *More to the Point: Buisness Aviation in Europe in 2007.* Eurocontrol Trends in Air Traffic Volume 4. Brussels, Eurocontrol.

Maslen, R. 2004. NetJets. Supporting the business community. *Airliner World*, February, 34-37.

Matthews, R. 2008. *Using Accidents and Incidents to Assess Anticipated Risks and Benefits Associated with Very Light Jets*, Paper presented at the Royal Aeronautical Society Conference 'Introducing Very Light Jets Into Europe' 26/03/2008.

McVeigh, K. 2008. Private jet sharing: It may assuage guilt, but is it really green? *The Guardian*, 19/05/2008, 14.

Merriman, P. 2004. Driving Places: Marc Auge, Non-places, and the Geographies of England's M1 Motorway. *Theory Culture and Society*, 21, 145-168.

Milmo, C. and Hickman, M. 2007. The world's least favourite airport. *The Independent*, 21/07/2007, 1-2.

Monbiot, G. 2006. *Heat: How to Stop the Planet Burning.* London: Allen Lane.

Nash, C. 2000. Performativity in practice: Some recent work in cultural geography *Progress in Human Geography*, 24: 653-664.

NBAA 2004. *NBAA Business Aviation Fact Book.* Washington DC: NBAA.

NetJets 2008. Corporate website, last accessed 11/07/2008.

O'Connell, D. 2008. Cheap jets lift private aviation. *The Sunday Times Business Supplement*, 03/02/2008, 8.

O'Kelly, M.E. 1998. A geographer's analysis of hub-and-spoke networks. *Journal of Transport Geography*, 6, 171-186.

Osley, R. 2008. Still not booked up? Then how about the first $1m holiday? *The Independent on Sunday*, 20/07/2008, 29.

Perrett, B. 2007. Ready to Blossom: China is opening up to business aviation. *Aviation Week and Space Technology*, 166(8), 45.

Pulford, C. 2004. *Air Madness Runways and the Blighting of Britain.* Second Edition. Woodford Hulse: Ituri.

Rothkopf, D. 2008. *Superclass: The Global Power Elite and the World They are Making.* London: Penguin.

Sarsfield, K. 2006. The New Frontier. *Flight International* (Business Aviation Special), 5057(170), 10-16 October, 46-49.

Sarsfield, K. 2008. European business aviation contributes €20bn to economy: Study. *Flight International*, 01/12/2008, retrieved from www.flightglobal. com/articles/2008/12/01/319570 on 01/12/2008.

Sheehan, J.J. 2003. *Business and Corporate Aviation Management. On-demand air travel.* McGraw-Hill Professional.

Smith, D. and Timberlake, M. 2002. Hierarchies of dominance among world cities: A network approach, in *Global Networks, Linked Cities*, edited by S. Sassen. London: Routledge, 117-141.

Steel, M. 2007. Why can't we stop flying when it's such torture? *The Independent*, 19/12/2007, 31.

Sunday Times 2008. Security searches 'too intimate'. *Sunday Times*, 17/06/2008, www.timesonline.co.uk/tol/travel/article193618.ece, last accessed 19/09/2008.

Thrift, N. 2004. Driving in the city. *Theory, Culture and Society*, 21, 41-59.

Urry, J. 2001. Transports of delight. *Leisure Studies*, 20, 237-245.

Urry, J. 2007. *Mobilities.* Cambridge: Polity.

Urry, J. and Sheller M., 2006. The new mobilities paradigm. *Environment and Planning A*, 38(2), 207-226.

Usborne, D. 2008. Travellers fly into clouds of misery. *The Independent*, 23/06/2008, 25.

Veevers, L. 2007. A £459,000 holiday for two. *The Independent on Sunday*, 08/04/2008, 18.

Walsh, C. 2005. We are all tycoons now (even if it is only by the hour). *The Observer Business*, 05/06/2005, 4.

Walsh, C. 2006. Private jets lose air of exclusivity. *The Observer Business and Media*, 23/04/2006, 6.

Warwick, G. 2006. Size sells. *Flight International*, 5037(169), 23-29 May, 30-31.

Webster, B. 2008. Boom in private jets with safety loophole raises risk of collision. *The Times*, 09/02/2008, 13.

Webster, B. and Watson, R. 2006. Private jets escape European carbon emissions proposal. *The Times*, 21/12/2006, 30.

Williams, Z. 2008. The security official at the airport stole my baby's dinner. Where else in the world would that be OK? *The Guardian*, 12/09/2008, www. guardian.co.uk/lifeandstyle/2008/sep/12/family, last accessed 17/09/2008.

Witlox, F. Vereecken, L. and Derudder, B. 2004. *Mapping the Global Network Economy on the basis of Air Passenger Transport Flows.* GaWC Research Bulletin 157, http://www.lboro.ac.uk/gawc/ rb/rb157.html, last accessed 17/12/2004.

Woods, R. 2006. Private jets for everybody. *The Sunday Times Business*, 08/10/2006, 13.

Zook, M and Brunn, S. 2006. From podes to antipodes: New dimensions in mapping global airline geographies. *Annals of the Association of American Geographers*, 96(3), 471-490.

PART 2
Business Travel and Mobility Regimes

Chapter 6

Business Travel and Portfolios of Mobility within Global Companies

John Salt[1]

Introduction

This chapter locates business travel within the portfolios of mobility which have been developed by large international companies. It is conceptualised as towards one end of a mobility continuum, the other being permanent movement. Companies use a range of types of mobility, long and short-term, to acquire and transfer expertise between their own sites and those of their clients or collaborators. Business travel is one form of this mobility. It is a moot point whether business travel should be regarded as labour migration. In the accepted sense of a move of home, it clearly is not. On the one hand, it might appear that business travel is better conceptualised as part of trade in goods and services rather than as migration. However, if we conceptualise international business travellers as 'equivalent workers' (Tani 2003) who spend time abroad and enhance the stock of knowledge at their destinations, then it is possible to include them in the broad compass of labour migration. The research reported on below tends towards the latter view and suggests that business travel is one element in a linked set of mobilities, which we term portfolios of mobility, used by international employers to conduct their business.

Study of corporate staff mobility sits at the junction of several literatures, notably those of migration and management. The migration literature has long been uncertain about how to treat short-term movements. For a long time the assumption was that migration necessarily involved longer-term movement, underpinned by a shift of home. Yet even in 1971, Zelinsky's 'mobility transition' final stage accepted that repeated 'circulation' would be a major characteristic in the 'super-advanced society'. That notwithstanding, it was not until the 1980s that migration scholars began seriously to place short-term moves into the theoretical canon of labour migration. Even then, interest focused mainly on longer-term (at least a year) assignments within corporate internal labour markets.

The management literature has adopted a similarly fragmented understanding of international corporate movements. Early literature on the mobility of staff in large organizations (Whyte 1956, Jennings 1971, McKay and Whitelaw 1977)

1   The research upon which this chapter is based was funded by the Leverhulme Trust. The project was carried out jointly with Dr. Jane Millar.

linked international mobility to the regeneration of management hierarchies. The growing internationalisation of companies meant that managerial transfer was increasingly seen as a control strategy designed to influence organizational structure and process (Edstrom and Galbraith 1977, Salt 1997, Edwards 1998). What expertise is required where within the global company, when and for how long became key issues. Further, as Goshal and Bartlett indicate (1998: 232), 'there is no such thing as a universal global manager. Rather, there are groups of specialists ... each of which much share a transnational perspective'. These specialists both draw upon and create different forms of mobility which unite to form global work patterns (Jones 2008).

During the 1990s there was a growing realization that economic globalization required new thinking about international labour movement. The speed and dense network of modern air travel had made it much easier to disseminate global expertise. Intuitively, it might be expected that the high costs of staff relocation (especially financial for the TNC, stress and family problems for the employee) or foreign recruitment might be obviated by increased levels of business travel. It would then follow that business travel might substitute for migration (Salt and Ford 1993). For example, modern air travel means that it may no longer be necessary to have a permanent expatriate presence with a major overseas customer: if something goes wrong a trouble-shooter can be sent out at a few hours notice. Similarly, and particularly within Europe where distances are relatively low, survey evidence at the time suggested that joint ventures were being serviced by frequent short-term trips rather than by secondment (see Ford 1992).

During the 1980s, the volume of business travel grew rapidly, revealed in analysis of data from 23 countries across five continents. Detailed breakdowns by destination revealed the business-driven nature of moves caused by the spatial and temporal specificity of organizations' needs to place expertise overseas (Ford 1992). For example, business visits to the UK increased by 90 per cent during the period 1978-1989. Unpublished data on the length of a business visit showed the increasing importance of short-term travel, especially one to two-day trips which accounted for 40-45 per cent of all those made (Ford 1992). More recent data have shown the continued growth of business travel and the central importance in it of movement by the highly skilled (Tani 2003, Faulconbridge and Beaverstock 2008, Beaverstock and Faulconbridge, this volume).

From the 1980s onwards, the application of new information technologies was also beginning to impinge more strongly on exchanges of global knowledge. Unlike the attributes of low-skilled migrant labour, which demand a physical presence in the performance of tasks, the main contribution of the highly skilled is knowledge, which can be transferred geographically in a number of ways not necessarily requiring a physical presence. Modern satellite and fibre-optic communications, faxes and e-mail meant that specialists could be in almost instant touch with each other, with tele- and video conferencing dealing with routine business. The disadvantage of not being in the same room as the person with whom one is conferring began to decline, although even then it was recognized that the ultimate advantage of physical contact would prevail in those sectors which traditionally place a premium on the quality of people and personality (O'Brien 1992). However, new information technology enabled a multiplication of possible meeting places, depending on the particular circumstances of the moment: to the modern professional, managerial and technical (PMT) worker, office support and files were only a fax or modem away. What was then uncertain was how far these facilities would make inroads into at least the growth of mobility among the highly skilled. This required systematic and detailed knowledge of the mobility practices of large employing organizations.

In recent years, knowledge has been considered as existing in an array of forms (Collins 1997, Williams 2007). It may be hypothesized that different patterns of movement might be related to different roles, for example those concerning the exchange of symbolic knowledge may be associated with shorter-term and virtual forms of mobility than those that relate to local business development or to global integration (Millar and Salt 2008). However, the link between international mobility and knowledge acquisition is not well understood (Koser and Salt 1997, Baganha and Entzinger 2004). The dynamics of production in transnational corporations focus attention on knowledge interchange, where the aim is to combine information from diverse sources and generate useful knowledge about designing, making and selling products and services in particular locales. The potential added value from accumulating internationally mobile expertise comes from their prior immersion in a range of cultural, institutional and project-related communities (Forsgren et al. 2005). Thus, from a company perspective, the learning imperative for international mobility is linked to a desire to create a cadre of executives and technicians who are able to think and act both globally and locally and also to develop the management mechanisms and resources available to mediate the transfer and assimilation of expertise and to support its synthesis with existing knowledge and integration with ongoing production in the receiving community (Millar et al. 1997). In order to do this, companies develop and deploy different forms of knowledge mobility at different stages in their operations.

The aim of this chapter is twofold. First, it shows that business travel is one of an interlinked set of mobilities used by international companies, where it fulfils a number of roles, including career development, project planning and implementation and a wide range of meetings. Second, it examines the particular role in corporate knowledge transfer played by business travel and the degree to which there is substitution between it and virtual mobility in an era of concern about carbon emissions. The evidence presented here is drawn from several sectors. It is acknowledged that specific sectoral characteristics are important in determining the relative frequencies of particular types (Millar and Salt 2008). For example, short-term assignments are a feature particularly of the ICT-sector, whereas rotation occurs largely in extractives companies. By including evidence from all sectors studied, the broad range of factors underlying business travel and its relationship with other forms of mobility may be elucidated.

Methodology

The chapter draws on the findings of a research project conducted during 2005-2006 which examined the range of mobility types used by over 30 companies in their global operations. Sectors of the economy studied included IT, aerospace, pharmaceuticals, electronic engineering, consultancies and extractives chosen to represent different degrees of industrial maturity and of capital and knowledge intensity, both of which were likely to influence their patterns of human resource mobility. Business travel and extended business travel were two of the types of mobility identified.

Semi-structured interviews, conducted with senior HR officials and with key actors in the selected sectors, were recorded and transcribed. The main thrust of the fieldwork was to ascertain how global employers acquire and move expertise internationally. Major issues arising in discussion included: the main and emerging types of mobility of expertise in modern TNCs; how TNCs combine skilled migration, organizational and process change and technological advance to survive in global markets; and what are the opportunities and the barriers associated with different patterns of mobility among skilled professionals.

Mobility Types

Companies are associated with different types of mobility (Cendant Mobility Services 2003, Mercer 2003, GMAC et al. 2004). There is no single accepted classification of international mobility and existing surveys use a wide range of classification criteria that include the degree of permanence, the regularity of return and the extent to which a mobile role can be supported virtually. From our companies, we were able to distinguish eight types of mobility: permanent recruitment through the external labour market (ELM) or the internal labour market (ILM); long-term assignments; short-term assignments; commuter assignments; rotators; extended business travel; business travel; and virtual mobility. Overall, the scale of mobility within each of these types varies, as does the rationale. Fuller details of how these forms of mobility are used in three sectors may be found in Millar and Salt (2007, 2008).

Use of the ELM and permanent ILM hires

In all companies, permanent international recruitment was rare, both through the ELM and the ILM. International ELM recruitment was used sparingly and mainly for senior positions. Permanent international transfer within the ILM was comparatively rare with local recruitment to fill vacancies preferred. A more common use of the ILM for a permanent hire was to move an individual from assignment to localization, usually after three years.

Long-term assignments

In both sectors, long-term assignments were usually defined as between one and four years in length with two to three years being the norm. Numbers at any one time varied with the peaks and troughs of business, stage of project lifecycle or phase in mergers and acquisitions. Long-term assignments fulfil particular roles, not necessarily related to the specific conditions of either sector. The first and more general role is career development for individual members of staff. Long-term assignments are seen as essential for upward mobility at all levels, although only for the more senior positions are they related directly to succession planning. In what are for the most part mature international firms, there is a requirement to develop international experience among staff in most functions. The other principal reason for long-term assignments is the transfer of knowledge and (often technological) skills. Beyond these two strategic roles for long-term assignments, other factors come into play. In some companies, long-term assignees are becoming more cosmopolitan with the increasing incorporation of staff recruited in emerging markets into the global workforce.

Short-term assignments

The most common definition of a short-term assignment was between three and 12 months. In most companies, numbers of short-term assignments were increasing, either absolutely or relatively to other assignments. The escalating use of this form of mobility does not seem to be a substitute for more expensive, longer-term forms on cost grounds, because the two fulfil different roles. Short-term assignments tend to be used for specific tasks, not necessarily related to the particular characteristics of the sector. Their significance in career development varies more from company to company than between sectors. In several cases, short term assignments allowed graduate trainees to gain experience in other parts of the company, typically in Europe or the USA. Elsewhere they were used to provide specific business or functional experience to high potential staff. Other circumstances for their use were related to project/product lifecycle stages that required physical co-presence for particular periods, for example, in the start-up phase of a new project when development teams were created to drive ventures forward. Where projects were collaborative and highly technological, short-term assignments were regarded as essential for brainstorming, producing solutions and building trust. From time to time short-term assignments were transformed into longer ones as projects developed and circumstances dictated.

Commuting assignments

Commuting assignments are relatively new phenomena and range from weekly commuting for periods of a few months up to one or two years. The numbers of international commuters per company are generally low and trends vary from one employer to another. The reason for international commuting almost always lies with the personal circumstances of the individual. Commuting assignments exist as substitutes for either long-term or short-term assignments and mainly occur within Europe. For example, someone offered an assignment for career development purposes may, for family reasons, opt to commute.

Rotation

Rotators are a peculiarity of extractive industries. One type consists of people who work on offshore or desert installations within the country on a shift cycle of several weeks on and several weeks off. A second type works internationally in remote or difficult locations on rotating shifts of one to two months on and one to two months off, with the company flying them to and from their home country. Usually this is because the work is at a location where it is neither feasible nor desirable to provide family accommodation for them in the country. The numbers of rotators may be considerable.

Extended business travel

An extended business trip of 30 to 90 days was normal, although one lasting up to six months was not uncommon. The general trend in extended business travel seems to be one of increasing volume and frequency. This is partly because shorter business trips are prolonged as projects demand, partly because they substitute for short-term assignments. The latter is less likely to be on cost grounds, more on a combination of the work required and individual preferences. For the most part, extended business travel is carried out by people in office functions and is almost always project related. There were examples in several companies where extended business travel was used in the pre-feasibility phase of acquisitions, mergers and divestments, necessitating staff on the ground frequently and sometimes for extended periods.

Business travel

Business travel, normally a trip of up to 30 days, provides a highly flexible form of corporate mobility. The trend in numbers was almost universally upward, with some variation across companies. Although there was a universal drive to restrain and reduce cost as much as possible, this was not a major issue. The main motive for business travel was for meetings relating to all aspects of business activity. Across each company, at any one time the full functional range was likely to be involved. Most meetings are project related, with spikes and troughs of mobility according to business activity. Without exception, companies recognized the need for face-to-face meetings. It was extremely rare for business travel to be seen as a substitute for longer-term assignments on a cost or any other basis.

Virtual mobility

Virtual mobility is the movement of knowledge without physical movement ('moving brains without bodies'). It relies on a series of tools such as teleconferencing, common databases and collaborative systems. These impinge upon business travel to varying degrees. There is some symbiosis between them, including both substitution and complementarity.

Summary

These different forms of mobility play different roles. They are formalized through benefits packages and allowable costs that are defined, at least initially, by the length of move and in some cases by the characteristics of the destination country. Generally, packages are more elaborate for long-term than short-term movements and for moves to comparatively inhospitable environments. However, there is considerable variation between companies in the ways that they define long- and short-term movements and what constitutes an inhospitable environment so that, in practice, the boundaries between the different types are not clear-cut.

Where does Business Travel Fit within Mobility Portfolios?

Although sometimes their roles overlap, these various forms of mobility are discrete. Companies use them in whatever combination is required according to business needs. Because there are certain elements of business operations that each type of mobility is particularly suited to, they are not easily substitutable one for another and hence cost alone is rarely the key factor in which type is used.

The amount of movement varies. In general it appears that for most forms of mobility it is increasing, either absolutely or relatively. Even where companies are downsizing there tends to be a less than proportionate response in the amount of movement. For example, an aerospace company reckoned that the level of business travel was about the same as ten years ago, despite a reduced workforce. In the same sector, another company with a long-standing joint operation at sites in the UK and on the continent estimated that about 100 people a day flew between the sites, mostly on day trips.

A common comment was that the scale of business travel is 'huge and very expensive'. While all respondents expressed concern about its cost, almost none were rigorously trying to rein in the amount of flying because it was recognized that global operations required mobile staff. However, most companies interviewed were hazy about exactly how much business travel there was. An electronics company admitted to paying for 30,000-50,000 air tickets per annum worldwide, but said 'we care don't whether that's for 200 people or 30,000'. A major difficulty in estimating the total volume of travel is that decisions to send someone abroad are distributed around the company and there is no central collection of information.

This is in contrast to assignments, responsibility for which is normally undertaken by the Human Resources department.

The factors involved in generating and orchestrating mobility portfolios and, within them, business travel are extremely complex. For the present purpose, they are reduced to four major groups, concerned with organizational structure and dynamics; client interface and trust; project, product and process; and market development. How each of these affects business travel will now be addressed.

Organizational structure and dynamics

All of the companies in our sample have evolved through a series of mergers and acquisitions (M&As) that gave rise initially to nationally focused, market-facing companies that operated independently, had devolved accountability and lacked integration. The ensuing consolidation demanded increasing volumes of international mobility in order to create an integrated corporate structure, replacing national focus with global identify and culture with common goals and visions. The early phase of such restructuring generates a surge of business travel, for example, to gain control over acquisitions, followed by a period of limited international mobility between decentralized entities. For example, after a merger one of our pharmaceutical companies went through a process of centralization as a precursor to offshoring and which spawned greater levels of business travel:

> With offshoring, you inevitably have meetings looking at what people are up to and if things go wrong, you're off trying to find out what's happening. (Pharmaceutical)

With greater internationalisation, firms look to business travel to provide the cement holding managerial control together.

> [It] oils the wheels, it's the lubricant that makes sure that the business continues to operate, that the leadership and control is provided, that the guidance in expertise is provided, that the strategy and operational excellence is provided. You know, it's just the way that we do business. (Pharmaceutical)

Managing international businesses as integrated entities often involves the development of matrix organizational structures and the creation of executive teams with global functional roles. Integration has increased business travel among senior executives associated with the need to create and spread common culture and practice throughout the business and it has increased both long and short-term mobility assignments among people who have skill sets that need to be spread throughout the corporation. One company reported operating a matrix organizational structure that created new global roles and multiple reporting lines spread between functional and project managers. This exerted two main demands for international mobility on senior level staff – first, international assignments to support project-leadership roles and second, extended business travel for global team management purposes.

> We're a matrix organisation anyway, so one person often has two bosses, and you then apply a project based organisation across that, and you've got a number of different individuals working for different project managers. (Consultancy)

> Within manufacturing, you tend to find that the head office people ... operate matrix teams .. so you would have a few people that would have the responsibility for going out and maybe passing information out to others or occasionally bringing people in to get knowledge. ... a lot of the mobility that you see in [company] is set up along those lines. It's not about sending somebody across there for three years. (Pharmaceutical)

Client interface and trust

Among manufacturing companies, customers' demands for closer contacts with their suppliers have also generated increasing volumes of business travel to attend meetings and build critical trust-based relationships. The penalties for inadequate relationship building in aerospace are high both in terms of loss of business and in terms of participation in those ongoing complex supply chain networks. Maintaining trust and goodwill generates high volumes of business travel.

> It's really important to be close to the customer and in a business where it's all about relationships; you get the relationship wrong means you don't get a big contract that lasts for 15 years, 20-30 years in terms of after-market. (Aerospace)

Client interface is also critical in the rather different world of consultancy. Corporate globalization among clients has presented consulting companies with major challenges for moving skills and expertise. However, the demands of achieving 'glocalised' operations include: global managerial oversight and extensive internal and external linkages and communications to filter, spread and accumulate knowledge and best practice. These increasingly demand frequent, and often extended, business travel – particularly among senior-level staff.

> There's definitely more, more sort of extended business travel than there is kind of secondment and international assignment moves, so we don't have a huge amount of international assignments on the go, at any one time. (Consultancy)

Regardless of the considerable potential for remote communications to support service delivery in this industry, face-to-face interaction was extremely important for relationship building – with clients as well as among teams.

> I think in the world of consulting, the ... face-to-face meeting is always still
> very, very key and on the sort of relationship building side of that as well.
> (Consultancy)

Project, product and process

Typically, the initial planning phase of a project or new product is associated with
extensive business travel. The early development phases, where risk and uncertainty
are high, demand specialized mobility among career expatriates or experienced
project managers 'who already know how to run billion dollar businesses'. In all
sectors, the more pragmatic demands of working on multiple projects – as well as
the characteristics of those projects – drive a desire for shorter-term movements,
assignments as well as business travel, supported by virtual communications.

> Sometimes if you've got a need for somebody and they've got to be covering two
> points or two areas, then they are going to have to do some travel so from that
> perspective you also have to take into consideration the needs of the individual,
> he will have a family, he will have a home, he doesn't necessarily want to, he
> physically can't move them backwards and forwards every three or four months
> so ... he's going to have to travel.

Where client-led networking and teaming was important, as in consultancy,
international mobility – typically short-term – as a response to client demands in
the context of a particular project was taken for granted.

> Here our consultants may very well be working on four, or five, or six projects,
> when things are tough and so they're having to juggle the project demands of
> bottlenecks. (Consultancy)

> I think what is growing dramatically are the number of short-term business
> visitors who are coming in, whether it's commuter or non-commuter it's coming
> in on projects. (Consultancy)

In extractives, project life cycles are of a different order to those in consulting.
The greatest volume of international moves are project-related. Upstream projects
are characterized by extensive lifecycles, long lead times to market, heavy
upfront capital investment, high risk, uncertainty, trial and error in development
and long payback times through development and upgrading through to eventual
decommissioning. These projects involve work on technologically complex
systems of component sub-project parts, each with their own project lifecycles
and particular skill requirements.

Different phases of project lifecycles generate different types of project-
related moves that may involve different people moving internationally 'different
specialists flying in at each stage of the asset and where it is in its lifecycle'.

You could have a project that would be in pre-feasibility for 2-3 years, you'd have one in a pre-feasibility study for a year, then from pre-feasibility study you get into the pre-operational phase which also starts off very much as a small project before it becomes operational and that can be up to four or five years. Then you move into life of a mine which then runs into anything from 20-30-40 years. (Extractives)

Markets and market development

The need to support a growing overseas presence from a remote location may drive international mobility among those with functional responsibilities that, hitherto, had been location specific, for instance, regular business travel among human resource managers. The bulk of international mobility in the IT-sector is characterized by very high volume, short-term movements – including business travel – among people with mid-level technical skills and lower volumes of longer-term moves among more senior staff.

Everyone is expected to be always mobile ... mobility is really key. The support functions, obviously, they don't move – like the finance guys, the HR guys and the infrastructure guys – although that, too, is changing because, as an organization takes on more and more responsibilities it needs more and more service from India. So they travel a lot – I expect my HR person in India to be here at least once a quarter for 2 weeks just visiting everyone and making sure things are in order. So they travel although, obviously, they don't get posted here. (IT)

Among consulting firms, where service delivery tends to be local, local team members may be supported by a distributed team of experts who may be brought in for very short periods to assist a project.

Typically you deliver locally, you pull in anyone from anywhere around the world. They can come from Australia, the States, they can come from ... across Europe and they will come straight in to the team and they will not be a problem. ... but we will move people in – if you need somebody for 3 days ... you put them in there to make it work. ... If you have a world class expert who in two days or a week can make a world of difference to the success of a project, you wheel them in and out again. (IT)

The patterns and directions of international mobility are influenced by business cycles that affect profit and investment opportunities. A decline in profitability generates cost-sensitivities that lead to reductions in assignments and a substitution of long-term with short-term, and short-term with business travel on cost grounds. One electronics company commented on the way in which all forms of mobility followed shifts in markets and technology developments.

> People only send ex-pats out when there's money available, so, we're on the top
> of this curve so there's more money to be spent in that discretionary spending
> space. So there's more business travel and there's more ex-pats. So it follows the
> cycle. If we were at the bottom of the cycle there would be less ex-pats and less
> business travel. (Electronics)

An increased volume of movement is typical in the initial stage of market
development. However, different types of people playing various roles may
be involved at each stage and each role may have different types of movement
associated with it. This limits the potential for substitution between, for example,
short-term and long-term assignments or between extended business travel and
short-term assignments. Short-term assignments or extended business travel
associated with winning business and building up markets.

> When markets are being built up and trust is being formed and you want to build
> a relationship that can rely on longer term contact. (Aerospace)

Business Travel and Virtual Mobility

Earlier it was suggested that there was more likely to be substitution between
business travel and virtual mobility than between other forms of mobility of
expertise. The degree to which this occurs is discussed in this section.

There is a lot of pressure on companies to substitute business travel with
virtual mobility, on both environmental and cost grounds. In reality, the two have
a symbiotic relationship. There are occasions when substitution is possible and
embraced; there are others when business travel alone will do. Several companies
commented that virtual was particularly poor at transmitting secure, secret or
sensitive information.

> And we also have restrictions for what you can do in restricted countries. We are
> a US corporation and Russia, China, etc. are restricted countries and we can only
> exchange certain data with those guys. We can't do some of the real teckie stuff,
> we can't exchange data with them because we're not allowed to because of the
> restrictions in the US law. (Electronics)

In consequence, the company had actually scaled back on some of its virtual
technology:

> We went through a big phase of having our own video conferencing technology
> – we had this dream that it was going to replace business travel. It never will
> and we've now got that realisation and we now have only one room equipped
> with video conference equipment. Prior to that we probably had 15. It's not as

effective as people think. You're as good on the telephone as you are on the video. (Electronics)

Undoubtedly, the main driver for substitution is cost, one firm for example claiming it had been able to halve its business travel bill through the use of virtual techniques. The reasons for changes in the balance between business travel and virtual mobility are not always obvious. One electronics company, with a new CEO more in favour of face-to-face contact than his predecessor, had insisted on a stronger focus on physical mobility that reversed an earlier tendency in the opposite direction:

Nowadays the focus is very much get out there, meet the people, do it in person. (IT)

There are a number of virtual technologies which are applied in varying degrees and circumstances. They include tele- and video conferencing, e-mail, mobile phones and connectivity networks. The value of a particular technology depends on the information to be transmitted. For the most part, virtual exchanges of expertise are used for more routine information sharing, 'for the back office' as one consultancy put it. E-mail and teleconferencing was most common – the latter, especially where teams were spread widely geographically; video conferencing was used where appropriate. The most successful technologies tend to be e-mail, mobile phones ('we wouldn't live without our Blackberrys these days') and shared connectivity sites with clients. Tele- and video conferencing have proved less effective 'because you never get that dynamic of what the person is really like'. However, symbiosis means that teleconferencing also creates the need for more business travel because it expands the range of contacts with the customer.

Teleconferencing has made a particular impact, particularly where business travel had previously been used to prepare for a meeting:

Teleconferencing has certainly reduced the number of business trips. In the past five to ten years ago, everyone would have had to get on a plane and go somewhere to have this conversation, which would cost the company a lot of money … but now you don't have to do that and you can also use it … almost like a pre-meeting. It does allow you to get a lot of the donkey work done before you [meet] … (IT)

Tele- and video conferencing have also had an impact on business travel for training purposes. Much of the initial training in companies is fairly standard so that recruits in several countries can receive training through video links rather than travel to an international centre.

So maybe seven years ago, we would all go off to somewhere in Europe and you know the same with Asia-Pac to have that training, whereas now we have

> video conferencing … So that kind of travel has been impacted by IT, certainly. (Consultancy)

In some cases, greater exposure to developments in technology can make a big difference. One of our pharmaceutical companies had recently merged with a larger competitor, already using a wide range of communications technologies:

> Because we've expanded and joined [a larger company], and we have now got that capability to have all this virtual conferencing and computer type support … now, we'll have the regular weekly T-Coms, whereas before we might have had a get together once every quarter, so there's much more virtual mobility that way. (Pharmaceutical)

This led directly to a reduction in business travel.

> Yes, we've got extensive video conferencing, telephone set ups so that you can get involved in sprint calls and other calls that bring various countries together. We've got computers set up on the basis that you can share servers, you can share processes. Everything is designed as far as possible to try and stop you travelling, or stop the need for you to travel. (Pharmaceutical)

The complementary nature of business travel and virtual mobility comes out time and again. Virtual mobility tended to be used to prepare for more effective meetings, increasing productivity by eliminating the need for business travel to prepare for meetings and possibly limiting the duration of eventual business moves.

> So you use all these facilities so that when you are face-to-face, it's going to be absolutely worthwhile and you're actually going to get something out of it because you've done all the preliminary work. (Pharmaceutical)

However, virtual techniques fail to compensate for the need for face-to-face meetings when complex interactions are involved and when non-verbal clues are important. Thus, in the early stage of a client relationship, when there are high levels of uncertainty on both sides, face-to-face is vital. This is especially the case where there is a need to manage the client interface for sensitive (risky and uncertain) activities like contract negotiations.

> I think it's very useful for, … getting the senior messages across to … the population, I think it's a tool … for delivering messages simultaneously, … but I don't think it's really kind of changed people actually still getting together and meeting their clients, meeting their teams. (Consultancy)

> You could do a lot of the preliminary work [virtually] but you wouldn't necessarily want to use that as a tool for negotiating with a client, you would use it as an internal process. (IT)

Later, once the relationship is established, the technology can take over:

> But nowadays once you have established a relationship, the communication systems are often so good that you can get around a video conference backed up by tools to communicate this material. (Consultancy)

This gives greater overall flexibility in working so that people can work from home or at client locations and still be connected back in the office, perhaps working on two or more things at once.

Conclusion

Business travel is a form of mobility of expertise. It interacts with other, longer duration moves to be a major element in the transfer of knowledge within global companies that is essential for their survival and development. Studies of labour migration have largely ignored business travel for well understood reasons. The move of home that underpins the concept of migration is not present in business travel.

Where business travel deserves consideration in the migration field is its place as one form of mobility among a set of movements that together constitute a mobility continuum. At one end of this continuum is permanent migration, at the other is business travel and between them is an array of shorter term moves including extended travel. Knowledge moves and is exchanged at all points along this continuum. Within global organizations each form of mobility has its own discrete role in knowledge accumulation and transfer. By and large the various forms of mobility complement each other but in some circumstances they may substitute. The particular role that business travel has within global companies has been discussed in this chapter. Multiple projects, multiple teams and, perhaps most important of all building trust, demand business travel.

Business travel has a close association with virtual mobility, adopted by companies for reasons of both cost and efficiency. Virtual mobility has proved a satisfactory substitute for business travel in many circumstances. It has allowed companies to operate globally through the exchange of routine information. Without virtual mobility of knowledge both information transaction and personal costs would rise. Indeed, there is a clear sense that globalization would not work without virtual teamwork.

Even so, it is also clear that there are many occasions when only face-to-face meetings will suffice. As the world economy becomes more global, the need for business travel can only increase. There is a cost for this and it falls particularly on the individuals who have to travel. Many are wedded to their airline gold cards, they enjoy being mobilcentric, but stress and declining efficiency take their toll.

For now, we need more empirical information from within companies about how they manage their mobility portfolios. Many of our companies lacked a central source of information on both permanent international recruitment and assignments. Information tended to be kept with the national arms of the global group as a whole. Information was even more fragmented with respect to business travel, permission and arrangements being left to individual managers. In consequence, at the level of the organization as whole it is impossible to know exactly how much business travel goes on and in what circumstances. Globalization may thrive on business travel but at the corporate level there is still much to be learned.

Filling this gap presents practical problems for companies and methodological ones for researchers. For the former, the sheer scale and diverse nature of business travel, together with its frequent unpredictability mean that tracking is an immense task. Some companies do now have recording systems in place, driven by both cost considerations and tax requirements, but from our evidence these are never at global corporate level. Even then, a problem for researchers is access because of the confidentiality that goes along with what are often regarded as market sensitive data. One potentially rich method of data acquisition is the use of 'diaries' for individual travellers to record the frequency and circumstances of their trips, along with personal assessments of their value. However, the complexities attendant on the seniority and occupations of the personnel travelling, the periods spent away and the reasons for movement mean that any research design must encompass a range of circumstances.

References

Baganha, M.I. and Entzinger, H. 2004. The political economy of migration in an integrating Europe: An introduction, in *Organisational Recruitment and Patterns of Migration: Interdependencies in an Integrating Europe*, edited by M. Bommes, K. Hoesch, U. Hunger and H. Kolb. Osnabrück: IMIS-Bietrage, 7-19.

Beaverstock, J. and Faulconbridge, J. This volume.

Cendant Mobility Services 2003. *Global Mobility Survey (2002)*. Connecticut: Cartus.

Collins, H.M. 1997. Humans, machines, and the structure of knowledge, in *Knowledge Management Tools*, edited by R.L. Ruggles. Boston: Butterworth-Heinemann, 145-163.

Edstrom, A. and Galbraith, J. 1977. Transfer of managers as a coordination and control strategy in multinational organizations. *Administrative Science Quarterly*, 22(2), 248-263.

Edwards, T. 1998. Multinationals, labour management and the process of reverse diffusion: A case study. *The International Journal of Human Resource Management*, 9(4), 696-709.

Faulconbridge, J.R. and Beaverstock, J.V. 2008. Geographies of international business travel in the professional service economy. *GaWC Research Bulletin*, 252, http://www.lboro.ac.uk/gawc/rb/rb252.html.

Ford, R. 1992. *Migration and Stress among Corporate Employees*. PhD thesis, University of London.

Forsgren, M., Holm, U. and Johanson, J. 2005. *Managing the Embedded Multinational: A Business Network View*. Cheltenham: Edward Elgar.

Ghoshal, S. and Bartlett, C.A. 1998. *Managing Across Borders: The Transnational Solution*, London: Random House.

GMAC, NFTC, SHRM Global Forum 2004. *Global Relocation Trends 2003/2004 Survey Report*, www.gmacglobalrelocation.com/ insight_support/grts/2003-04_GRTS.pdf, last accessed 18 July 2007.

Jennings, E.E. 1971. *The Mobile Manager: A study of the new generation of top executives*. New York: McGraw Hill.

Jones, A. 2008. The rise of global work. *Transactions of the Institute of British Geographers*, NS33, 12-26.

Koser, K. and Salt, J. 1997. The geography of highly skilled international migration, *International Journal of Population Geography*, 3(December), 285-303.

McKay, J. and Whitelaw, J.S. 1977. The role of large private and government organisations in generating flows of inter-regional migrants: The case of Australia. *Economic Geography*, 53(1), 28-44.

Mercer Human Resource Consulting 2003. *International Assignments Survey*, London.

Millar, J. and Salt, J. 2008. Portfolios of mobility: The movement of expertise in transnational corporations in two sectors – aerospace and extractive industries. *Global Networks*, 8(1), 25-50.

Millar, J., Demaid, A. and Quintas, P. 1997. Trans-organizational innovation: A framework for research. *Technology Analysis and Strategic Management*, 9(4), 399-418.

Millar, J. and Salt, J. 2007. In whose interests? IT migration in an interconnected world economy. *Population, Space and Place*, 13, 41-58.

O'Brien, R. 1992. *Global Financial Integration: The End of Geography*. London: Pinter.

Salt, J. 1997. International movements of the highly skilled. *International Migration Unit Occasional Papers*, No. 3, OECD, Paris.

Salt, J. and Ford, R. 1993. Skilled international migration in Europe: The shape of things to come? in *Mass Migration in Europe*, edited by R. King. Belhaven: London, 293-309.

Tani, M. 2003. International business travel and Australia's skills endowment. *Agenda*, 10(3), 245-258.

Whyte, W.H. 1956. *The Organization Man*. New York: Simon & Schuster.

Williams, A. 2007. Listen to me, learn with me: International migration and knowledge transfer. *British Journal of Industrial Relations*, 45(2), 361-382.

Zelinsky, W. 1971. The hypothesis of the mobility transition. *Geographical Review*, 61, 219-249.

Chapter 7

Hierarchies in the Air:
Varieties of Business Air Travel

James Wickham and Alessandra Vecchi

Introduction

Although business air travel appears to be one of the most visible and tangible aspects of globalization, until recently it received surprisingly little attention from academic research. This is all the more unfortunate because contemporary theories of social structure involve implicit assumptions about the consequences of extensive physical mobility, assumptions which are unencumbered by any encounter with empirical research. This chapter uses a case study of business travel in the Irish software industry in an attempt to reduce this gap between theorizing and empirical investigation.

The chapter begins with those theories of social structure which claim to identify new dominant groups in society ('symbolic analysts', the 'creative class', the 'new service class') – groups which are alleged to have new forms of mobility. The second section of the chapter sketches the social structure of the Irish software industry, focusing on the importance of professional and technical workers, putative members of the 'service class'. After a brief account of the actual research, the chapter then develops a taxonomy of business travellers in the industry: commuters, explorers, nomads and visiting tradesmen (the choice of gender is deliberate). We use this to explore the extent of autonomy enjoyed by different groups of travellers. We stress the extent of routine 'commuter' travel in the industry and, focusing on the role of visiting tradesmen, conclude that business travel replicates rather than destabilizes managerial hierarchies.

Business Travel and Social Hierarchies

Early accounts of the 'network society' (Castells 1996) ascribed a key role to information technology and in so doing built on a long tradition of research going right back to the 1970s (e.g. Kraft 1979) on 'computers and society'. By contrast, there was little attention paid to the physical movement of goods, the physical mobility of workers and the expansion of work-related travel. Air transport has largely remained taken for granted and outside the purview of social research.

One recent challenge to this silence has been the development of research on business travel. Initial work on the use of video conferencing and other forms of 'virtual travel' (Urry 2002) suggested the paradox that business travel and the use of information and communication technologies (ICT) by business have not only grown in parallel, but appear to be in general complementary rather than substitutes (for review of the small technical literature, see Mokhtarian 2003). The spread of video conferencing and other newer communication technologies continues to have had little impact on the growth of business travel (Denstadli 2004, Denstadli and Gripsrud, this volume). At the macro level Choi et al. (2006) have shown that the networks of air transport and internet backbone have the same structure. Just as in the nineteenth century the telegraph wires ran alongside the railway lines, so in the twenty-first century the electronic linkages parallel the airline routes.

Most business travel is driven by the need for face-to-face meetings. As we shall see, travellers believe that only by physically meeting someone can they build up trust, acquire detailed knowledge and carry out complex negotiations. A long research tradition has stressed that physical proximity in economic clusters or 'industrial districts' enables the development of trust and informal knowledge between local firms (e.g. Giuliani 2005). Only relatively recently however has it been noticed that the *temporary* proximity of meetings, conferences and trade fairs has a very similar function (e.g. Maskell et al. 2006, Wickham and Vecchi 2008). Similarly, senior staff of large corporations make short-term visits (and hold intensive face-to-face meetings) to transfer expertise or acquire knowledge (Millar and Salt 2008). Research on business elites has shown how business travel creates personal links between global cities and is used by firms to manage the distribution of skills and knowledge (e.g. Beaverstock 2004). Such an approach begins to treat business travel as a form of mobility and so links transport technology with the broader study of migration.

Opening up air travel to research could also mean exploring its implications for social structure. For writers such as Manuel Castells it is axiomatic that in the 'network society' enterprises are themselves de-layered and flexible. Because information technology allows everyone to contact everyone, then enterprises become de-hierachialized. Although this is rarely explicitly discussed, it could be assumed that air travel would have the same consequence. Just like virtual travelling, easy physical travelling facilitates contacts across traditional organizational structures. Organizations can become loose and shifting networks of individuals, rather than rigid command-and-control bureaucratic structures in which communications only flow vertically. Yet here we encounter a second paradox. Especially but not exclusively in the USA, the growth of such new and allegedly egalitarian organizational forms has coincided with growing social inequality (e.g. Ryscavage 1999). Everywhere the income of the upper decile has been moving away from that of the rest of society. At least to date therefore, loose network structures have been associated with greater social inequality.

A coherent explanation for this contradiction was put forward by Reich's (1993) account of 'symbolic analysts'. This suggested that employment in the USA could be divided into three broad categories: routine production work, in-person services, and symbolic-analytic services. For the first and second categories globalization is a threat. Routine production work can be outsourced to cheap labour areas, in-person services can be provided by new low-paid immigrants. By contrast, not only does globalization increase the demand for 'symbolic analysts', but communication and transport technologies also facilitate their mobile forms of working. As such the working conditions – and the incomes – of the symbolic analysts diverge from those of the other two groups.

For Reich symbolic analysts are 'knowledge workers' who 'broker' information and identify, analyse and solve problems. Reich estimates that these symbolic analysts now represent approximately 20 per cent of the US workforce, up from about eight per cent in 1950. They are rarely in direct contact with the clients who benefit from their work and their principal products are 'reports, plans, and proposals'. Teamwork is often critical to them, and 'when not conversing with their team-mates, they sit before computers, spend long hours in meetings or on the telephone and even longer hours in jet planes and hotels' (Reich 1993, 122). The most important reason for this expansion has been the dramatic improvement in worldwide communication and transportation technologies:

> Symbolic-analytic services can be transported at no cost. When face-to-face meetings are still required, and video conferencing will not suffice, it is relatively easy for symbolic-analysts to travel and meet directly with their worldwide clients. (Reich 1993, 222)

For Reich symbolic analysts are inherently mobile. Much of their work involves meeting and briefly interacting with those who pay for their services – who may be anywhere in the globe. The sheer normality of travel for them apparently arises because the work of the symbolic analyst involves making brief connections between different groups of differently knowledgeable people. The more important are these connections, the more travel will be involved.

If travel is thus an obligation for symbolic analysts, for Reich they are remarkably unconstrained in where they are actually based, since their more static work can be done anywhere. More recently Florida (2004) has argued that it is the location choices of members of the 'creative class' (broadly analogous to Reich's symbolic analysts) that determine economic growth. If a city wishes to attract innovative and creative industries, what matters now is its diversity and tolerance and the quality of life it can offer the new elite. Symbolic analysts and members of the creative class are thus seen as uniquely unconstrained in their choice of workplace.

Reich's account of the work of symbolic analysts has two further themes which resonate with subsequent accounts of these occupations. Firstly, such people now also enjoy unprecedented autonomy in the workplace in terms of how they organize their own work, and secondly (and interwoven with this) the work organization itself is 'flat' and relatively egalitarian. Thus, whereas Reich provides an account of overall social inequality *between* his three social groups, he posits an almost communitarian situation *within* his dominant group.

Other studies of the social structure of contemporary market societies have defined the dominant class as the 'service class'. In the 1980s British sociologists developed Renner's original formulation to conceptualise the service class as comprising occupations at the peaks of large scale bureaucracies. Subsequent work has however focused on the transformation of these groups (for overview see Bidou-Zachariasen 2000). However the concept of the service class is essentially an aggregation of occupations. Certainly those who use the term have stressed the contemporary de-bureaucratization of the large-scale capitalist enterprise, while also highlighting changes in the profession and in the public sector (e.g. Hanlon 1998). Nonetheless, while the 'service class' is defined as the same occupations as those which allegedly comprise Reich's symbolic analysts or Florida's creative class, the term itself does not depend on claims about new forms of work – claims which are intrinsic to the arguments of Reich or Florida.

As we have seen, for both Reich and Florida mobility is doubly linked to autonomy: not only can 'creatives' or 'symbolic analysts' choose where to live, but because their work involves travel they are free from the constraints of the traditional office workplace. However, what is unclear is the extent to which mobility and autonomy are actually linked, and the extent to which they, singly or together, are defining features of *all* 'symbolic analysts', *all* 'creatives' or *all* members of the 'service class'. One way to answer this question is to focus on the relationship between business travel and inequality within the service class in general and within business organizations in particular. Instead of assuming that mobility is simply a natural part of work, we need to ask *who* travels and with what extent of autonomy. What is the relationship between the hierarchies of business organizations and the mobility of business travel? At its simplest, who decides whom is to travel?

Physical mobility was not a theme in the initial discussion of the service class, but the more specialist literature on skilled migration shows that highly skilled managers and professionals are especially likely to live away from their country of birth, have career paths that take them through a variety of countries, and furthermore are especially likely to be involved in various forms of short-term migration such as 'expatriation' or two-city living (Salt 1997, Beaverstock 2005). Because air travel allows such people to travel easily, firms can create portfolios of skill which they can deploy across the globe (Salt, this volume). However, such studies tend however to be confined to relatively elite groups of managers often moving between a few global cities. At the same time, air travel data has been used to identify 'global cities' within world communication networks (e.g. Smith and Timberlake 2001, Derudder and Witlox 2008). Since such studies focus on relations between cities, they say relatively about mobility and relations *within* enterprises: the search for hierarchies amongst cities paradoxically occludes hierarchies within enterprises. To understand the role of mobility in the service class more generally, we need to move beyond the study of business elites and the study of global cities.

Here the software industry – the subject of this chapter – is an interesting contrast to financial services. Although software production is relatively concentrated in global terms, the centres of production are not the global cities of the financial services industry. At least in Ireland, the industry is notorious for its high levels of business travel. Conversely, access to Dublin airport has been crucial for the growth of the Irish software industry. Extensive travel (always involving air travel) is a normal part of many different occupations in the industry.

A case study of travel in the software industry is therefore well suited to exploring the role of business travel within the new service class. Such a case study can disaggregate both the service class and business travel. It can identify who travels to what destinations and for what purpose. This in turn allows an investigation of the relationships between travel, hierarchy and autonomy within the dominant groups of contemporary society. How is business travel related to the nature of work and the business strategy of individual enterprises? How is business travel related to individuals' position within the managerial hierarchy? Does it offer an escape from organizational hierarchies or contribute to their re-affirmation? In what ways is business travel interwoven with use of electronic communication?

The Service Class and the Irish Software Industry

According to Florida (2005, 136) Ireland now has a larger proportion of employment in 'creative class' jobs than any other country in the world (over 30 per cent of jobs if technicians are excluded); it also has had the fastest rate of growth in these occupations in recent years. Indeed Boyle (2006) uses Ireland's capital city as a test of Florida's thesis that the quality of life which a city can offer is now a major determinant of economic growth. Ireland is therefore also well suited for a case study of the role of business travel in the work of what is here termed the service class.

One preliminary point is needed. Reich's own account of 'symbolic analysts' implied that their independence was partly because they were often self-employed. Indeed, the growth of the self-employed independent consultant was a constant theme of popular business literature at the turn of the century (e.g. Pink 2002). Florida himself explicitly rejected such claims and they certainly do not apply to Ireland. Analysis of the census micro-data shows that amongst 'professional' and 'managerial and technical occupations' the proportion who were employees (as opposed to self-employed) actually *rose* between 1996 and 2002, from 72.3 per cent to 76.1 per cent and from 75.7 per cent to 80.4 per cent respectively.[1] The service class is predominantly a class of employees.

To measure the size of the 'creative class', Florida simply takes the number of people in professional and managerial *occupations*. This ignores the crucial question of economic sector. In Ireland much of the growth in these occupations has come from the public sector, from rather traditional state services (especially education and health) and the civil service itself. Here Ireland is hardly unique. However, the 'Celtic Tiger', the Irish economic boom which began in the late 1980s, did generate professional and managerial jobs in industries that had hardly existed before. In sectors such as software 'service class' jobs were created which could be expected to be close to those of Reich's symbolic analysts or Florida's creative class.

The Irish software industry was a key element of the 'Celtic Tiger'. For more than half a century, Irish economic growth has depended on a continual inflow of foreign direct investment. The emergence of the foreign-owned software sector can be seen as a continuation of the successes – and the failures – of this policy. Large international (almost entirely US) companies initially set up plants in Ireland in order to export to the European market. By the mid-1990s Ireland was the world's second largest software exporter and produced more than 50 per cent of all software packages sold in Europe for personal computers (O'Gorman et al. 1997, 1). This in turn enabled Ireland to also rapidly become the European centre for software localisation for such companies. In 2005 there were a total of 140 such foreign-owned software firms in Ireland employing a total of 13,000 employees. In the foreign-owned software sector the markets are international and the production process in Ireland is itself part of a global process. Both factors, we can assume, make business travel important.

Employment in the indigenous software sector is almost as large as in the foreign owned sector. Whereas a few Irish firms can be traced back to the 1970s, in the 1990s a significant number of new Irish firms emerged. The total number of indigenous software companies rose from 291 in 1991 to 770 by year 2000. In 2005 the number of firms had fallen back slightly to 750 and total employment was 11,100. Irish software firms are not micro-enterprises, but they are significantly smaller than the MNCs (the average number of 15 employees is 15, that of the MNCs 92) (NSD 2007). Like the MNCs these Irish-owned firms are export-oriented, but totally unlike the MNCs, the Irish firms developed new highly specialized products and services centred on specific technologies. For such firms, the Irish market was of little importance and almost from the beginning they depended on exporting to niche markets abroad, including the USA (Wickham and Vecchi 2008). As Table 7.1 shows, even very small Irish software companies have offices abroad. For the indigenous sector too, business travel is important.

---

1   We acknowledge permission for the use of the COPSAR data set from the Central Statistics Office – Census of Population Sample of Anonymised Records © Government of Ireland.

The vast majority of the employees in the industry are clearly skilled. Thus one source reports that in 1999/2000 19 per cent of those employed in the industry were 'managers', 20 per cent 'professionals' and 34 per cent 'associated professionals and technical workers' (Wickham and Boucher 2004). Taking these proportions as a base line would mean that the 'service class' of the software industry comprises at most about 19,000 people. Given however that in Ireland in 2006 some 700,000 people were working in 'professional, managerial and technical' occupations (approximately 33 per cent of the workforce) the software industry contributes at most 3 per cent of the total service class.

Managers and professionals in the software industry are important not because of their numerical significance within the broader service class, but because they work in jobs which are new, are in globally oriented firms and which involve extreme levels of mobility. Although business and leisure travel is increasingly difficult to differentiate, growth in business travel has been one factor which has made Dublin airport one of the world's fastest growing airports, currently the ninth largest airport in Europe and indeed the 16th largest in the world (DAA 2007). Amongst these business travellers, many work in the Irish software industry. A study of travel in the software industry therefore is a study of a sector where work should closely resemble the descriptions of Reich and Florida.

Researching Business Air Travel

The rest of this chapter analyses the nature of business travel by looking at the travel patterns of individuals within Irish software firms. The chapter uses case studies of ten companies based in Dublin, three foreign-owned, seven indigenous, identified here by the letters A through J (Table 7.1). The companies were also selected to reflect the range of products in the sector, differentiated into 'middleware' and 'end-user' products. In each company we collected basic background data: history, size, ownership (indigenous vs. foreign), range of activities, extent of outsourcing, organizational structure, market and external relations.

In each company we asked to interview the senior manager best able to give an overview of the company's business travel; in small companies this was usually the Chief Executive Officer (CEO). We asked our respondents about the amount of business travel undertaken within the company and the use of ICT-mediated communication; we asked them to identify the people in the company who travelled most. The second part of the interview examined the travel pattern of the interviewee in order to obtain a more accurate picture of their individual travel patterns, both in relation to places that are regularly visited as well as trips that are more infrequent and often undertaken on the basis of *ad hoc* arrangements as illustrated in Table 7.2. Respondents were prompted to discuss their individual travel patterns: the purpose of their own travel, the destinations and frequency of their journeys, the discretion and the freedom they enjoy over the journey as well as the extent to which they use ICT.

Table 7.1 Case study firms

Firm	Ownership:	Employment in Dublin	Foreign offices (Irish firms)	Product: Middleware vs end-user
A	Irish	130	5	Middleware
B	Irish	25	None	End-user
C	Irish	25	3	End-user
D	Foreign	600	n/a	End-user
E	Foreign	120	n/a	Middleware
F	Irish	200	2	End-user
G	Irish	50	2	Middleware
H	Foreign	350	n/a	Middleware
I	Irish	16	3	Middleware
J	Irish	40	1	End-user

Table 7.2 Managers' travel in the case study firms

Interviewee	Position	Places regularly visited	Places visited occasionally	Product
A	Marketing Manager	UK/Ireland	None	Software for Telecom
B	Commercial Manager	Ireland/UK States The Netherlands	None	Business Software Solutions
C	Customer Relations Manager	Ireland/UK	None	Software for Universities
D	Managing Director	Europe US	China Asia	Business Software Solutions
E	Customer Relations Manager	None	Many	Software for Financial Sector
F	Customer Relations Manager	UK/Ireland Finland US	Norway Russia South Africa + 'ad hoc trips to the usual countries'	Software for Telecom
G	Chief Technology Officer	US Germany	2 conferences	Middleware software for game developers
H	R&D Manager	Sweden Canada India	*Ad hoc* trips to US Europe	Software for Telecom
I	Chief Executive Officer	UK US	2 conferences	Middleware software for game developers
J	Customer Relations Manager	UK Germany	None	Software for Financial Sector

Interviews were carried out during 2005 and supplemented by background information on the companies, in particular from company websites. In three companies additional interviews were carried out during 2007.

A Travelling Life

Modalities of travel

Our interviews showed that in the software industry travel is a fact of life, but it takes different forms for different companies and for different individuals. It would be absurdly pedantic not to make statements such as 'Manager A travels less than Manager B', even though our measurements are hardly very precise. The diagram (Figure 7.1) attempts to formalize such statements by showing a graphical representation of individuals' travel patterns. It should be stressed that our 'variables' (travel reach, new places visited) are at most ordinal level data and we do not claim that the measures are anything more than an initial sketch. On the Y-axis we measure the number of places that our interviewees visit on a regular basis (individual traveller's reach). On the X-axis we measure the number of novel places that they visit. On the basis of these two parameters we mapped out the travel patterns of the most travel intensive individuals for each company.

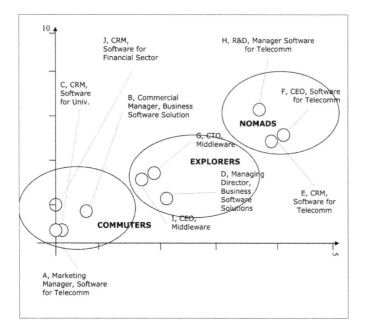

Figure 7.1 A taxonomy of travellers

Even though all our interviewees spent much of their time travelling, Figure 7.1 shows how their travel patterns tend to cluster along three main modalities. We have named these 'commuters', 'explorers' and 'nomads'. Commuters are business travellers who – on average – routinely travel, but do so to relatively few destinations and hardly ever travel to new places. Located in the lower left of the diagram, they are low on both the reach axis (number of places visited) and on the novelty axis (number of new places visited). Explorers travel to more destinations and some of these are novel; they therefore score higher on both reach and the novelty dimensions. Finally nomads travel to even more places, to many of which they have never been before. Located in the upper right of the diagram, they score highest on both dimensions. We now examine each of these three types of traveller, along with the 'visiting tradesmen' who are reported in these interviews but not interviewed directly.

Commuters

Interviewee A works as the Marketing Manager in an Irish-owned company based in Dublin. The company specializes in internet protocol mediation software for global telecom companies; it employs around 130 people spread throughout the world. The CEO is based in the company's head office in Dublin, though he actually lives in France; other senior staff are based in Dublin but live in the UK, as does interviewee A.

 Given that the company has a number of smaller offices throughout the world, our interviewee explained that the staff of the company get together very rarely, but phone and e-mail were sufficient for keeping in touch. He explained that even though he is a manager of product marketing he does not travel extensively, but does travel every week or so between the UK and Ireland:

> Unlike in other companies, the Marketing Manager [of a company specialised in the telecommunication sector] is part of the communication process rather than meeting to finalise sales. (Interview A)

When asked about the freedom and discretion he enjoys when deciding his travel, he explained that there was a formal travel policy in place:

> A few years ago travel costs were getting out of hand, and it couldn't carry on like that. Now all travel has to be authorised, you need to explain where you need to travel to and why. All travel is economy class, well, with the exception of trips to Australasia, and this includes senior managers. The costs have declined dramatically and there is more attention to travel costs, for example a trip that used to involve three people will be just one person: fewer people, travelling more cheaply with maybe slightly fewer trips, though this would be marginal. Since I arrived here, travel has changed a lot. Travel was a lot easier, frequent and less controlled. (Interview A)

Interviewee C, the Customer Relations Manager of a company providing software for universities, travel means regular trips to the UK to maintain contact with existing clients. As she explained:

> Project managers and technical staff travel more often (4-5 days per week on average), where I personally travel "only" 2-3 days per week. They travel to solve practical issues of implementing the software on-site, where I go over more "to visit people". (Interview C)

Despite the intensity of her travel, its fairly routine nature defines her as a commuter.

B works as the Commercial Manager in the transport and telecom division of a company specialized in providing bespoke business solutions to corporate clients. He is also a commuter but his more central location in the graph requires some explanation. B regularly travels to Amsterdam and 'other places in Europe and in the US' and on average he is away for three days out of ten. When prompted to discuss his travel pattern, he identified the need to travel as involving:

- Prospecting for new clients
- Delivering expertise and consulting
- Managing projects at the site of partners and the point of sales to end users,
- Checking that everyone is happy with progress or products though brief personal updates
- Clarifying details through customers coming to Ireland, virtual communication, or 'though it's more unusual, shipping out a few techies over to them' (Interview B).

B explained that he controls his own work travel and this flexibility enables him to organize meetings at convenient times and with stay overs that make the trip more enjoyable. For him travel involved a lot of networking, and might involve 'contacts through contacts', cold calling, or meeting people through introductions from some of the state support organizations, such as Enterprise Ireland. Travel might be arranged around a specific customer who wants to get together with him, but to make the most of the trip it is then filled up with other contacts, prospecting and networking.

The defining feature of 'commuters' is the regular trip to one or two destinations. As our interviews show, one reason is simply the distance between home (or at least the main residence) and the workplace. In Company A for example, both our interviewee and the CEO do not live in Ireland, but travel regularly to Dublin from their homes in England or France respectively. They will usually stay in Dublin for several nights, so that cheap and frequent air travel has not only extended the physical distance over which it is possible to commute, it has also enabled people to maintain several distinct living places. Such commuting is an extension of the traditional journey from home to work. However, air travel also enables regular travel between different work destinations, as when interviewee C travels regularly to the UK from Dublin to visit a small number of existing clients. Here the regular and almost routine journey occurs in order to maintain an existing customer base.

Some of our other interviewees also made regular journeys between their companies' different offices. Just as air travel enabled some of our travellers to have multiple living places, so some of them also had multiple workplaces. While this generated regular commuter *journeys,* all those who travelled in this way also made many other journeys, so that none of them have been classified as commuter *travellers.*

Explorers

For commuters the key journey is one between two distinct places, between home and work or between two different homes. Such journeys are regular and familiar. By contrast, the defining feature of explorers' journeys is their *novelty.* Explorers frequently travel to places where they have not been before. Yet whereas explorers travel to new places, they always come home, they always report to base. Like the heroic European adventurers of the past, explorers return home with news of strange and wonderful places – which they are opening up for business.

One example is interviewee I, the CEO of a software company, He is based in Dublin but travels to Los Angeles every 3-4 weeks and stays there for at least a week. He also travels to London every two weeks for a couple of days. He also regularly attends several conferences a year. Most of I's journeys are therefore commuting journeys, but his frequent conference visits make him an incipient explorer:

> The people who travel the most are the CEO, the CTO and the Sales Director. The CEO goes to LA every 3-4 weeks and he stays there for at least a week, he goes to London every two weeks for a couple of days. The CTO goes to LA every 5-6 weeks and he stays there for ten days. The Sales Director travels extensively all around the US to meet up with potential publishers and he on average gives a presentation every three weeks. The entire team goes to two main trade-shows: one, the Game Developers Conference in March, which is very technical, therefore the entire team needs to attend "to keep everyone in the loop" the other one, E3, is held in May in LA and is open to the public. (Interview I)

Again, when prompted to discuss his travel pattern our interviewee pointed out how this has to do with his activity along with the company size:

> Obviously when you have simple products, you have easy sales and the amount of business travel that you have to do becomes less. But for a small company it is very important to have people close to the customers – the CEO and the CTO have to be there, out, all the times next to the bigger customers. When

the partnership with X [a large multi-national] began after briefly discussing a proposal over the phone, they asked to get someone there straight away and they were very impressed by Sean who immediately flew there (LA) on the following day, I think that's how we got the deal. (Interview I)

He also clarified this point by explaining the importance of business travel for a small company if compared with the use of ICT:

Phone calls, e-mails and instant messaging are extensively used to provide support. Video conferencing has no use for products with a sophisticated technical content. When the customer wants to evaluate a product you have to send people there. When I go over as I am the CEO, we all get visibility: sending a senior manager is very important to finalise a deal, to meet customers, to meet potential customers and for networking in general. It has to do with prestige and it makes us look bigger than we actually are. (Interview I)

Who travels and when is decided by himself as CEO and by the CTO. In this small company the two most important executives have autonomy, but nobody else.

Interviewee D is the Managing Director of a foreign-owned company providing business software solutions. Like interviewee I, he too has regular journeys: he has many routine visits within Europe and some to the USA. However, he is an explorer because he is now beginning to travel to China and to the Asia Pacific region:

Most business travel is around Europe, but there is a lot to USA and the amount elsewhere is beginning to grow, particularly to China. The areas of Europe, USA and the Asian Pacific are three zones that are served by individuals that while based in Ireland will travel to and throughout that zone. (Interview D)

Solving conflicts and smoothing out difficulties with customers means 'we deal with a customer's difficulty on a one-to one and face to face basis' and contract negotiations need to be done in person so that 'you can see the whites of their eyes' (interview D). In addition, clients have to be taken to operations and even brought to meet other clients. This was typically between Ireland, the UK and Germany:

For example, one client we have is a bank in Ireland, and we arranged for them to meet another customer which, as they need to meet a non-competing bank, means that we take them to Germany. (Interview D)

Although D's company had a centralized booking procedure, he considered that he was not the only person with discretion over his travel plans. Flights are usually booked electronically through a travel company, though where need be, people can make their own travel arrangements either directly or through their office assistants. Nonetheless, D maintained that the procedure operated more to control costs than as a means of closely supervising other employees.

Overall explorers tend to be strategy-oriented, often executives such as Managing Directors, CEOs and CTOs. Like the commuters, they travel to familiar places to attend internal meetings of the company. Such travel usually involves a 'command and control' role, co-ordinating the different activities of the firm (recall that even the small Irish firms usually have offices overseas). Crucially however, they also visit novel and still unexplored places to conduct negotiations and establish links with new customers and new suppliers. Our explorers' continued stress on the importance of face-to-face contact in these situations recalls the role of 'hand-shakes' (physical interaction) in creating trust and shared understandings in long-distance business relationships (Leamer and Storper 2001); their insistence that only by meeting people in the flesh can they really understand the technical possibilities of co-operation recalls the role of human 'pipelines' in transmitting knowledge between high technology clusters (Bathelt et al. 2004). This need for a physical corporeal presence in strange places creates explorers. Almost by definition, as they venture out into the unknown world, they make their own decisions and organize their own travel.

Nomads

Even if explorers spend much of their time 'on the road' (or more accurately, in the air), they have a clear sense of base, of home. However, we have noticed that some of our travellers have multiple workplaces and/or multiple residences, all facilitated by ubiquitous electronic communications and cheap air travel. Potentially at least, these might allow the emergence of *nomads* who really are at home nowhere and who are able to work anywhere.

Amongst our interviewees the three individuals in the upper right hand side of Figure 1 come close to this type. Compared to our other interviewees, they travel both to more places (high on the reach dimension) and to more new places (to the right on the novelty dimension). Thus interviewee F is the CEO of an Irish-owned company providing a range of software solutions for both the wholesale and retail telecommunications markets. He lives in the UK, but commutes regularly to Ireland. However, he also travels to Finland and the US, while making some '*ad hoc* trips to the usual countries' which here means China, India, Japan, and the rest of the Asian Pacific area.

The company is still relatively small, with only fifty employees. However, it has been growing steadily, partly through acquisitions, and now has a small research and development centre outside Dublin as well as regional offices in the US and Europe. As the company's sales have grown, so has his travel:

> The customer expects the supplier to visit them, if not they don't think that we can take care of them. Sometimes they need to see the CEO to know you are a serious company; it's reassurance for them. (Interview F)

Interviewee F described people in the software industry who seemed to delight in what he termed the 'masochistic perversion of endlessly following one trip from hell with another', although according to him, such 'airport warriors' are still relatively rare, rather than industry standard:

> Having said that, recently I was called by my first name by someone who works at Heathrow Airport just on the basis of the amount of times I pass through the place. I don't know how many millions of passengers pass through the airport each year, but it's pretty scary to be known in Heathrow, to stand out as a regular. (Interview F)

The other two nomads were the Marketing Communications Manager of Firm E (and one of the two women amongst our interviewees) and the R&D Director of Firm H. Even more so than the explorers, they travel to many destinations, some of which they are visiting for the first time. Furthermore, their relationship to any base in Ireland is tenuous. Not only are they physically out of the country for long lengths of time, but for both of them their 'home' reference point is essentially the global company rather than its operations that happen to be located in Ireland.

Below the radar: Visiting tradesmen

Our interviewees frequently commented on the importance of other travellers whom we describe as visiting tradesmen (the gender is deliberate). The simplest case is where people travel to visit customers' sites to solve technical problems. The more complex situation is where the product has to be installed and customised at the customer's site. This is often effectively project work and can involve the temporary migration of employees of the supplying firm to the customer's site. Although such work has a high technical content, it also requires the 'migrants' to have a range of social skills in order to interact effectively with the customer's employees with their very different concerns and experiences. Finally, people may be members of a development team which is spread over several workplaces (which or may or may not be part of the same firm) but held together by frequent physical visits, sometimes just of managers but often also of team members. The latter case is an example of the importance in the software industry of what we have elsewhere called the 'co-located project' (Wickham and Vecchi 2008, see also O'Riain 2000).

Our interviewees were all senior managers. For them the purpose of travel is essentially to meet with other people to exchange information and, more or less explicitly, to increase the level of trust within the business relationship. By contrast, for visiting tradesmen the purpose of travel is to work (often for days and sometimes for weeks) at the client's site. While we have classified Interviewee G as an explorer (Figure 7.1), he contrasted his travel with that of sales staff and technical staff:

Sales people make frequent short trips. They are not salesmen in the traditional sense but provide a range of skills to customers. The service and support people travel less frequently but for longer duration, maybe a few days, maybe a week or so. (Interview G)

Equally in Firm A sales staff make short visits, but the service staff stay longer at any one site:

We are a technology driven company. Sales people make frequent short trips. They are not salesmen in the traditional sense but provide a range of skills to customers. The service and support people travel less frequently but for longer duration, maybe a few days maybe a week or so. (Interview A)

And in Firm J:

Project teams generally spend 50% of their working time on site … out of a project of six months they will be spending on site more than three months. The Support Team, made up of 18 people amongst which developers and leading support personnel travel for 40% of their working time. Developers are responsible for quarterly reviews on site, where leading support personnel travel slightly more – five-six times per year for each project … (Interview J)

The software industry is hardly unique in having sales people who are frequent travellers. A more distinctive feature of the industry is the importance of support staff and of project members whose work also involves extensive travel. For all three groups, their actual work may be relatively autonomous, but they have little choice over where they work. Unlike their managers, they do not choose when and where to travel, they are essentially simply dispatched to their new destinations. For them, frequent travel is hardly the same as autonomy. Indeed, despite the alleged importance of technical knowledge in theories of the new workforce, it is those whose work has the highest technical content who have less autonomy – and who, according to our respondents, often travel the most.

Conclusion

Examining the travel patterns of individuals allows us to disaggregate the generic category 'business traveller'. As in particular Millar and Salt (2008) have also shown, there are very different types of business travellers even (or perhaps especially) in an industry where frequent travel is the norm for managers and professionals. To understand business travel we have to move beyond aggregate journey statistics and locate individuals within the enterprises for whom they fly.

Focusing on the different journeys our interviewees made, we distinguished between commuters, explorers and nomads. For commuters all their journeys are routine: they travel to relatively few destinations and hardly ever travel to new places. Explorers usually also have routine journeys, but always travel to more places, some of which they have never visited before. Explorers 'report back' their findings, for although they are frequently on the move they are linked to a clearly defined base. Nomads have even more destinations more of which are novel. However, nomads are essentially defined by the fact that they have cut the umbilical cord which links explorers to their base. As such nomads are close to the heroic cosmopolitan business traveller whose adventures in sophisticated eateries and boutique hotels are described in the leisure pages of the global business press. Interestingly, the more nomadic of our interviewees were especially aware of such images, but tended to treat them with considerable irony. Finally, our interviewees also reported numerous other travellers with very different journeys whom we classified as visiting tradesmen. These comprised sales staff, technical support staff and project workers. They all travel in order to carry out technical work at a foreign destination (recall that in software even sales staff provide technical skills to customers). Their journeys usually involve just travelling to one destination, staying for anything up to several weeks, and then returning back to base.

The different travel patterns of our interviewees are partly explained by their different jobs. Commuters are all in various roles in customer relations and sales. This is unsurprising, since the rationale for the normal regular journey in the industry is to maintain contact with existing customers. We have seen however that some sales managers have become explorers, for in addition to this routine task they also 'prospect' for new clients. Both explorers and nomads are however less clearly defined since each group includes both technology managers and chief executives. By contrast, the journeys of visiting tradesmen are directly linked to their jobs – to take a job in the software industry in sales or customer support will entail this sort of travel, while to the extent that technical staff working on a project travel, it will also take this form.

In the software industry extensive business travel and high use of information technology has ensured that for many people work is no longer uniquely linked to a specific workplace. Work occurs at multiple workplaces, including that of the customer, and also while travelling. Equally the managers and owners in the industry often have multiple residences, so that for them the notion of 'home' as a unique place becomes blurred. In these terms our interviewees do appear to resemble Reich's freewheeling symbolic analysts who can work anywhere and Florida's creatives who can choose where to live.

Yet this is simplistic. For most of our interviewees most of their journeys are routine trips, visiting existing customers to maintain the firm's customer base. By definition our commuters only make such commuter journeys, our explorers do make exploratory journeys but usually these are in addition to (rather than instead of) more routine trips. Such journeys are hardly the expressive individual choice of Reich's symbolic analysts. Certainly, our interviewees themselves do largely make their own travel decisions, even if this has to be within a company defined purchasing policy. However, talking about their own travel is very different to talking about the travel of the sales, support and technical staff in the company. For these – who are frequently reported to actually travel more than the managers – the realm of choice is much more constrained. For the visiting tradesmen, when they travel and what they do at their destination is hardly their decision. In this sense, business travel articulates the hierarchies of the business enterprise – in the air.

References

Bathelt, H., Malmberg, A. and Maskell, P. 2004. Clusters and knowledge: Local buzz, global pipelines and the process of knowledge creation. *Progress in Human Geography*, 28(1), 31-56.

Beaverstock, J. 2004. 'Managing across borders': Knowledge management and expatriation in professional service legal firms. *Journal of Economic Geography*, 4, 157-179.

Beaverstock, J. 2005. Transnational elites in the city: British highly-skilled inter-company transferees in New York. *Journal of Ethnic and Migration Studies*, 31(2), 245-268.

Bidou-Zachariasen, C. 2000. A propos de la 'service class': Les classes moyennes dans la sociologie britannique. *Revue Francaise de Sociologie*, 41(4), 777-796.

Boyle, M. 2006. Culture in the rise of tiger economies: Scottish expatriates in Dublin and the 'creative class' thesis. *International Journal of Urban and Regional Research*, 30(2), 403-426.

Castells, M. 1996. *The Rise of the Network Society (Vol. 1 of the Information Age)*. Oxford: Basil Blackwell.

Choi, J., Barnett, G., and Chon, B. 2006. Comparing world city networks: A network analysis of internet backbone and air transport intercity linkages. *Global Networks*, 6(1), 81-99.

DAA (Dublin Airport Authority) 2007. *Annual Report 2006.*

Denstadli, J. 2004. Impacts of videoconferencing on business travel: The Norwegian experience. *Journal of Air Transport Management*, 10(6), 371-376.

Denstadli, J. and Gripsrud, M. This volume.

Derudder, B. and Witlox, F. 2008. Mapping world city networks through airline flows: context, relevance, and problems. *Journal of Transport Geography*, 16(5), 305-312.

Florida, R. 2004. *The Rise of the Creative Class: And How its Transforming Work, Leisure Community and Everyday Life.* New York: Basic Books.

Florida, R. 2005. *The Flight of the Creative Class: The New Global Competition for Talent.* New York: HarperCollins.

Giuliani, E. 2005. Cluster absorptive capacity: Why do some clusters forge ahead and others lag behind? *European Urban and Regional Studies*, 12(3), 269-288.

Hanlon, G. 1998. Professionalism as enterprise: Service class politics and the redefinition of professionalism. *Sociology*, 32(1), 43-63.

Kraft, P. 1979. The industrialisation of computer programming: From programming to software production, in *Case Studies in the Labor Process*, edited by A. Zimbalist. New York: Monthly Review Press, 1-16.

Leamer, E. and Storper, M. 2001. The economic geography of the internet age. *Journal of International Business Studies*, 32(4), 641-665.

Maskell, P., Bathelt, H. and Malmberg, A. 2006. Building global knowledge pipelines: The role of temporary clusters. *European Planning Studies*, 14 (8), 997-1013.

Millar, J. and Salt, J. 2008. Portfolios of mobility: The movement of expertise in transnational corporations. *Global Networks*, 8(1), 25-50.

Mokhtarian, P. 2003. Telecommunications and travel – the case for complementarity. *Journal of Industrial Ecology*, 6(2), 43-57.

NSD (National Software Directorate) 2007. *Software Industry Statistics*, http://www.nsd.ie/htm/ssii/stat.htm, last accessed 16 November, 2007.

O'Gorman, C., Omalley, E. and Mooney, J. 1997. *Clusters in Ireland: The Irish Indigenous Software Industry*. Dublin: NESC (National Economic and Social Council).

O'Riain, S. 2000. Net-working for a living: Irish software developers in the global workplace, in *Global Ethnography*, edited by M. Burawoy. Berkeley: University of California Press, 175-202.

Pink, D. 2002. *Free Agent Nation: The future of working for yourself.* New York: Warner Books.

Reich, R. 1993. *The Work of Nations: Preparing Ourselves For 21st Century Capitalism*. London: Simon & Schuster.

Ryscavage, P. 1999. *Income Inequality in America: An Analysis of Trends*. Armonk, New York: M.E. Sharpe.

Salt, J. 1997. *International Movements of the Highly Skilled*. Paris: OECD International Migration Unit Occasional Paper No. 3.

Salt, J. This volume.

Smith, D. and Timberlake, M. 2001. World city networks and hierarchies, 1977-1997: An empirical analysis of global air travel links. *American Behavioral Scientist*, 44(10), 1656-1678.

Urry, J. 2002. Mobility and Proximity. *Sociology*, 36(2), 225-274.

Wickham, J. and Boucher, G. 2004. Training cubs for the Celtic Tiger: The volume production of technical graduates in the Irish educational system. *Journal of Education and Work*, 17(4), 377-395.

Wickham, J. and Vecchi, A. 2008. Local firms and global reach: Business air travel and the Irish software cluster. *European Planning Studies*, 16(5), 693-710.

Chapter 8

'… Travelling, where the Opponents are': Business Travel and the Social Impacts of the New Mobilities Regimes

Sven Kesselring and Gerlinde Vogl

Introduction

Uli Hoeness, the business manager of the Bayern München professional soccer club, recently commented on his team's trip to play in Japan as follows: 'Markets can only be opened in person by going there. If you decide to be a global player, then you must go to where the international opponents are' (Münchner Merkur, 30 July 2008).

What Hoeness states here for his soccer team seems to be a good analysis of the sociological relevance and the economic importance of business travel in general. The physical mobility of company employees, or of a professional soccer team, creates a market-compatible regime based on physical travel and the corporeal presence of its members. This regime requires – quasi the duplication of that regime inside the company – the creation of a corporate mobility regime geared not to the freedom and autonomy of individual employees but rather to deploying the mobility of those employees to the desired end, namely dominance over territories and markets. The company's mobility regime thus radiates inwardly and outwardly and ultimately describes the boundaries of the company. The question of who travels for the company where and when to visit whom in what mission is constitutive for the structuring of social relationships and networks within a company and to its outside. In-person customer contacts create social relationships that constitute important assets for the company.

Business travel thus reflects the general trend towards mobility in modern societies. Travel and particularly international travel has been on the rise for years. In air travel, roughly a billion arrivals are anticipated by 2010, a quadrupling since 1950 (Urry 2007: 3). There is no end in sight. The same holds for business travel. In Germany, the volume of business travel for companies with between 10 and 250 employees increased 2 per cent in 2007. Unlike vacation travel, total expenditures for business travel rose. German vacation travellers spent about 50.9 billion euros in 2007, about 3 billion euros less than in the previous year, while firms boosted their travel outlays from 47.4 to 48.7 billion euros (VDR – Verband Deutsches Reisemanagement 2008: 7). According to the yearly statistics gathered by the German Travel Management Association VDR, the business travel trend since 2002 is for the length of time away to decrease while the number of business trips increases. No fewer than 166 million business trips were made in Germany in 2007. Every third employee was on the road at least once in 2007, with about 15 per cent of all trips involving an overnight stay outside the country (VDR – Verband Deutsches Reisemanagement 2008: 8).

The topic of spatial mobility touches in general on one of the central questions in sociology, the question as to the stability of social networks over distance, 'relations at a distance' (Urry 2004: 27). Coping with absence and having to conduct social relationships at a distance and maintain them in structure and significance over longer periods has always been a manifest social problem and is one of the hallmarks of modernity. The question whether geographical distance must lead to social distance is fundamental in a world in which social networks are detached from a common locale and must exist above and beyond the spatial dimension (Kellerman 2006). In Germany today, one worker in five experiences extended periods of mobility at least once in the course of a working life (Schneider 2008). Mobile lifestyles are neither unusual nor exotic. On the contrary, mobility is part of the standard repertoire for modern couples (Schneider and Limmer 2008).

Mobility is both a consequence and a precondition of individualisation. Towards the end of the nineteenth century, Georg Simmel predicted that 'the necessity and the inclination to reach out beyond one's original spatial, economic and intellectual borders' would grow and become 'a centrifugal force building bridges to other groups' (Simmel 1990: 47). Individualisation 'loosens the bond to what is close-by, weaving instead a new bond – real and ideal – to what is further away' (Simmel 1990: 48). As a result, social relationships come about in which closeness must be managed in order to overcome physical distance. Globalization processes in the economy, in politics and society have dramatically intensified this necessity.

Cosmopolitan social networks are no longer the hallmark of highly educated or monied elites. Increasingly, individuals from all walks of life are frequent travellers. Globalization has become 'democratised' and normalized in the professional and personal routines of everyday people. Even housework has become transnationalized in an international division of labour, with highly mobile domestic workers moving back and forth between the countries where they live and the countries where they work (Lutz and Schwalgin 2007). Such mobility attests to the emerging phenomenon of 'banal cosmopolitanism' (Beck 2008) in modern life. Just as the supermarkets are filled with international goods, managers, engineers, consultants, service technicians and cleaning women telephone and e-mail and travel all over the world (Salt, this volume). The business trip is emblematic for the mobility imperative in professional life.

In this investigation the business trip is subject to an analysis which questions the everyday character business travel has become today. This study questions the processes which make spatial corporate mobility a strategic instrument in business activities. We want to deconstruct the social impacts of two ongoing processes of normalization and rationalization which transform the character of modern business travelling irretrievably. Mobile work and the mobile worker as such are key elements in these processes where the mobility burdens and loads for the business travellers constantly increase.

Mobile Work and Mobile Workers

Mobile work is nothing out of the ordinary any more. 'There will be over one billion mobile workers by 2011' according to a recent prognosis (IDC Report 2008). Mobile work as defined by the ECaTT norm (Electronic Commerce and Telework Trends) is work totalling ten or more hours per week performed away from the normal place of business or the home and utilising online data transmission. On a global scale, the extent of such mobile work is estimated at about 25 per cent of all jobs (Pearn 2007: 8). 'In Europe, 47.1% of the working population are in jobs that are potentially mobile. As early as 2010, 20% of all workers will be doing mobile work – with more expected' (Hess 2007: 17). Since the term mobile work, strictly speaking, only covers jobs involving computerised data transmission, the effective potential for mobile work (in a broader understanding) is much greater if we take away data transmission.

In the networked society of globally interlocking communications and transport systems, dealing with distance is a far cry from what it was in the nineteenth and early twentieth centuries. The temporal structures have changed radically. At the beginning of the twentieth century letter-writing between East India and the Netherlands was a dialogue with postponed echo, with a reply coming after seven weeks at the earliest (Mak 2003: 154). An e-mail takes seconds. The social problems, however, have remained the same: how can mobile individuals maintain the stability of their social networks over distance? How can social proximity be maintained when face-to-face interaction is impossible? In principle, there are two ways. First, one overcomes spatial distance physically and comes to visit. Modern travel makes it possible to communicate and interact directly and without any technical mediation. Or, second, modern communication technologies are used so as not to have to travel, because it is inconvenient or otherwise inopportune. Social relationships are thus maintained purely by communication, most directly by telephoning. But virtual forms of communication such as e-mail and other script-based exchanges (chat, SMS, MMS, etc.) have become increasingly important. Recent developments make it possible to see one another as well, internet telephoning in connection with a webcam, Skype, and so forth. Virtual mobility, i.e., communication via internet and telephone, can be substituted for actual travel.

The technologically possible creation of 'immediacy' (Tomlinson 2003) over great distances gave rise to the idea that a new kind of sociality might supplant travel and visits and overcome distances. The 'death of distance' (Cairncross 1997) was thus not an absurd or wildly futuristic idea; in many cases it has become a reality. 'Electronic mobility' (ALCATEL 2002) has become a major influence on the design of production processes and will continue to determine the future configuration of work. Ever more jobs and production processes will be virtualized, delegated to so-called agents and proceeding without human involvement. The internet makes it possible to work on the same product round the clock regardless of time zone. When the work day ends in Europe, the job can continue on another continent.

Virtual and geographical spaces overlap and blend, but the 'compulsion of proximity' (Boden and Molotch 1994) is unbroken because creative processes, complex decisions, and tough negotiations demand direct interaction. Businesses have not eliminated meetings in favour of video and internet conferencing; meetings are a fixture in modern business culture, with companies relying on physical rather than virtual mobility.

> The scale of business meetings is enormous. Even back in 1988, the USA's major 500 companies are said to have held between 11 and 15 million formal meetings each day and 3-4 billion meetings each year. Managers spend up to half of their time in such face-to-face meetings and much of their time involves working with and evaluating colleagues through long and intense periods of physical co-presence and talk. (Larsen et al. 2006: 29)

The situation that presents itself is the following: individuals today possess great competence in the management of media- and technology-based social relationships (Kesselring and Vogl 2008). Immobile mobility exists, with extensive use of virtual mobility and electronic mobility especially in business (Vogl 2008). Nevertheless, physical travel continues and is on the increase. As communication increases, social networks become denser and provide more and more necessity for face-to-face meetings. Virtual activities stimulate real activities and interaction: '[t]he more virtual, the more real' (Woolgar 2002: 18).

Consistently Sennett (2007: 589) says 'modern capitalism is unthinkable without physical mobility', confirming Marx's observation that '[t]he need for ever-greater markets for its products chases the bourgeoisie all over the globe' (Marx and Engels 1848, 1977: 465). The physical movement of labour, goods and raw materials, Sennett is saying, is as much a part of the capitalist system as the circulation of capital. Business travel is thus a strategic element in capitalistic business activity and relevant to the total system. Seemingly marginally important business travel is in fact a strategic instrument of business, generating and securing presence, marking out territories and spheres of influence and markets. But nevertheless, the character of modern travelling has changed still as to the boxing of physical and virtual spaces, the interpenetration of geographies by communication on mobile devices has brought up a new quality of what Sennett following Marx states. Physical has not lost its major relevance for the modernization of societies. But the intermingling of spaces and the immediacy of here and there, absent and present, on the move and accessible, private and public have changed the nature of travelling (Hislop 2008).

The Mobile Individual

It is easily overlooked what complex social skills are demanded of business travellers. Early results from the New Mobility Regimes research project[1] show that the social integration of highly mobile employees depends greatly on their individual 'mobility competence'. Most companies simply take for granted that employees possess the skills needed to cope with the social consequences of their mobility and do not fully appreciate the specificity of the social situation of such employees.

The demands on employees' mobility willingness and competence seem to be undergoing a process of normalization. Mobility and the ability to harmonise demanding travel with the requirements of the job, likewise the abilities needed to cope with unexpected and sometimes uncertain situations, to make decisions and act independently, etc. are seen in human resource departments as essential qualities of a successful employee (Boltanski and Chiapello 2005). Employees are expected to deal successfully with frequently changing new projects in dynamic networks and to come to grips positively with constant change and high risks. Social and mental flexibility and the willingness to be mobile are decisive success criteria. To be successful, an employee must eliminate everything that stands in the way of full application of his or her productive capacity.

> Demands for lightness presuppose the rejection of stability, rootedness, bonds to persons and things. (...) The "light" individual cannot become rooted because living in a complex, mobile and uncertain world is the last secure feeling remaining to him.[2]

Sennett (1998) tells us that the increasing flexibilization of working life causes individuals to lose their social rootedness. He sees a process of inner flexibilization that makes people rootless. On the personal level, flexibility is characterized by a lack of long-term bonds. Frequent job changes and frequent moves are hard on friendships at work and off the job. Constantly adapting to new circumstances, the individual is divorced from social traditions and origins and becomes a 'drifter'. These processes of inner flexibilization are closely connected with mobility. The mobile individual, we are led to believe, has the world on a string, whereas the

---

1   The project is funded by the German Hans Boeckler Foundation. It is conducted by Gerlinde Vogl and Sven Kesselring and is a cooperation between the Department of Sociology and the mobil.TUM – interdisciplinary project group for mobility and transport at Munich Technical University.
2   Translated from Boltanski and Chiapello (2005: 466).

immobile individual is potentially excluded from power and the cosmopolitan society. But obviously employees who are mobile for the sake of the company and expect thanks in the form of a career boost may be often disappointed (Paulu 2001). Social mobility processes within companies are no longer vertical movements up or down the career ladder. Horizontal mobility processes are becoming more important, whereby it is increasingly hard to distinguish between vertical and horizontal mobility processes. The upshot is a kind of opaque 'non-directional mobility' (Kesselring 2008: 88).

Corporate business is increasingly moving production and other activities to locations where circumstances are most favourable. It has become important for capital to be geographically independent, mobile, liquid and fleet-footed. This trend has been accelerated and radicalised by network technologies which enable capital to act globally and in concert. This gives international corporations a distinct advantage over geographically bound players such as governments and trade unions:

> [C]apital has gained extraterritorial status, becoming light, unfettered and unbound to an unprecedented degree, and its mobility is easily sufficient to outmanoeuvre territorially bound political entities in pursuing its own interests. (Bauman 2003: 176)

This amounts to a profound transformation of the relationship between capital and labour. Even if labour as a factor of production can be moved around the world, work is bound up with the person of the worker. Work is socially and spatially rooted and thus necessarily in contradiction to the mobility of capital. The consequence is a new social imbalance in which the burden of market uncertainties is borne by employees who must increase their geographical and employment mobility in a job market characterized by discontinuities, precarious employment and the risk of unemployment. Few employees are able to avoid such mobility pressure.

> Corporations breaking out of the nation-state framework expect their employees to get on board, who then have no choice but to be mobile or be replaced. (Schroer 2006: 119)

The social consequences of this mobilization of labour have not been sufficiently researched nor even fully registered in their problematic dimension. Not only has 'the process chain of mobility (...) in most companies not been sufficiently investigated' (Arnaud and Allais 2004: 2), neither have the social consequences of mobility for the corporate structure and social cohesion in the company. High mobility surely does not imply only an accumulation of suffering. Surely there are empirically verifiable lifestyle successes for those who are able to feel at home in mobile ways of life. Initial results from interviews with personnel managers, union officials and mobile employees undertaken by the Corporate Mobility Regimes research project point in this direction. They support Axtell and Hislop's (2008) observations of the ambivalent character of mobility in mobile working lives.

Corporate Mobility Regimes

The research project on Corporate Mobility Regimes is concerned with the consequences of increasing mobility on the part of employees. The project concentrates on business trips, i.e., travel lasting from one to several days. A business trip can last up to three months. Longer job-related absences do not fall within the purview of the project.

Mobility, especially in the context of one's job, is not necessarily free and autonomous but rather socially prefigured and thus subject to power and authority structures. In a business, the decision as to which employees travel and how and who stays home reflects hierarchic power structures and hegemonies. We use the term 'mobility regime' to denote the institutional pre-structuring of job-related mobility.

The term mobility regime is generally used by sociologists in connection with social mobility. It denotes career movement and changes in hierarchies and social stratification. The (Western) German institutional system, characterized by a close correlation between educational level and job status, gave rise to a mobility regime typified by stable career paths and low individual mobility. The concept of a mobility regime is thus closely connected with the social construction of normal employment, which however is now undergoing rapid change. The term is not entirely suited to describing present changes in working life.

We use the term 'regime' in a political-science sense, meaning 'an institutionalised set of principles, norms and rules which fundamentally regulate the actions of individuals in a certain framework' (Nohlen 1998: 548). Thus a mobility regime in our sense is the set of principles, norms and rules regulating the physical mobility of individuals employed by corporate business. Principles, norms and rules are interlocking but point to differing social levels. We shall look at principles, norms and rules individually in order to identify the individual dimensions of the mobility regime.

Principles are philosophies, laws or guidelines overarching other laws or instructions and possessing greater recognition and authority than norms and rules. Principles place decisions and actions in a social framework. The central principle of the mobility regime is the social necessity and desirability of mobility. Along with such principles as rationality, individuality and equality, the orientation of thinking on the necessity and desirability of mobility is a constituent element of modern experience and of the modern way of looking at the world (Beck 2008, Kesselring 2008).

In working life, this means that the demand that workers be mobile has become a matter of course. Employers assume that employees are mobile, and employees usually accept this assumption unquestioningly. A concrete consequence is that the mobility principle has already found expression in many employment agreements. Personnel managers in international companies explain the inclusion of mobility expectations in employment agreements as resulting necessarily from the company's presence in the international marketplace. As a human resource manager from a multinational company located in Germany puts it:

> Of course we have had it in our employment agreements for a longer time now that people must be mobile, must be ready to go to other locations if theirs is closed down. We have a clause saying (…) that mobility may be necessary in case of changes [in the company]. That clause didn't used to be in all agreements. (34: 126-130)

Employees are thus forewarned as to mobility expectations, even if their job does not at first glance seem to require it. Mobility, then, is a principle, an imperative and as such a normal factor in working life.

Norms are standards of behaviour for individuals. 'Be mobile!' is the central norm of corporate mobility regimes. Here the mobility principle becomes an almost paradoxical demand on employees. On the one hand, the company demands flexibility and readiness to identify oneself totally with the aims of the organization, but on the other hand the company demands creativity, initiative and autonomous activity to exploit individual innovative potentials.

Indeed, the etymological roots in the Latin word *mobilitas* has more to do with agility than with 'mobility as a brute fact' (Cresswell 2006: 3). Mobility thus implies directionality, the ability to channel developments in desired directions, not merely travel in the interest of the employer. When companies demand mobility, they demand agility, mental and physical. That means that employees, especially those in international projects, are constantly on call. Business trips are often necessary on short notice as this statement from a manager in mechanical engineering signifies:

> When there's a problem, the people in Munich have to drop everything, no matter where the problem is. When the customer calls, they have to get up and go. Even if they are having dinner with friends in a restaurant, they have to excuse themselves and leave. (23: 85-90)

In this case the mobility imperative can mean that a member of this firm has spontaneously to leave to China, Australia or any European country. The mobility norm subordinates private life to job requirements. Employees generally accept this as legitimate and normal. Asked how he reconciled job-related mobility with his personal life, an engineer answered,

> It's not easy. You're always at the mercy of your appointment calendar. It's hard to plan things. You have to arrange things to fit your calendar. (22: 249-251)

Rules translate the norms of a mobility regime into concrete procedures and directives, making it possible to reward conformity and punish deviation from the norm. The rules of a mobility regime structure and circumscribe the mobility of company employees. This takes the form of written guidelines for business trips, mobility management, expense account criteria, and supervision and evaluation of mobility practices. The result is a framework for business travel which lends itself to close company control.

Mobility having become a general fact of business life, companies seek to organize and manage it to make it efficient (VDR – Verband Deutsches Reisemanagement 2008). In particular, increased mobility has led to increased mobility cost-cutting. Recent revisions of travel rules have brought about a significant reduction in travel standards. A management consultant who spends half of her time travelling complains about gradual downgrading of travel comfort on orders from higher up:

> We used to be able to fly business class sometimes, if we could justify it or the boss allowed it. But now even the head of our unit must go by the rules. That didn't used to be the case. He used to be able to decide how I flew. That came about gradually. (...) now there are rules, and he has less to say about it. (24: 269-276)

The interaction of principles, norms and rules in a mobility regime replicates the structure of the various levels of society, making the company's mobility policies seem all the more powerful, almost ineluctable. The resulting mobility stress represents a new burden on workers which sociologists have yet to pay sufficient attention to.

The analysis of interviews with business travellers and other experts suggests two hypotheses as to the basic structure of mobility regimes: the one is that mobility is robbed of all romance and becomes normalized, the other being that job-related travel is subjected to comprehensive rationalization. If travel is a normal cost of doing business, it can be rationalized with an eye to cutting costs.

Normalization

In the older type of mobility regime named by Paulu (2001) as the 'old world' it went more or less without saying that the willingness of employees to spend a longer time abroad or do a lot of travel had to be rewarded. Going on a business trip represented a kind of distinction and was in itself a gratification. Having to travel signalled to others that one was important to the company and did not have to be supervised by a superior. One was autonomous to a certain extent, and especially in the days before mobile phones on one's own at least until the destination was reached. Travel thus was an experience of freedom and autonomy.

Today a business trip is rarely seen as a privilege, perhaps with the exception of the exalted few who travel business class or even first class. With the prognosis that a quarter of all employees will soon be travelling personnel, it is not surprising that business travel has lost the aura of privilege. A union official at an international chemical company puts it this way:

> There's a clear trend away from the philosophy, "Oh, wow, a business trip is a privilege and an honour!" This idea is history. Now and in the future the situation is that people especially in the functions that require a lot of business travel see it more as a burden than as a distinction. (31: 296-299)

This 'disenchantment' (Weber 1995) of the modern mobility myth is not taking place only in corporate business. It is rather symptomatic for a general change in social attitudes towards mobility. The European Union's 'Year of Labour Mobility', declared in 2006, is a good example. We read in an official folder that '[m]obility [is] good for labour and good for business' and that '[t]he future prosperity of Europe depends on the ability of European labour to react and adapt to change'. The European Union must develop a 'mobility culture', we are told, in order to compete with other economic blocs. This is the tenor of the report on 'Mobility in Europe' (European Foundation for the Improvement of Living and Working Conditions 2006), which asserts that the mobilization of Europe is only just beginning.

What the authors of the report ignore and most publications on the subject overlook is that the mobility culture they call for consists largely in the fact that the everyday practices and processes of corporate business are increasingly tied up with mobility. Mobility is reduced to its significance as an economic factor. They neglect the 'cultural' effects of this structural change on the living and working conditions of travelling personnel. Not only has the economy become global, the social and professional networks of individuals and families have also lost much of their geographical specificity (Urry 2003, Schneider and Limmer 2008). The topography of social networks has undergone irrevocable change under the impact of globalization. Global business activity means more travel for the individual worker almost regardless of status:

> Nowadays we also send union guys abroad. We distinguish between union and salaried employees. In the past we only sent our salaried people, whether it was a business trip or a longer stay somewhere. But now union employees are making business trips more and more frequently, for example to China, or have to stay somewhere for half a year to train and supervise the people we recruit on location. (32: 38-44)

Almost unnoticed, mobility has become a basic necessity for success in finding a job. The normalization of mobility requirements has been a gradual process without the hullabaloo that usually accompanies major changes in economic life. The social consequences of these changes have been individualised, as the following excerpt from an interview with a human resource manager shows:

> We just assume (…) that we can expect more mobility and flexibility from a salaried person. It goes without saying that someone who is paid a salary must bring along more mobility. But this is changing too maybe. Now we expect, well, not really expect, but we are happy when a union person says that travel is an interesting challenge and is good for his resumé and is maybe good for his development in Germany. (32: 47-53)

Travel in general and particularly the increase in business travel is a manifestation of globalization. Increasing mobility demands are accepted by business and labour as inevitable in the global economy. The mobility imperative is clear in the following quotation from an interview with a sales manager:

> I travel a lot. You have the most success when you are where the customer is, when you can have a drink together. That's the secret, the personal relationship, the confidence in one another. It's a totally different approach. Building relationships like that on the phone or in video conferences is impossible. It just doesn't work. Especially in other cultures where people put so much emphasis on personal presence. (20: 27-32)

There seems to be no alternative to Uli Hoeness's observation that markets must be opened in person. The normalization of mobility demands means that the employee's willingness to travel is no longer appreciated as a positive feature in the employee's personnel file. Have job, will travel. Must travel. Resistance to having to travel must be justified and can result in a black mark on one's personnel record.

Rationalization

The second factor in the structure of a mobility regime is the rationalization of job-related travel. Increasing travel costs lead to cost-cutting:

> The accounting department is on its toes and is always looking at travel costs for ways to save money. It is a big cost factor, and they naturally wonder whether so many of us have to travel so often. There's a kind of a contradiction there. On the one hand we want to be globally present (…). But on the other hand we see the increased costs and wonder whether a trip is really necessary and the problem couldn't be taken care of in a video conference. (31: 289-295)

And so it is not surprising that 'the average cost of a business trip is going down' (VDR – Verband Deutsches Reisemanagement 2008: 4). The rationalization of business travel has led to a 'concentration of travel', with the number of trips increasing but the duration of each trip diminishing.

> There is quite a lot of pressure to make a trip, if at all possible, on a single day.
> Leave early, see the customer, then go back the same evening, with as little
> time as possible on location. This is a real chore. Leave the house at 4:30 in the
> morning and get back around midnight. (35: 86-90)

In 2006 every third employed person in Germany took a business-related trip lasting an average of 2.2 days. In 2003, average duration was 2.6 days, with 84 per cent of all trips lasting three days or less. Seventy per cent of all business trips were one-day trips without overnight in 2006, as compared with 67 per cent in 2003 (VDR – Verband Deutsches Reisemanagement 2007: 6).

These figures show how employee mobility has become the object of cost-cutting rationalization, the insight having made itself felt that 'travel costs are not "peanuts"' (VDR – Verband Deutsches Reisemanagement 2008: 4). Gernot Zielonka, the editor-in-chief of the German trade magazine *Der Mobilitätsmanager*, says that business travel is the third-largest personnel cost factor in most companies. In Germany, 490 million trips are driven in company cars each year. The German Association for Materials, Purchasing and Logistics BME estimates that German companies spent about 180 billion euros on business travel in 2006.[3]

The advent of systematic mobility management is fairly recent, at least in Germany. Sometimes specialized travel agencies are used. So-called travel managers – a new job description in mobility management – have the task of identifying potential savings and taking advantage of them. Travel rules increasingly insist on economical travel practices. According to the travel service provider Carlson Wagonlit CWT, the stringent application of travel rules can save companies as much as 20 per cent on their mobility costs (www.carlsonwagonlit.com).

A further strategy for reducing mobility costs is the increased use of telephone and video conferencing. But care is taken not to overdo it. Not all person-to-person meetings can be replaced by virtual means:

> There was a wave of cost-cutting. But we found that face-to-face meetings really
> were more efficient and more effective and that the savings potential with video
> conferences was not as great as expected. So now there is a pendulum movement
> back to investing in talking to the customer in person. (24: 167-173)

The rationalization of business mobility is not taking place only on the part of management. The normalization of mobility also leads to self-rationalization on the part of the employee and to rationalizations in lifestyle. Voß and Pongratz (1998) show that workers assume certain management functions of their own

---

3   See http://www.fachtagung-tourismusmanagement.de/Dateien/Vortraege%20Refer enten%202006/Herr%20Zielonka.pdf (last accessed 17 December 2008).

accord and supervise themselves in an effort to be more productive. This also happens in the organization of travel. Business travellers sacrifice off time in order to arrive at their destination rested and ready to do business. Sometimes they even choose bad connections and accept long travel times in order to save money for the company.

> Cost consciousness is always stressed and you have to go along with it. If you fly to Japan, Korea, China, or the US on a weekend, the flight is cheaper. Instead of 1.800 euros, it costs only 700. There are differences that you can't just sweep under the rug. (21: 509-514)

A further self-optimisation variant is shortening the stay at destination in order to minimise jet-lag on return, as does this management consultant:

> It's a physiological fact that short trips really are less of a burden than long trips. You are tired is all. The body adjusts to the new time only about one hour per day. I notice it myself. If I am only in New York for a day or two, I have no problem at all with jetlag. But if I come back after a week, I am jetlagged. As a rule you need two weeks before your inner clock is back to normal. (24: 380-388)

As a conclusion we can say that the rationalization of business travel takes place on to levels: first, on the structural level, where cost cutting and the compression of time is on top of the agenda; and second on the body scale, where employees internalize the structural logic of the company and its economic goals and intentions.

But nevertheless, the next section of the article shows that this is not an unidirectional process where the individual is suppressed by the company and its rationalization strategies. Much more, systematic ambivalences dominate the empirical data and exemplify the strained relationship between autonomy and heteronomy which is characteristic for mobility as a social process and phenomenon.

Ambivalent Mobilities

With mobility being normalized and rationalized and an everyday experience for workers at all levels, it becomes a challenge for everyone in the company.

> In modernity, to be mobile not only means to move but also to be moved. Therefore mobility unfolds its ambivalent character: It extends the individual room to manoeuvre and the opportunities of movement, while at the same time the social expectations increase to use these opportunities. (Schneider 2005: 92)

As a consequence workers have to deal with mobility demands, and they have to think about how to cope with the mobility imperative. Human resource departments have registered that mobility demands on employees have risen and thus also new burdens and challenges. To date the response in terms of programmes for the development of employee mobility competence and support in coping with the attendant social problems has lagged behind. This means that labour representatives, unions and shop stewards, are called upon to take action. A recent study by the German Trade Union Association DGB points this out (Fuchs 2006).

The DGB study comes to the conclusion that mobile workers are less happy with their jobs than stationary workers.

> Mobile workers judge all aspects of their job more negatively than or at best equally so as workers with a stationary job. Their assessment of their job future is more negative, likewise of their income outlook, physical demands, work rules and work intensity, chances for promotion, opportunities for further qualification and personal development, and the company culture. (Fuchs 2006: 7)

On the assumption that mobility will continue to increase and that mobile workers will continue to be less happy with their work than their 'immobile' co-workers, the need for specific solutions to address this problem will also become more acute.

Notwithstanding the burdens of job-related mobility, many business travellers see the positive side of not having to be in the office or in the shop all of the time. Our interviewees, like the engineer in the following quotation, frequently stress how nice it is not to be under someone's direct supervision:

> Sure, travelling is fun. Especially because no one is there looking over my shoulder when I am with the customer. I work independently and am my own boss. (23: 138-140)

But in fact, workers judge their working situations as very ambivalent: on the one hand business travels become more and more rationalized and temporally compressed. Mobile phones and blackberry technologies are considered as a sort of hidden panopticon to control the moves and steps of mobile workers. But at the same time interviewees talk about the advantages of being ones 'own boss', just loosely coupled to the company's headquarter and remote from direct control. The citation above is characteristic for this as the engineer continues with his reflection by saying *'for that I can put up with travelling. It's worth it'*. Obviously it is a high value for many of them not to be routinized and forced to travel to the same working place every morning. This seems to be something worthwhile to manage the burdens and strains of a mobile working life.

Mobility means escape from the company's internal structures and – notwithstanding the rules – experiencing autonomy in one's work. Even with the technological means of supervision in use today, business travellers describe working with the customer as an expansion of their sphere of action and discretion. A high degree of responsibility and problem-solving competence is needed at the customer's. Many interviewees stress as positive the need to improvise and solve problems in suboptimal circumstances. This is also part of the appeal of mobility, as our interviews repeatedly show.

The main problem seems to be not mobility but the summation of burdens. Work pressures are very high, companies are often short-handed, and work piles up when the traveller is away as the following statement of a sales manager shows:

> Let me put it this way, I have reached a point where I have to pull the rip cord. Not stop travelling, but reduce the total work I have to do. Because 24/7, that is getting to be too much, that can't go on. (21: 569-572)

Conclusions

Business travel is undergoing substantial structural changes. It is an essential element of the 'portfolios of mobility' (Salt, this volume) companies develop to compete in global markets and to mark presence and power. Along with the globalization of economic activities we observe significant intensifications as well as extensifications of corporate travel activities. Mobile work as a particular form of corporate mobility is a key indicator for the mobilization of business life in general. Nevertheless, the social consequences of the increase of mobility and travel demands for employees are often neglected and they are often unseen in their relevance for the social cohesion within companies and the work-life balance of personnel. The worldwide accessibility and availability of communication and transport devices and technologies make 24/7 a real time phenomenon. In our study on the social impacts of the new mobility regimes we observe that the boundary management and the negotiations about the conditions of work and travelling usually are in the responsibility of the individual workers. The forms and the shape how mobile working occurs, how availability and technologically based immediacy are interpreted and handled is mostly reported as a matter of individual standing and the single employee's capacity to negotiate with superiors.

Obvious was the highly ambivalent character how people talk about their mobility experiences as business travellers. On the one hand travelling is considered as a burden and must; on the other hand the experience of autonomy and the opportunities to learn new aspects and to be treated as a relevant and a recognized person was strongly emphasized.

For a critical analysis of business travel which intends to motivate socially sustainable corporate strategies of mobility management the ambivalent character is problematic. Companies' management stuffs need to respect the social limits of the rationalization, intensification and compression of travel activities. But from the standpoint of current research it is very hard to say where the limits are and how regulation should be shaped. The empirical examples in our study show that business travel is highly rationalized and structured by economic necessities and logic. But beyond business travelling is an opportunity space and a reservoir of freedom and autonomy which employees are willing to defend and want to be respected by the company as well as trade unions and other colleagues, too.

Against this background our considerations basically focus the self-empowerment and the strengthening of peoples' potentials to structure travelling in a socially sustainable way to take care for their own working forces as well as their capacities to maintain social networks and contacts. Needed for the future are instruments and tools to make visible the risks of frequent travelling for the business travellers themselves but for the companies and their human resource management as well. The normalization of mobility and business travelling includes that both sides, the working force as well as the capital side, currently neglects the socially risky character of increasing mobility in corporate life. Frequent travelling leads in some cases to disintegration and weak social ties within the company as well as in private life. To strengthen the social cohesion and the embedding of people is a joint task for all actors in business life. Thus, our study on the social impacts of the new mobilities regimes can only be a beginning for a research on the social sustainability of business travel and corporate mobility in general.

References

ALCATEL-SEL-Stiftung für Technische und Wirtschaftliche Kommunikations-forschung 2002. *Mobile Arbeits-Welten: Soziale Gestaltung von 'Electronic Mobility'*. Mössingen-Talheim: Talheimer.

Arnaud, A. and Allais, G. 2004. *Mobility Benchmarking Study*. Ergebnisse. Bremen: TQ3 Mobility Solutions.

Axtell, C. and Hislop, D. 2008. The lonely life of the mobile engineer, in *Mobility and Technology in the Workplace*, edited by D. Hislop. New York: Routledge, 105-119.

Bauman, Z. 2003. *Flüchtige Moderne*. Frankfurt am Main: Suhrkamp.

Beck, U. 2008. Mobility and the cosmopolitan perspective, in *Tracing Mobilities*, edited by W. Canzler, V. Kaufmann and S. Kesselring. Aldershot: Ashgate, 25-36.

Boden, D. and Molotch, H.L. 1994. The compulsion of proximity, in *NowHere. Space, Time and Modernity*, edited by R. Friedland and D. Boden. London: University of California Press, 257-286.

Boltanski, L. and Chiapello, E. 2005. *The New Spirit of Capitalism*. London: Verso.

Cairncross, F. 1997. *The Death of Distance: How the Communications Revolution Will Change Our Lives*. Boston: Harvard Business School Press.

Cresswell, T. 2006. *On the Move. Mobility in the Modern Western World*. New York: Routledge.

European Foundation for the Improvement of Living and Working Conditions 2006. *Mobility in Europe*. Analysis of the 2005 Eurobarometer Survey on Geographical and Labour Market Mobility. Dublin: Eurofound.

Fuchs, T. 2006. *Mobile Arbeit im Spannungsfeld der wahrgenommenen Arbeitsqualität*. Eine Auswertung auf Basis des DGB-Index Gute Arbeit. Herausgegeben von INIFES-Internationales Institut für Empirische Sozialökonomie. Augsburg.

Hess, K. 2007. Mobile Arbeit: Erfahrungen, Anforderungen und Gestaltungsbedingungen für die Interessenvertretung. *Gute Arbeit*, 4, 17-18.

Hislop, D. 2008. *Mobility and Technology in the Workplace*. New York: Routledge.

IDC Report 2008. *Worldwide Mobile Worker 2007-2011*, Forecast and Analysis Doc #209813.

Kellerman, A. 2006. *Personal Mobilities*. New York: Routledge.

Kesselring, S. 2008. The mobile risk society, in *Tracing Mobilities*, edited by W. Canzler, V. Kaufmann and S. Kesselring. Aldershot: Ashgate, 77–102.

Kesselring, S. and Vogl, G. 2008. Networks, scapes and flows – mobility pioneers between first and second modernity, in *Tracing Mobilities*, edited by W. Canzler, V. Kaufmann and S. Kesselring. Aldershot: Ashgate, 163–180.

Larsen, J., Urry, J. and Axhausen, K. 2006. *Mobilities, Networks, Geographies*. Aldershot: Ashgate.

Lutz, H. and Schwalgin, S. 2007. *Vom Weltmarkt in den Privathaushalt. Die neuen Dienstmädchen im Zeitalter der Globalisierung*. Opladen: Budrich.

Mak, G. 2003. *Das Jahrhundert meines Vaters. Genehmigte Taschenbuchausgabe, 1*. Aufl. München: Goldmann.

Marx, K. and Engels, F. 1848, 1977. Manifest der Kommunistischen Partei. *MEW*, 4, 459-493.

Nohlen, D. 1998. *Wörterbuch Staat und Politik. Neuausgabe 1995*. Bonn: Bundeszentrale für politische Bildung.

Paulu, C. 2001. *Mobilität und Karriere*. Wiesbaden: Deutscher Universitäts-Verlag.

Pearn, K. 2007. *A Study: Understanding and Managing the Mobile Workforce*. Unter Mitarbeit von Stuart Duff, Holly Jones, Emma Trenier. Herausgegeben von Cisco Systems Inc., http://newsroom.cisco.com/dlls/2007/eKits/MobileWorkforce_071807.pdf, last accessed 29 July 2008.

Salt, J. This volume.

Schneider, N. and Limmer, R. 2008. Job mobility and living arrangements, in *Tracing Mobilities*, edited by W. Canzler, V. Kaufmann and S. Kesselring. Aldershot: Ashgate, 119-140.

Schneider, N.F. 2005. Einführung: Mobilität und Familie. Wie Globalisierung die Menschen bewegt. *Zeitschrift für Familienforschung*, 17, 90-95.

Schneider, N.F. 2008. Heimatverbunden, aber hoch mobil. In Deutschland hat jeder Zweite im erwerbsfähigen Alter Erfahrungen mit Mobilität, www.jobmob-and-famlives.eu/download/pressemappe.pdf., last accessed 5 July 2008.

Schroer, M. 2006. *Räume, Orte, Grenzen. Auf dem Weg zu einer Soziologie des Raums*. Frankfurt am Main: Suhrkamp.

Sennett, R. 1998. *The Corrosion of Character: The Personal Consequences of Work in the New Capitalism*. New York: Norton.

Sennett, R. 2007. *Kulturmaterialismus*. Dankesrede Richard Sennetts anlässlich der Verleihung der Hegel-Preises in Stuttgart am 27. März 2007, in 'Blätter für deutsche und internationale Politik', H. 5, S. 585-590.

Simmel, G. 1990. Über sociale Differenzierung. Sociologische und psychologische Untersuchungen. Reprint der Ausgabe von 1890, in *Staats- und Socialwissenschaftliche Forschungen*, G. Schmoller. Leipzig: Dunker & Humblot.

Tomlinson, J. 2003. Culture, modernity and immediacy, in *Global America. The Cultural Consequences of Globalization*, edited by U. Beck, N. Sznaider and R. Winter. Liverpool: Liverpool University Press, 49-66.

Urry, J. 2003. Social networks, travel and talk. *British Journal of Sociology*, 54(2), 155-175.

Urry, J. 2004. Connections. *Environment and Planning D: Society and Space*, 22(1), 27-37.

Urry, J. 2007. *Mobilities*. Cambridge: Polity Press.

VDR – Verband Deutsches Reisemanagement 2007. *VDR Geschäftsreiseanalyse 2007*. Frankfurt (Main), www.geschaeftsreiseanalyse.de, last accessed 13th February 2009.

VDR – Verband Deutsches Reisemanagement 2008. *VDR Geschäftsreiseanalyse 2008*. Frankfurt (Main), www.geschaeftsreiseanalyse.de, last accessed 13th February 2009.

Vogl, G. 2008. Selbstständige Medienschaffende in der Netzwerkgesellschaft. Boizenburg: Hülsbusch.

Voß, G. and Pongratz, H. 1998. Der Arbeitskraftunternehmer. Eine neue Form der Ware Arbeitskraft. *Kölner Zeitschrift für Soziologie und Sozialpsychologie*, 50, 131-158.

Weber, M. 1995. *Wissenschaft als Beruf*. Stuttgart: Reclam (Universal-Bibliothek, 9388).

Woolgar, S. 2002. Five rules of virtuality, in *Virtual Society*, edited by S. Woolgar. Oxford: Oxford University Press, 1-22.

PART 3
The Production and Meaning
of Business Travel

Chapter 9

Business Travel and Leisure Tourism: Comparative Trends in a Globalizing World

Aharon Kellerman

Introduction

Airplanes carry on board business travellers and leisure tourists alike, seated next to each other in both economy and business classes. Hotels, mainly in downtown or in hotel districts of major cities, serve indiscriminately business and leisure guests, which is true also for restaurants and other entertainment establishments. Still, distinctions are normally made, by laymen as well as by professionals, between business travellers or business tourists, on the one hand, and leisure tourists, on the other. The objective of this chapter is to compare these two classes of travellers at the international level from several basic perspectives: motivations and goals; relative magnitude; spatial patterns; and interrelationships between the two classes of travellers. However, before delving into elaborations on these four perspectives, business travel has to be defined and business travellers classified, in order to see whether business travel constitutes merely a form of travel or if it constitutes also a distinct form of tourism. The definition and classification of business travel by trip objective and nature which we will elaborate on will lead us to focus on one specific form of business travel for our following comparative discussions of leisure and business travels.

Definition and Classification

The contemporary rather significant increase in international leisure tourism has received much attention in tourism studies as well as in cognate fields. However, the no less considerable growth in international business travel, mainly as a result of and as an expression of expanding globalization trends, has gone by with little treatment in relevant literatures. This lacuna might hint to one of two contrary options: either business travel is considered similar to leisure tourism, or maybe the other way around, namely that business travel is viewed as a form of work for business persons, which does not require special and separate attention: it is similar to domestic office work, just being performed at a distance from home, and located in foreign countries.

Business travel has been variously defined as both travel and tourism. Ironically, in a book entitled *Business Travel*, Davidson (2000: 1) provided the following definition: 'Business *tourism* is concerned with people *travelling* for purposes which are related to their work ... general business travel, meetings, exhibitions, and incentive travel' (italics are by the author). In a later text, Davidson and Cope (2003: 3) noted the confusion between 'travel' and 'tourism' regarding business trips, and they distinguished, therefore, between business travel as individual business travel *versus* business tourism, which refers to business persons going for meetings, exhibitions, and incentive travel. Whereas the latter three classes usually include, *a priori*, elements of leisure by their very nature, individual business travel seems to constitute 'pure' business travel, involving foremost office meetings and, thus, this class of business travel may seem, at a first glance at least, as distinct from leisure tourism. The blurring of boundaries between business and leisure tourism at large has been recently noted also by Lassen (2006) and by Faulconbridge and Beaverstock (2007).

In the past incoming international passengers were normally asked for the purpose of their visit. Noting the blurring of differences between leisure and business travel and experiencing a growing number of multipurpose visits have brought many countries to stop asking incoming passengers about their visit purposes. Coupled with the almost free moving of Europeans within the EU, without any entry documentation, has brought about a reduced and rather constrained availability of comparative data, as we will notice later on.

Given the diversity of business travel, our following conceptual discussions will, thus, focus mainly on a comparison between individual business travel and leisure tourism, attempting to highlight the touristic elements in business travel, and the business-like elements in leisure tourism. Corporate travel of the form of 'general [or individual] business travel', as a sub-class of business travel, will exclude 'travelling workers' (i.e. workers whose very work includes travel, such as pilots), and 'working tourists' (such as travel agents) (see Cohen 1974, Uriely 2001). The emerging class of international work mobility of all kinds, performed through airplanes, was called by Lassen (2006) 'aeromobility'.

Comparing individual business travel with leisure tourism, strikes out travel *per se* as the non-routine activity for business persons *versus* touristic activities (e.g. swimming, museum visits, etc.) as the non-routine activity for leisure tourists. Through this differentiation we refer to business trips as non-routine international travel experiences of business people for the purpose of business meetings, which is the major type of office activity for these people in their routine work at their domestic offices. This stands in contrast to leisure trips which constitute for tourists foremost an opportunity to be engaged in some non-routine touristic activities at some remote destination, an opportunity which can be materialized only through travel. Taking this difference one step further, we may note that business travel may be considered as constituting means for making business whereas leisure tourism may be viewed as an objective by itself. Lassen (2006) pointed to self-determination as the aspect which traditionally divided between leisure tourism, for which self-determination is highest, and business travel, for which self-determination was considered at its lowest, because employers were assumed to determine the various parameters of business travel for their employees. Lassen (2006) was able to show that this distinction has been blurred, since contemporary employees share with their employers the determination of their travel, involving jointly both business and pleasure elements. These differences between business and leisure tourisms may lead us to a comparative examination of motivations and goals for these two types of trips.

Motivations and Goals

Business mobilities may be considered as rather stratified and complex in a globalized world, consisting of both virtual and corporeal mobilities. Virtual mobilities, performed through the telephone and the internet, may offer substitutes for corporeal travel, at least for routine business, such as for sales maintenance and its routine boosting. However, the establishment of new business contacts and contracts, involving the creation of mutual trust, would normally involve face-to-face meetings (see Boden and Molotch 1994, Urry 2000, Kellerman 2006), something which Urry (2003) termed as 'meetingness'. Thus, business deals are not necessarily any more direct and straight forward outcomes of face-to-face meetings only, as they reflect virtual contacts, as well. As Tani (2005) noted, it is 'head-content' rather than 'headcount' that is of importance in contemporary business contacts.

Urry (2002) categorized the motivations for individual travel at large around the three elements of people, time and place: potential travellers need either to meet other people, attend events in time, or see places (or some combinations among the three elements). Applying this categorization to a comparison between business travel and leisure tourism, we can see that travelling for business persons always implies meeting people, but it may less frequently involve visiting sites/ places or attending events. Business persons might occasionally visit sites, for the development of a new project for instance, and they might attend events, such as an inauguration of a new service or production line, but they always aim at meeting people, formally and informally. On the other hand, leisure tourism always implies tourists visiting places, and this is also why tourists normally change their overseas vacation destinations from time to time. In addition to visiting places, for leisure tourists a vacation may or may not optionally involve a desire to meet other people, and/or it may or may not involve attendance of events (Table 9.1).

Table 9.1 Goals of business travel and leisure tourism

Goal	Leisure tourism	Business travel
Seeing places	Always	Infrequently
Meeting people	Sometimes	Always
Attending events	Sometimes	Sometimes

Source: Urry (2002).

Relative Magnitude

How many international business travellers and leisure tourists are there? This question may be asked for all the three relevant geographical scales: global, national and local. For global and national measures, data on the number of tourists are published by WTO (World Tourism Organization), and these may be helpful for the calculation of a percentage ratio of leisure to business tourists, in order to assess the relative magnitude of the two classes of tourism. Such a simple ratio is, thus, sensitive to changes in the numbers of both leisure and business tourists. However, for measuring the even more intriguing shares of leisure and business tourists at the city level, only the percentage of business tourists has been available, and even this measure could be found for only a handful of cities for which such data have been published, normally by city governments or agencies.

There is some problem of data reliability concerning the statistics at all the three geographical levels, since WTO collects and publishes national data produced by relevant national authorities, whereas city data may constitute only estimates made by municipalities or other local agencies. As we noted already, it turns out that the traditional classification of tourists into business and leisure ones has not been provided any more at all in recent years by several countries, given the complexity of travel motivation, which mixes business with pleasure within same trips.

At the global level, business visitors comprise some 15-20 per cent of total visitors (Law 2002), and the value of the global ratio of leisure to business tourists was 315.6 per cent in 2002; 314.6 per cent in 2003; and 321.1 per cent in 2004. These ratio levels seem to remain constant in recent years so that globally there are three leisure tourists for every business visitor. The constancy of this ratio may mean that the global growth in leisure tourism has been coupled with a similar growth in business tourism. However, the possible interdependence between the two classes of tourism is only partial, as we will see later on. Interestingly enough, the most growing world tourism class has been neither leisure nor business tourists, but rather the third class of 'VFR (visiting friends and relatives), health, religion, and other'! The highest growth levels reached by this class might be related to the growth in immigration, bringing about more family visits in the old motherland by the immigrants, side by side with visits to the new countries of residence by family and friends of the immigrants still living in the country of origin.

The relative magnitude of business tourism at the national level is presented here through the ratio of leisure to business tourists 2001-2005 (in per cent) for various countries (Table 9.2). The missing data for leading countries in leisure tourism, such as Austria, France, Germany, Greece, The Netherlands, and Switzerland, stems from the lack of differentiation between leisure and business visitors in their national statistics, presenting a difficulty in distinguishing between the two classes, when visitors enter countries for both business and leisure planned for a single trip. It further presents a lack of interest by countries in maintaining such a differentiation when both forms of tourism use similar infrastructures (such as transportation) and services (such as hotels). As we noted already, this tendency of non-differentiation between business and leisure visitors is typical to European countries, since no entry forms are required for EU residents moving among EU countries.

Table 9.2 Ratio of leisure to business tourists 2001-2005 (in per cent)

Country	2001	2002	2003	2004	2005
Australia	296.8	275.0	271.2	268.8	267.3
Austria	–	–	–	–	–
Belgium	163.2	174.3	189.6	199.4	185.2
Canada	446.4	449.3	433.4	248.3	379.5
China	–	172.7	148.4	192.0	203.2
France	502.1	–	–	–	–
Germany	–	–	–	–	–
Greece	–	–	–	–	–
Hong Kong	–	–	–	–	–
Italy	275.2	259.2	280.4	309.7	282.8
Japan	219.8	240.5	238.5	277.7	295.8
Korea	1769.5	1708.4	1392.6	1567.4	1429.9
Netherlands	–	–	–	–	–
New Zealand	400.4	426.2	413.4	392.7	373.7
Singapore	217.9	226.4	208.9	–	–
Spain	1154.1	1057.3	710.4	782.8	739.0
Sweden	114.6	144.8	140.4	–	–
Switzerland	–	–	–	–	–
Taiwan	111.7	110.3	89.2	103.1	133.8
United Kingdom	102.7	98.7	105.0	115.1	109.9
United States	149.0	141.3	161.5	184.4	181.5
World		315.6	314.6	321.1	

Source: UNWTO (2007a, b).

Though the data set used here is partial, it still permits some interesting observations and interpretations. Generally, the countries for which data were available, present stability in the relationship between the two classes of visitors, so that the global stability in this relationship, which we mentioned before, reflects wide national ratio stabilities. This simultaneous growth in business and leisure visits attests once again to the basic element in globalization, that when international movements at large are facilitated and enhanced they would affect all types of transactions and human movements (see e.g. Appadurai 1990, Kellerman 1990, Kulendran and Wilson 2000, Kulendran and Witt 2003).

Most countries enjoy a larger number of incoming leisure visitors than business ones, which is true even for countries which may be called 'business states', such as Singapore. One cannot discern a general relationship between the level of popularity of countries as leisure destinations and their ratio values, and the ratio may attest to domestic trends. For example, Spain, which is a leading country in leisure tourism, presented lower ratio scores than Korea which is considered more of a business destination. By the same token both the UK and Taiwan reached ratio levels attesting to an equal number of leisure and business tourists, despite a major difference in their level of attraction for leisure tourists, with the UK being a popular leisure destination, as compared to the more business-oriented nature of visits to Taiwan. Furthermore, similar ratio values have also been shown by the US and Sweden, probably excluding visitors from Canada and Mexico to the US, possibly attesting to an insensitivity of the leisure/business tourism ratio to country size. Some other countries exhibit a special business status. Thus, the low ratio values of Belgium which hosts the EU headquarters in Brussels, and thus attracts many business tourists, and the higher levels of Australia as compared to those of New Zealand, attesting to a higher business attractiveness of Australia.

As it turns out, rarely do cities collect or release data on the categorization of international visitors, so that data could be found through the Web for only five major world cities, albeit in four continents (Table 9.3). The range of the percentage value of business tourists among these five cities is high, ranging from 28 per cent in London to 66 per cent in Frankfurt. Thus, these rates may be related to local business specialties as well as to the degree of leisure attractiveness of cities. For instance, the high value of Frankfurt attests to its financial centrality, side by side with its lower leisure attractiveness, whereas Boston enjoys visits by some special business communities through its leading health services and universities.

In many cases, however, and similarly to nations, cities may be attractive to both business and leisure visits. Thus, Faulconbridge and Beaverstock (2007) were able to show that the leading European cities for business visits were London, Paris, Frankfurt and Geneva, and three out of these four cities are simultaneously also major leisure-tourism havens. Still, however, leisure-attractive cities may present varied rates of business visits as compared to their respective national values. For example, the ratio of business to leisure visitors into London is 1:4, as compared to the UK national ratio of 1:1, attesting to the high attractiveness of London to leisure tourism as compared to the rest of the country. In Sydney, the local ratio is similar to the national one, 1:3, which is true also for Singapore in which the two values are similar, given the nature of the country as a city-state (1:3/1:2). London was ranked in 2006 much higher than Sydney and Singapore, as far as the populations of the urban areas of these cities were concerned: London was ranked 28 (with a population of 7.61 million), as compared to Singapore's rank of 55 (4.47 million), and Sydney similar rank of 57 (4.45 million) (Citymayors Statistics 2008). This difference might add to the explanation of the differences among the ratios of business/leisure tourists for these cities, so that a larger city in a larger nation might attract more international leisure tourists. As we noted earlier, possibly the ratio of business to leisure tourists at the national level is less sensitive to population size, but it seems that for cities size matters, assuming that larger cities provide more tourist attractions of various sorts.

Table 9.3 Percentage business visitors and expenditure among international tourists in selected cities

City	Percentage visitors	Percentage expenditure	Year
Boston	46	N/A	2000
Frankfurt	66	N/A	2006
London	25*	33	2003
Singapore	28	35	2006
Sydney	35.5	N/A	2005

Note: * Percentage of overnight visitors.
Source: Boston: New York, Boston, Washington DC-Media Kit Request (2007). Frankfurt: MPI (2007). London: City of Westminster (2006). Singapore: Newscentral 24 (2007). Sydney: Sydney Media (2007).

For the two cities for which data on percentage expenditure of business visitors out of total visitors' expenditures were available, business travel expenditures were higher than the percentage of business visitors among the total number of visitors. This additional contribution to local incomes from business tourism looks as if business tourism 'cross-subsidizes' leisure tourism, though it does not necessarily have to be so, as leisure tourism may be profitable by its own operation.

Spatial Patterns

Spatial touristic patterns present mixed and complex trends when it comes to a comparison between business and leisure tourisms. Normally leisure tourists make use of business infrastructure and services. Thus, business tourism infrastructures (i.e. hotels, restaurants, etc.) may be useful for leisure tourism, but usually not *vice versa.* For instance, beaches, historical sites and museums, which serve as major leisure activities and attractions, are normally not visited by 'pure' business travellers. In addition, business services for travellers have become important for leisure tourism, for example hotel 'business centres', providing access to the internet, and airline business class, providing higher flight comfort, both of which may be used by leisure tourists, as well.

Preferred locations for business hotels within metropolitan areas have expanded, so that the coincidence of the locations of business hotels with leisure-oriented ones is not restricted any more to downtowns only. Business-oriented hotels have expanded their locations to outlying, suburban and even exurban business centres or 'edge cities', and these outlying areas might coincide with leisure areas and attractions (see Garreau 1991). Business hotels have also been built next or even within major airports, providing diversified amenities for travellers on the road, and obviously these hotels are also attractive to leisure passengers on transit.

Even more striking are transitions in the specialties of cities, as far as incoming tourism is concerned. Cities which originally functioned as purely business cities have become also leisure-oriented ones, for example UAE cities such as Dubai, and Abu Dhabi or Doha in Qatar. Such a transition may also happen the other way around, so that cities which originally functioned as leisure cities have turned into business centers, as well, such as Orlando and Las Vegas becoming centres of high-tech R&D and production. However, whereas in the Gulf countries the locations of business and pleasure activity areas are mixed, in American cities business areas and their hotels may develop in separate areas from the previously developed tourist attraction areas of such cities as Orlando and Las Vegas.

Interrelationships

The blurring of distinction between business and leisure tourisms is not only spatial but it relates also to the travellers themselves. The attitude and use of time by travellers presents some interesting interrelationship between business and leisure tourists. Thus, the business accent on time as a resource has become important in leisure as well, as leisure tourists plan the time frames for their various vacation activities, being aware of the rather restricted time availability for their vacation, and being used to efficient time use from their daily time use at work. The use of business services by leisure tourists, mainly hotel business centres, may facilitate a more efficient time use when on vacation. On the other hand, the accent on pleasure in leisure tourism has become important for business, as well, so that relaxed dining has turned into an integral part of business-making itself, and this may apply also to other forms of entertainment, depending more on local cultures.

The complex interrelationships between the two classes of business and leisure travels come into expression through two special groups of visitors: *returners* and *extenders.* Returners are leisure tourists who happen to like their vacation destination and who decide to return there for some business development (Davidson and Cope 2003: 261). Extenders are visitors who *a priori* conduct multipurpose travel to a specific destination, involving both business and pleasure (Davidson and Cope 2003: 257). Studying exports and imports in an Australian longitudinal context it has been shown that levels of international trade were related to international travel at large. Furthermore, leisure tourism may bring about business tourism and *vice versa* (Kulendran and Wilson 2000, Kulendran and Witt 2003).

Conclusion

Clear-cut differentiations between business and leisure tourisms have blurred for all the three major dimensions of tourism: people, places and activities. For people, business meetings by business people may yield leisure visits by these business persons and *vice versa*, leisure visits may bring about business ideas and opportunities yielding future business visits by vacationers. As for places and activities, leisure tourists and business visitors may share the same transportation, lodging and entertainment facilities. This blurring of boundaries between business and pleasure tourisms is similar to the emerging blurring of distinctions between daily home and work activities, so that mobility at large, domestically and internationally, routine and non-routine alike, evolves as a rather continuous and permanent state of life involving in a rather integrated way both business and leisure (see Urry 2000, Kellerman 2006). Obviously this integration implies also contradiction and conflict between business and pleasure, but these aspects deserve separate treatments.

Cities, notably major ones, serve as the joint spatial platforms and meeting arenas for business and leisure tourisms and tourists, and hence the importance of urban tourism. As a starting point for an examination of cities as joint platforms for business and leisure tourism, one could assert that there might possibly emerge three phases of leisure/business relationships in cities. The first phase could be called spillover, in which one well-established class of tourism makes room for the use of its facilities by the other class through the offering of available services; for example, business hotels which become available also for leisure tourists. In the second phase, both types of tourism in a certain city may have become well-established and sizeable, and the two classes complement each other in the creation of demand for infrastructures, such as expanded airports and land transportation. In the third phase, the two categories of tourism may fuse into each other, and it becomes difficult to separate hotels and other urban touristic services by their served markets. Alternatively, it may also occur that all three phases, or forms of relationships, may operate simultaneously within one city, so that there are spillover effects between the two categories of tourism, side by side with complementarities and fusions between them taking place, with these different relationships taking place in distinguished types of urban services or facilities which serve tourists.

References

Appadurai, A. 1990. Disjuncture and difference in the global cultural economy. *Theory, Culture and Society*, 7, 295-310.

Boden, D. and Molotch, H.L. 1994. The compulsion of proximity, in *NowHere Space, Time and Modernity*, edited by R. Friedland and D. Boden. Berkeley: University of California Press, 257-286.

Citymayors Statistics 2008. http://www.citymayors.com/statistics/urban_2006_1.html, last accessed 15 August 2008.

City of Westminster 2006. http://www.westminster.gov.uk/leisureand, last accessed 15 August 2008.

Cohen, E.1974. Who is a tourist? A conceptual clarification. *Sociology*, 22, 527-555.

Davidson, R. 2000. *Business Travel*. Essex: Longman/Pearson Education.

Davidson, R. and Cope, B. 2003. *Business Travel: Conferences, Incentive Travel, Exhibitions, Corporate Hospitality and Corporate Travel*. Harlow: Prentice Hall.

Faulconbridge, J.R. and Beaverstock, J.V. 2007. Geographies of international business travel in the professional service economy. *GaWC Research Bulletin* 252, http://www.lboro.ac.uk/gawc/rb/rb252.html, last accessed 15 August 2008.

Garreau, J. 1991. *Edge City*. New York: Doubleday.

Kellerman, A. 1990. International telecommunications around the world: A flow analysis. *Telecommunications Policy*, 14, 461-475.

Kellerman, A. 2006. *Personal Mobilities*. London and New York: Routledge.

Kulendran, N. and Wilson, K. 2000. Is there a relationship between international trade and international travel? *Applied Economics*, 32, 1001-1009.

Kulendran, N. and Witt, S.F. 2003. Forecasting the demand for international business tourism. *Journal of Travel Research*, 41, 265-271.

Lassen, C. 2006. Aeromobility and work. *Environment and Planning A*, 38, 301-312.

Law, C.M. 2002. *Urban Tourism Second Edition: The Visitor Economy and the Growth of Large Cities*. London: Continuum.

MPI 2007. http://www.gccoe.mpiweb.org/CMS/mpiweb/mpicontent.aspx?id=10060, last accessed 15 August 2008.

New York, Boston, Washington DC-Media Kit Request, 2007. http://www.vgp.com/advertising/adv_splash.html, last accessed 15 August 2008.

Newscentral 24, 2007. http://www.a2mediagroup.com/?c=164&a=17845, last accessed 15 August 2008.

Sydney Media 2007. http://www.sydneymedia.com.au/html/2285-city-visitors.asp, last accessed 15 August 2008.

Tani, M. 2005. On the motivations of business travel: Evidence from an Australian survey. *Asian and Pacific Migration Journal*, 14, 419-440.

UNWTO (United Nations World Tourism Organization) 2007a. *Compendium of Tourism Statistics: Data 2001-2005*. Madrid, UNWTO.

UNWTO (United Nations World Tourism Organization) 2007b. *Facts and figures*. http://www.world-tourism.org/facts/eng/inbound.htm, last accessed 15 August 2008.

Uriely, N. 2001. 'Travelling workers' and 'working tourists': Variations across the interaction between work and tourism. *International Journal of Tourism Research*, 3, 1-8.

Urry, J. 2000. *Sociology beyond Societies: Mobilities for the Twenty-first Century*. London: Routledge.

Urry, J. 2002. Mobility and proximity. *Sociology*, 36, 255-274.

Urry, J. 2003. Social networks, travel and talk. *British Journal of Sociology*, 54, 155-175.

Chapter 10
Individual Rationalities of Global Business Travel

Claus Lassen

Introduction

(...) [W]e don't forget that frequent business travellers are often the most frequent leisure travellers, so we examine where to escape on your next break and what to do if you are lucky enough to get time off when travelling on business. With editorial staff based in our offices around the globe we are uniquely placed to ensure that our different editions reflect the needs of our readers locally. We can also use this expertise to produced first-class editorial insights wherever we need to report. (www.businesstraveller.com)

In the wake of economic globalization, a transformation of work has taken place which means that for many professionals today their working lives take place on the global stage. The creation of 'global work' (Jones 2008) means that international business travel by airplanes has increased significantly in recent decades. Figures from the World Tourism Organization (2005) show that 19 per cent of all international travel is work-related and that this type of travel more than doubled between 1990 and 2001. In relation to this increase in air travel, knowledge workers and knowledge organizations especially seem to be important players (Høyer and Næss 2001). A number of studies have emphasized the importance of face-to-face communication and social obligations as elements that necessitate people to travel in relation to work (Boden and Molotch 1994, Urry 2007). Likewise, in various transport and tourism research fields, business travel has traditionally been seen as a structural output of work and business with only little individual influence by business travellers themselves, and as opposed to the freedom of the tourist. Based on a study that explores international business travel among knowledge workers in two Danish knowledge organizations,[1] this chapter shows that international professionals travel within a globalized labour

---

1   A 'knowledge organization' is defined as one with a high level of either the production or consumption of knowledge (see Castells (1996) for a more detailed description). I use the term 'knowledge organization' in this chapter because it varies from the traditional Fordist organizations and Fordist labour market. Knowledge has, of course, always played an important role in industry, but today we see that units or agents in the new economy

market in order to cope with a number of social obligations and face-to-face needs. However, the knowledge workers are also members of an individualised labour market in which a number of non-work elements from other spheres of everyday life function as important rationalities for travelling internationally as well. It is therefore argued that international work travel cannot just be understood as reflecting employers' demands and expectations, since it is produced through a complex interplay between many different components and rationalities coming not only from work, but also from the very different spheres of everyday life, family, consumption, tourism leisure and play. These various elements influence how professionals construct and assess the demand of business and air travel at the individual level. In conclusion, therefore, the chapter points out that research into business travel needs a much stronger focus on the individual social motives for business travel if it is to acquire a more in-depth understanding of the way such types of movement have increased.

In the following, I will present some of the main results from the case studies of the two Danish organizations, exploring the perspective described above. First, the research design, theories and methods of the study will be laid out. Secondly, the main results of the study will be presented and summarized. Finally, in the conclusion the chapter will end by pointing out some challenges for further research into international business travel.

The Mobilized Knowledge Worker

The study of '*the mobilized knowledge worker*' that this chapter draws on focuses on explaining the ever increasing number of international business trips taken every year. Concentrating on international trips made by aeroplane as part of one's professional activities that is paid for by one's employer, it aims to shed light on the driving forces, patterns of meaning and incentives behind long-distance business travel. The aim is to understand why this form of travel has increased markedly in our modern society, especially in the knowledge industries, and what this type of mobility means for knowledge workers' social lives, environmental problems, etc. (see Lassen 2005 for a further discussion of the research project). The notion of the knowledge workers refers particularly to the so-called 'knowledge industry', i.e. highly-skilled organizations which are players in what has been described as the 'new globalised, knowledge and network based economy' (Castells 1996). The knowledge workers have been termed the 'creative class' (Florida 2002) or 'knowledge workers in the net sector' (Wittel 2001), and they form a group which includes scientists, engineers, architects, teachers, writers, artists, and entertainers as well as any businessmen who are working in new and different ways. They are members of the new labour market of the economy, and as many authors have pointed out, they can be characterized

---

fundamentally depend upon their capacity to generate, process and apply efficient knowledge-based information (Castells 1996: 77).

by their flexible working behaviour. Compared with previous generations of the industrial society, they are liberated from clocking-on, production lines, and monotonous routines (Sennett 1999, Eriksen 2001). Wittel (2001) argues that knowledge work is organized around a 'network sociality' which involves a number of social obligations to be co-present in relation to places, events, and people, which often involves air travel (Urry 2003, 2007). Klok (2003) stresses that in a network sociality, mobility becomes a necessity of life for knowledge workers and that this type of sociality is therefore deeply embedded in communication technology, transport technology and technologies to manage relationships (Wittel 2001: 69-70). Mobility functions for the knowledge workers as capital that links with, and can be exchanged for, other forms of capital (social, economy and cultural capital) (Kaufman et. al. 2004, Urry 2007). Furthermore, as Wittel (2001: 69-70) points out, working lives in knowledge organizations are not characterized by a separation of work and play, but rather by a combination between work and play. Moreover, a life on the move in knowledge organizations seems to be related to a number of social consequences (see Lassen 2009, Kesselring and Vogl, this volume) In terms of the environment, knowledge work has been seen as an example of a 'dematerialisation', which is assumed to make continuous economic growth compatible with reduced material consumption and pollution (Heiskanen and Jalas 2000). However, there has been a great deal of work on this issue suggesting that, in practice, strong 'material' impacts arise from supposedly 'immaterial' industries (Graham and Marvin 2001: 335, Kaplan 2002: 34). International flying especially seems to be related to more serious environmental impacts than travel at ground level (Høyer and Næss 2001). This means that the analysis of knowledge workers is also linked to a consideration of more sustainable knowledge work (Lassen 2006) by reducing physical travel through increased use of different forms of virtual communication (see Denstadli and Gripsrud, this volume).

Theory

The study of knowledge workers is based on the new 'paradigm of mobilities' (Kaufmann 2002, Kesselring 2006, Lassen 2006, Canzler et al. 2008, Sheller and Urry 2006, Urry 2007) and challenges the 'predict and provide' tradition as a way of exploring air movement (see Whitelegg 2000: 88). The starting point is instead to understand the sociology of international work-related travel and aeromobility. As a consequence of this approach, this chapter addresses the social basis of aeromobility and international work-related travel. The study of work and aeromobility in knowledge organizations rests on a model of understanding that covers mobility, identity and work. The model of understanding must capture the production of work travel and its consequences as a phenomenon that transcends the traditional demarcation of work in industrial society. International business travel cannot only be understood as reflecting employers' demands and expectations. The model of understanding must therefore include a perspective on mobility and identity as well as work, and it must focus on the employees' coping strategies when they combine these different elements. The model examines how individuals create and cope with strategies that give them meaning in their everyday lives and that express a meaningful and manageable handling of external demands and internal intentions (Lassen and Jensen 2004: 252). Apart from the demands and expectations of the workplace and labour market, the employees' theme of reference in relation to individual choice is also deeply rooted in personal circumstances such as lifestyle and identity and these elements are closely connected with decisions about travel. In light of the phenomenon of mobility, the model of understanding also explores how employees within networks assess and manage the necessity for 'co-presence' and face-to-face communication and, by using different strategies, transform or do not transform their motility into different types of mobility. Moreover, as a consequence of this approach, the study does not only focus on actual mobility, but also on the potential mobility of individuals, examining how a potential is transformed into different forms of physical, virtual, and social mobility (Høyer 2000, Kaufmann 2002, Kesselring 2006), where the mobility strategies of individuals and their practices are considered to be in a causal or material relationship with their surroundings (Bhaskar 1975, Sayer 2000).

Methods and Sample

The social basis of international business travel is explored through in-depth research that seeks to understand and interpret the patterns of meaning, rationalities and mechanisms attached to international business travel in knowledge organizations, with a particular focus on individual employees. This implies a qualitative research design based on methodological pluralism (Bourdieu and Wacquant 1996: 209; see also Danermark et al. 2002 on methodological pluralism). The analytical approach therefore focuses on both the production of meaning and causalities. Drawing on this theoretical approach, the analyses are primarily based empirically on a multiple-case study (Flyvbjerg 2001) involving two Danish knowledge organizations:

- Aalborg University, a Danish institution whose primary activities are research and teaching (in total 1,200 employees).
- Hewlett-Packard Denmark, a division of a global provider of products, technologies, solutions and services to consumers and businesses. Its core areas are IT infrastructures, personal computing, access devices, global services, imaging and printing (in total 600 employees).

There are different arguments for choosing these two specific cases. Flyvbjerg (2001) argues that, when the objective is to achieve the greatest possible amount of information on a given problem or phenomena, a representative case or random sample may not be the most appropriate strategy to adopt (Flyvbjerg 2001: 78).

This is because the typical or average case is often not the richest in information. From an understanding-orientated perspective, it is often more important to clarify the deeper causes behind a given problem and its consequences than to describe its symptoms and how frequently they occur. The idea is that, by choosing two very different cases when it comes to the private-public dichotomy, organizational structures, work cultures, tasks, reasons for travelling, etc. are likely to vary and, therefore, it is reasonable to assume that, if shared mechanisms and rationalities are found, they might also be found in a range of other organizations. Hopefully, this will help us achieve a deeper understanding of the reasons for the increase in international business travel in recent decades. The case study used the following data-collecting techniques: (1) a web-based questionnaire was distributed to all the employees in the two Danish cases[2] (in total 1,800 employees), (2) qualitative research interviews were conducted with selected employees in the two cases (in total 11 employees), and (3) qualitative research interviews were conducted with top management in the two cases (in total two managers).

A Set of Social Work Obligations

In the following, I will present the main results of the study, exploring why international business travel takes place in two Danish knowledge organizations. The study shows that from time to time employees have to be co-present in relation to people, places and events to manage the obligations of their jobs (there is a need for situations that Urry (2002) describes as face-to-face, face-to-place and face-the-moment). There exists a core of social obligations where the employees, through culturally embedded expectations, need to travel. It is very difficult for individuals to refuse such obligations if they want to keep their present positions (and make a career), and for many it can be felt as a burden (see also Nowicka 2006: 111). There are both similarities and dissimilarities between the cultural expectations which the employees at Aalborg University and Hewlett-Packard face. Globally, Hewlett-Packard is divided into a number of regional working areas. This is reflected in the fact that 67 per cent of journeys have been to other European countries, and only 7 per cent to countries outside Europe. Many employees are responsible for specific activities within a region and therefore need to work across

---

2 The response rate to the web questionnaire at the first organization, Hewlett-Packard Denmark, was 32 per cent, or 193 out of 600 employees. The answers show that 75 per cent of these had made a trip abroad within the last year. The employee who had travelled the most had been on 43 international trips, while 49 employees had not made any international work-related trips at all. The total response rate at the second organization, Aalborg University, was 46 per cent, or 547 out of 1,200 employees. Here, 69 per cent of those surveyed who participated in the analysis had been on work-related trips within the last year. The employee who had travelled the most internationally had carried out 22 trips within the last year, while 168 of respondents had not travelled at all.

national borders in Europe. Likewise, the company functions through autonomy and internal networking between employees. Hewlett-Packard is project-driven, which means that each individual employee is committed to a set goal for a minimum income to the organization, and therefore its employees are 'forced' to participate in any available project, whether nationally or internationally. This is organized through an internal market place:

> We have something we call "Resource Market Place", where vacant jobs are posted. If there is a project there, you can apply if you are interested. If a person doesn't have any assignments, you suggest they take a look at it, and you say: "Hey, there is a project somewhere which might be of interest to you". Obviously people without any commitments at home have more opportunities and might also be more interested. (41-year-old male Consultant at Hewlett-Packard)

This can also be illustrated by the fact that the two most common reasons for travel at Hewlett-Packard are 'internal journeys to other departments' and 'sale, purchase and negotiation with business partners' (see Figure 10.1).

Aalborg University is organized into a number of departments that function autonomously. Staff members in the various faculties are expected to carry out research, publish their work internationally, create international relations with other universities etc. Each individual employee decides how to perform his or her duties in this respect. In 2003, Aalborg University had the largest travel budget among universities in Denmark, which the top management of the university sees as a sign of success because it indicates the university's strong integration into global knowledge flows. Compared to Hewlett-Packard, travelling patterns at Aalborg University are much more individualised, as can be seen from the fact that work-related trips are spread over many more countries and continents (22 per cent of trips are to countries outside Europe). The reason for this is that employees' mobility at Aalborg University is not organized along the lines of a multinational company structure, as is the case with Hewlett-Packard, but instead relates to loosely connected and individualised network collaborations which are established and maintained by each individual employee, especially through participation in conferences and congresses (see Figure 10.1).

In both cases, the organization's employees are in various ways dependent on different sorts of network that create the demand for mobility within the organization because they provide access to knowledge and resources. Internal and external networks open doors when it comes to everyday problems at work, and this strengthens one's personal career. The web-survey showed that 90 per cent of respondents at Aalborg University and 81 per cent at Hewlett-Packard cited network obligations as an important driving factor for international business travel (see Lassen 2005: Chapters 5, 9, for a more detailed description of this subject).

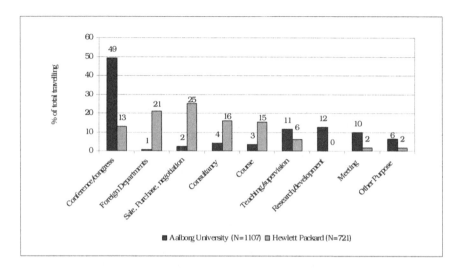

Figure 10.1 Reasons for travelling among residents at Hewlett-Packard and Aalborg University

Note: N = Total number of journeys.
Source: Lassen (2005).

Is it Only a Matter of Co-presence?

Before moving on, it is important to make a theoretical point with empirical implications in relation to the need for co-presence and business travel. In social science, there exist a number of studies showing the importance of co-presence in human socialization. As Goffman (1963) showed decades ago, face-to-face contacts, or what he terms 'face-work', play a fundamental role in social relations. For example, he stresses how 'Eye to eye looks, then, play a special role in the communication life of the community, ritually establishing an avowed openness to verbal statements and a rightfully heightened mutual relevance of acts' (Goffman 1963: 92). Another, more recent example is represented by Boden and Molotch (1994: 264), who argue that co-presence is still the fundamental mode of human intercourse and socialization in modern society. Such types of interaction require participants to be present at a specific time and place, and the face-to-face meeting provides evidence of commitment. For example, business meetings often begin with preliminary meetings involving 'small talk' where participants update one another on both work and leisure. Items such as 'Just sent you a message regarding the things which we talked about yesterday' are interwoven with informal remarks about appearance, weather, lunch, plans, overwork, family news, etc. Small talk tells the listener how to cope with the business meeting that will follow because it depicts what types of person you will be dealing with (Boden and Molotch 1994: 269).

Although the type of research presented above emphasizes the importance of face-to-face communication in business life too, it does not say anything about how often face-to-face meetings are necessary in order to cope properly with the work task and live up to job expectations in the global work market. However, at first sight, the interview transcripts from the present research project leave the impression that the need for co-presence in its various forms is the only rationale for going on international business journeys. However, further examination of the interview material and survey data reveals that other, more individual but less work-related types of rationalities and mechanisms also seem to play a role in certain situations, as will be demonstrated in the following section.

The Individualisation of Work and Business Travel

The knowledge workers in these two cases belong to a transformed labour market (Sennett 1999, Eriksen 2001, Castells 1996). In relation to business travel, this transformation of work means that employees have a high degree of self-determination when it comes to deciding the destination and frequency of international work-related flying according to both the qualitative interviews and the web-survey (see Figure 10.2). Work-related journeys are not only a question of employees facing demands from the employer about going to specific places within a set period of time. Work mobility is created through a process in which the individual is influenced by external demands to be mobile, though the employee's requests, choices and priorities also play important roles in the construction of his or her patterns of mobility. The individualization of work means that business travel should not only be researched in relation to work and work-related rationalities, but should also cover other aspects of employees' everyday lives.

Business Travel as a Part of One's Identity

One of the aspects not exclusively related to work is identity. Identity is seen as 'increasingly fragmented and fractured; never singular but multiple across different, often intersecting and antagonistic, discourses, practices and positions' (Hall 1996: 4). Here international work-related journeys through a system of corridors (see Lassen 2006, 2009, for further descriptions of corridors), founded in the logic of a space of flows (Castells 1996), offer material support for a cosmopolitan identity. Work is not only about earning money, it also has a symbolic value in the way the employees choose to present themselves to the world. The business journey seems to deliver an important material and symbolic contribution to the employee's identity which is shaped on an international scale.

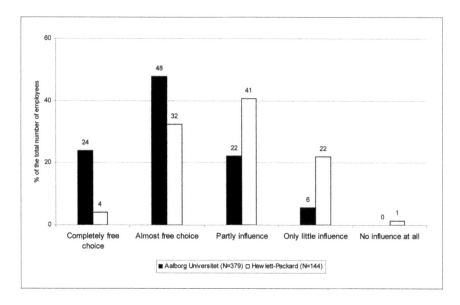

Figure 10.2 Extent to which employees surveyed decide the frequency of work-related journeys

Note: N = Total number of respondents.
Source: Lassen (2005).

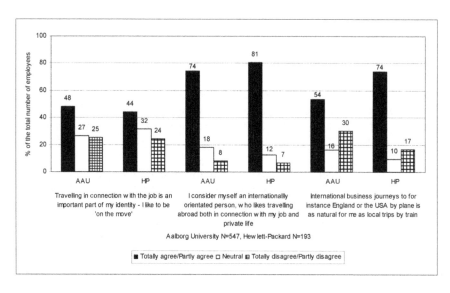

Figure 10.3 Employees' attitude to international business travel

Note: N = Number of employees surveyed.
Source: Lassen (2005).

As Figure 10.3 shows, there are a number of questions from the web-survey concerning travel and identity in which the majority of the respondents in both cases say that identity is important to them in relation to business travel. Most of the respondents consider themselves to be international persons who like to travel globally, and long-distance travel by airplanes is as natural to them as local trips by trains or car. This indicates that travel has an influential meaning for employees' ways of looking at themselves (see Lassen [2005] for more details on the web-survey attitude questions). Although the web-survey questions do not say anything about the specific meanings of business trips for employees' identities, they do indicate that such trips play a role in the employee's self-concept. For a hyper-mobile 'way of living' or 'way of working', the 'consumption of distance' is fundamental, and there is a connection between this type of consumption and particular lifestyles and identities. A cosmopolitan identity puts the spotlight on the prevalence of this new kind of cosmopolitanism or post-national situation in which global civil society is the frame of reference for solidarity and identity (see Habermas 2001, Stevenson 2003, Urry 2003, Beck 2008). There are increasing streams of cosmopolitanism coming from television, airplane trips, mobile phones and internet connections. This transforms the relationship between co-presence and mediated social relations, between proximity and remoteness, and between the local and the global (Harvey 2000: 85-86 in Urry 2003: 138). As Urry (2003: 137) states, 'cosmopolitan fluidity thus involves the capacity to live simultaneously in both the global and the local, in the distant and the proximate, in the universal and the particular'. However, as shown in the following, employees cope with the demands for global air travel in different ways.

Different Ways of Coping with Business Travel

As I have shown elsewhere (Lassen 2005, 2009), three different coping strategies can be identified from the qualitative interviews when it comes to handling work, mobility and identity (see Table 10.1).[3] In the following, these strategies will be summarized briefly.

The *first* is the career strategy. These employees live a single life or have a partner who functions as a backer and takes care of the home. Life is work, and mobility is a fundamental and necessary element of one's working life. The employee lives the life of a cosmopolitan tourist (Bauman 1999). A high level of work mobility and an international orientation are core elements in one's self-conception and identity. Employees using this strategy practise a de-centred (see

---

3   The development of the categories 'career strategy', 'juggling strategy' and 'family strategy' is inspired by an analysis of working life, family life and stress produced by the Danish Society of Engineers (IDA) in 2002. Previously available at: http://ida.dk/Ansat/ Ansaettelsesvilkaar/Arbejdsmiljoe/Publikationer.htm (last accessed 3 December 2007).

Kesselring 2006: 272) handling of mobility where the home centre is less clear than for the other strategies.

Table 10.1 The different coping strategies that can be found at Aalborg University and at Hewlett-Packard in terms of mobility, identity and work

Coping strategy	Mobility	Identity	Work
Career strategy	De-centred	Cosmopolitan	Work is life-style
Juggling strategy	Centred	'Glocal' (juggler)	Work and family are equally important
Family strategy	Centred	'Glocal' (balance)	Family before work

Source: Revised from Lassen (2005).

The *second* is the juggling strategy. In these cases, both family and work have high priorities, without either one of them being chosen over the other. The strategy is based on a 'glocal' identity (Urry 2003) in which employees try to combine and juggle their international working lives with a locally rooted family life. These employees use a centred mobility strategy (see Kesselring 2006: 271) through which they travel back and forth between home and abroad in hub–spoke patterns of movement.

The *third* strategy is the family strategy. In these cases, the employee gives a high priority to his family above work, and work-related mobility is planned taking the needs of the family into account. This way of coping is more locally oriented, but work trips may be seen as an exciting and exotic part of the job, provided they can be fitted in with everyday life and obligations. Also here the employees practise a centred strategy of mobility with a clear centre (see Kesselring 2006: 272).

That different coping strategies that can be identified show that mobility is not homogeneous, but is produced differently depending on personal circumstances. The answers to the web-survey also show that the needs of business travel are affected by the personal situations of individual employees. The web-survey shows that the cosmopolitan tourist (Bauman 1999) with many annual business trips is most often a man without any family obligations (men travel on average 4.3 times a year compared to 2.7 for women). The family factor is the most important brake on international mobility. At Hewlett-Packard, single employees in their thirties, with children living at home, travel the least (at Hewlett-Packard single employees with children travel annually 3 times, while those without children travel 9.6 times). When employees marry and start families, they are often compelled to choose another strategy than the career strategy (e.g. the juggling strategy or the family strategy). At Aalborg University, this pattern is not so evident because international work travel increases throughout one's career, which can probably be explained by the fact that people in general travel less globally, and start out on a lower level of travelling in general (employees at Hewlett-Packard take 3.8 trips per year compared to two trips per year at Aalborg University). This finding seems to be supported by other studies. Gustafson (2006) explores national travel surveys from Sweden and examines the relationship between family situation, gender and work-related overnight travel. His study indicates that family obligations have an impact on travel activity, but also that women and men differ in this respect (Gustafson 2006: 513). He therefore argues that the relationship between work-related travel and family obligations involves both individual and structural factors. Likewise Kesselring (2006) identifies different types of mobility management among the different types of employees in the study of the mobility of pioneers in the IT and media industries, the service sector and the armed forces.

Escape Journeys and Formative Journeys

Two other mechanisms also seem to play a role in relation to international business travel in the two cases. As Adey et al. (2007: 876) point out, long international air travel offers an escape from everyday life. One female employee from Hewlett-Packard illustrated this aspect of business travel:

> (…) [S]ometimes I feel that it is actually nice that I can have a break; tonight I only have to take care of myself. I am staying in a hotel room, where I can read a book which I have longed to read, or I can do something else which I have longed to do, because I am alone during such an evening. (38-year-old female Chief Consultant at Hewlett-Packard)

The female employee with small children finds that going on a business journey offers her a break from everyday problems: taking children to the kindergarten, shopping, everyday transport, cleaning, cooking, the time pressures of everyday life, etc. For such a woman, the trip abroad, being alone in a hotel room, offers her a break from everyday problems. Like this woman, a number of the knowledge workers live a hectic and stressful everyday life in which it is difficult to cope with and co-ordinate various tasks of everyday life in relation to work, family and leisure-time activities. In some cases, an international work-related trip can feel like a holiday from the time-pressures of everyday life (see Rojek 1993).

Secondly, business travel functions as formative journeys which historically has played a role in the cognitive and perceptual education of the upper class (Urry 1990), and which still seems to be a factor for the new elite of knowledge workers (Florida 2002). Business travel in the two cases involves an element of both professional and cultural education. The journeys provide an opportunity to develop professional skills and acquire access to new knowledge. For example, it makes it possible to participate in highly specialized courses, which are only held at a few places around the world. This can be illustrated by the following example:

> It is hardcore training in, for example, a tool for some of the things which we are implementing, but it could also be training in the processes I told you about; actually this week we are organizing a three-day-course here, where one of my colleagues is the instructor. This is an example of the kind of training courses for which I would go abroad if they weren't available in Denmark. There is a very wide range of courses. On the one hand there are the more or less theoretical courses, where there are, of course, some lectures, and maybe some workshops or similar with group exercises, but no technical training. On the other hand, there are the hardcore technical courses, where you are taught some technical skills with integrated hands-on exercises. (41-year old male Consultant at Hewlett-Packard)

In the same way, a conference or a congress may help employees to develop professionally in their job, as well as exchanging experiences with colleagues in various other countries and cultures etc. Moreover, seen from a cultural perspective, business travel also delivers an 'exotic touch' (Nowicka 2006: 192), which means that employees want to experience something new and unusual. If they were not able to travel, they would miss the physical experiences of the smell, the food, the air and the people during their stay in another place. Therefore, journeys always involve small pockets of new and exotic experiences, some unplanned or unconscious (see also the next section). As De-Botton (2002: 69) has also shown, the exotic elements of a journey are an important driver of travel. Objects and symbols that we meet during our journey can give us cultural information, as well as new knowledge of ourselves.

Tourist and Experience Practices

In relation to international travel, the analysis also shows that employees combine work with non-work activities, e.g. sightseeing, family visits or a vacation. Especially at Aalborg University, the employees use the possibility of a holiday in relation to work travel, usually linked to participation in congresses and conferences abroad. This accounts for 55 per cent of all journeys at Aalborg University, where employees indicated that they have gone on a holiday related to conference and congress participation. This type of work trip is also that on which employees at the university most frequently bring their families along, and 23 per cent of all trips with the aim of going to a congress or conference were to a location situated directly on the Mediterranean coast, not only in large cities but also in small towns, which tend to be popular tourism destinations. The fact that the employees at the university more often take holidays in relation to work travel does not mean that pleasure activities are absent at Hewlett-Packard, but people's working lives are even more intensive and fast-paced there, which means that employees have fewer opportunities to take a holiday. Instead, pleasure activities such as day trips activities and small adventure trips are integrated into the Hewlett-Packard work trip whenever possible, for example, between two meetings or a weekend trip between two working days.

As I have shown elsewhere (Lassen 2006), in relation to mixing work trips and tourism, three main practices can be identified in the two cases (see also Lassen (2005) for a further description of these practices). The *first* practice is what can be termed 'day-tripper activities'. In both cases, employees carry out such activities when they are on international work-related trips. The *second* practice can be termed 'tourist activities'. Some employees occasionally use the opportunity to extend a normal working trip for a few days or maybe use it as a launch pad for a vacation. That is, they extend their trip by some extra days or start their holidays at the end of an international working trip. In this respect, employees sometimes travel to interesting places and want to explore these more than would be possible within the ordinary working period abroad. As Nowicka (2006) describes it, knowledge workers are experts and tourists at the same time (see also Lassen 2006). The *third* practice can be termed 'family activities', which includes both 'bringing and visiting family and friends' abroad.

Conclusion

This chapter has shown that, to a very large extent, knowledge workers in an individualized and globalized labour market are responsible for interpreting their own needs for business travel and for deciding whether to travel or not. There exists a core of social obligations where the knowledge workers, through culturally embedded expectations, need to travel (see also Beaverstock and Faulconbridge, this volume). It is very difficult for individuals to refuse such obligations if they want to keep their present positions (and make a career) and as Kesselring and Volg stress (this volume) mobility becomes a key element to be success at work (see also Jones 2008). However, international work travel in knowledge organizations cannot only be understood as reflecting employers' demands and expectations, since it is produced through a complex interplay between many different components and rationalities coming not only from work, but also from the very different spheres of everyday life, family, consumption, tourism, leisure and play. Business travel in knowledge organizations is not something given or fixed, as it is constructed differently by each employee, depending on the balance between structural demands and more individual wishes, needs and dreams, and it is also associated with questions of identify and life-style (see Wickham and Vecchi (this volume) on travel decision-making in the Irish computer software industry). As Kellerman (this volume) also stresses, the clear-cut differentiations between business and leisure tourism have become blurred, which is similar to the amalgamation between home and work (see also Wittel 2001).

Theoretically, these findings from the knowledge organizations challenge the traditional understandings of business travel. In transport research based on a 'predict and provide' way of thinking (see Whitelegg 2000: 88), work travel has often been considered as the opposite of tourist travel (Davidson 1994), and in connection with this, the degree of each individual's self-determination is regarded as one of the parameters which separate work travel from tourist travel. Tourist travel is here seen as related to the individual's sphere of self-determination, while the work trip is considered to be a result of the employer's needs and demands on the employee (Urry 1990). This separation can also be found in a traditional understanding of tourism (Urry 1990: 2-3). Here tourism is understood as the opposite of regular and organized work, and it often involves movements of people to new places. Tourism sites are outside the normal places of residence and work, and there is a clear intention to return 'home'. It is different, and separate, from our day-to-day lives; we tour in order to see and experience something different. Tourist sites are of 'a different scale or involving different senses', and they are separated from everyday experiences and are 'out of the ordinary'. Based on the analysis in this chapter, it can be argued that there is a need to re-think this notion of business travel (see also Graham, this volume).

A number of studies focus on opportunities to replace international business travel with virtual communication (see Armstrong 2007). However, Denstadli and Gripsrud, (this volume) show that various forms of telecommunication have only had a minor effect on travel. In the light of the findings in this chapter, it can be suggested that these studies overlook the strength of a number of the individual rationalities and mechanisms when they list the personal advantages to employees of travelling less. The question asked by Adey et al. (2007: 786) still remains unanswered: '[w]hy do people still feel the need to fly in an era when many forms of business and sociality can be conducted at arm's length?' In conclusion, therefore, this chapter ends by arguing that a rethinking of business travel must include 'a new sociology of business travel' focusing on the factors that make business more or less travel-intensive (Haynes et al. 2006). There is clearly a need for much more theoretical and empirical research in order to understand the social motives for business travel and the relationship between travel, work and the potential for increased use of virtual communication (see also this volume). A new sociology of business travel needs especially to address flying as a core object, and as Budd and Hubbard (this volume) point out, the many different ways people fly in relation to work (and one could add why people fly). In addition, the connection between systems of mobility and the practises and rationalities in traveller's mobile everyday life must also be addressed (Richardson and Jensen 2008). Moreover, in relation to methodology, elements from ethnography and anthropology might be able to open doors to new types of knowledge regarding workers actual travel. Finally, new data collection techniques such as GPS-mapping and video technologies might provide new insight to social motives of business travel.

Acknowledgements

I would like to thank Erik Jensen of Roskilde University for valuable comments on this chapter.

References

Adey, P., Budd, L., and Hubbard, P. 2007. Flying lessons: Exploring the social and cultural geographies of global air travel. *Progress in Human Geography*, 31(6), 773-791.

Armstrong, C. 2007. *Business Air Travel Demand in the Light of Conferencing Alternatives and Pressure for Responsible Practice*. Master's thesis, School of Engineering, Department of Air Transport, Bedfordshire: Cranfield University. https://dspace.lib.cranfield.ac.uk/handle/1826/2444, accessed 5 November 2008.

Bauman, Z. 1999. *Globalisering: de menneskelige konsekvenser*. København: Hans Reitzels Forlag.

Beaverstock, J. and Faulconbridge, J. This volume.

Beck, U. 2008. Mobility and the cosmopolitan perspective, in *Tracing Mobilities: Towards a Cosmopolitian Perspective*, edited by W. Canzler, V. Kaufmann, and S. Kesselring. Aldershot: Ashgate, 25-36.

Bhaskar, R. 1975. *A Realist Theory of Science*. Leeds: Leeds Books.

Boden, D. and Molotch, H. L. 1994. The compulsion of proximity, in *NowHere: Space, Time and Modernity*, edited by R. Friedland, and D. Boden. Berkeley: University of California Press, 257-286.

Bourdieu, P. and Wacquant, L. 1996. *Refleksiv Sociologi – mål og midler.* København: Hans Reitzels Forlag.

Budd, L. and Hubbard, P. This volume.

Canzler, W., Kaufman, V. and Kesselring, S. 2008. *Tracing Mobilities: Towards a Cosmopolitan Perspective*. Aldershot: Ashgate.

Castells, M. 1996. *The Information Age: Economy, Society and Culture, Vol. 1: The Rise of the Network Society*. Oxford: Blackwell.

Danermark, B., Ekström, M., Jackobsen, L. and Karlsson, J.C. 2002. *Explaining Society: Critical Realism in the Social Sciences*. London: Routledge.

Davidson, R. 1994. *Business Travel*. London: Pitman Publishing.

De-Botton, A. 2002. *The Art of Travel*. London: Penguin Group.

Eriksen, T. H. 2001. *Øyeblikkets Tyranni: Rask og langsom tid i informationsalderen.* Oslo: Aschehoug.

Florida, R. 2002. *The Rise of the Creative Class: And How it's Transforming Work, Leisure, Community and Everyday Life*. New York: Basic Books.

Flyvbjerg, B. 2001. *Making Social Science Matter: Why Social Inquiry Fails and How it can Succeed Again*. Cambridge: Cambridge University Press.

Goffman, E. 1963. *Behavior in Public Places: Notes on the Social Organizations of Gatherings*. New York: The Free Press.

Graham, B. This volume.

Graham, S. and Marvin, S. 2001. *Splintering Urbanism: Networked Infrastructures, Technological Mobilities and the Urban Condition.* London: Routledge.

Gustafson, P. 2006. Work-related travel gender and family obligations. *Work, Employment and Society*, 20(3), 513-530.

Habermas, J. 2001. *The Postnational Constellation: Political Essays.* Oxford: Polity Press.

Hall, S. 1996. Introduction: Who needs identity?, in *Questions of Cultural Identity*, edited by S. Hall and P. du Gay. London: Sage, 1-17.

Harvey, D. 2000. *Spaces of Hope.* Edinburgh: Edinburgh University Press.

Haynes, P., Vecchi, A. and Wickham, J. 2006. *Flying around the globe and bringing business back home?* IIIS Paper No. 170/2006, http://ideas.repec.org/p/iis/dispap/iiisdp173.html, accessed 9 November 2008.

Heiskanen, E. and Jalas, M. 2000. *Dematerialization Through Services – A Review and Evaluation of the Debate.* Helsinki: Ministry of the Environment.

Høyer, K.G. 2000. *Sustainable Mobility: The Concept and its Implications.* PhD dissertation. Roskilde: Roskilde University.

Høyer, K.G. and Næss, P. 2001. Conference tourism: A problem for the environment, as well as for research? *Journal of Sustainable Tourism*, 9(6), 541-570.

Jones, A.M. 2008. The rise of global work. *Transactions of the Institute of British Geographers*, 33(1), 12-26.

Kaplan, C. 2002. Transporting the subject: Technologies of mobility and location in an era of globalization. *Proceedings of the Modern Language Association of America*, 117(1), 32-42.

Kaufmann, V. 2002. *Re-thinking Mobility: Contemporary Sociology.* Aldershot: Ashgate Publishing.

Kaufmann, V., Bergman, M.M. and Joye, D. 2004. Motility: Mobility as Capital. *International Journal of Urban and Regional Research*, 28(4), 745-756.

Kellerman, A. This volume.

Kesselring, S. 2006. Pioneering mobilities: New patterns of movement and motility in a mobile world. *Environment and Planning A*, 38(2), 269-279.

Kesselring, S. and Vogl, G. This volume.

Klok, J. 2003. *Knowledge Workers NL: Developments and Trends.* Delft: TU Delft, https://doc.freeband.nl/dsweb/Get/Document-39450/Ontwikkelingen%20kenniswerkers.pdf, accessed 2 November 2008.

Lassen, C. 2005. *Den mobiliserede vidensarbejder: en analyse af internationale arbejdsrejsers sociologi.* Ph.D. dissertation, Institut for Samfundsudvikling og Planlægning, Aalborg: Aalborg Universitet.

Lassen, C. 2006. Work and aeromobility. *Environment and Planning A*, 38(2), 301-312.

Lassen, C. 2009. A life in corridors: Social perspectives on aeromobility, in *Aeromobilities*, edited by S. Cwerner, S. Kesselring and J. Urry. London: Routledge.

Lassen, C. and Jensen, O.B. 2004. Den globale Bus: om arbejdsrejsers betydning i hverdagslivet, in *Arbejdssammfund? Den beslaglagte tid og den splittede identitet*, edited by M.H. Jacobsen and J. Tonboe. København: Hans Reitzels Forlag, 241-279.

Nowicka, M. 2006. *Transnational Professionals and their Cosmopolitan Universes*. Frankfurt: Campus Verlag.

Richardson, T. and Jensen, O.B. 2008. Constructing mobile subjects. *Built Environment*, 34(2), 218-231.

Rojek, C. 1993. *Ways of Escape: Modern Transformation in Leisure and Travel*. London: The Macmillan Press.

Sayer, A. 2000. *Realism and Social Science*. London/Thousand Oaks/New Delhi: Sage Publications.

Sennett, R. 1999. *Det fleksible menneske, eller arbejdets forvandling og personlighedens nedsmeltning*. Højbjerg: Hovedland.

Sheller, M. and Urry, J. 2006. The new mobilities paradigm. *Environment and Planning A*, 38, 207-226.

Stevenson, N. 2003. *Cultural Citizenship: Cosmopolitan Questions*. Berkshire: Open University Press.

Urry, J. 1990. *The Tourist Gaze*. London: Sage.

Urry, J. 2002. Mobility and proximity. *Sociology*, 36(2), 255-274.

Urry, J. 2003. *Global Complexity*. Oxford: Polity Press.

Urry, J. 2007. *Mobilities*. Cambridge: Polity Press.

Whitelegg, J. 2000. *Aviation: The Social, Economic and Environmental Impact of Flying*. London: Ashden Trust.

Wickham, J. and Vecchi, A. This volume.

Wittel, A. 2001. Toward a network sociality. *Theory, Culture and Society*, 18(6), 51-76.

World Tourism Organization 2005. *Inbound Tourism: Tourist Arrivals by Purpose of Visit*, www.world-tourism.org, accessed 1 October 2006.

Chapter 11

Understanding Mobility in Professional Business Services

Andrew Jones

Introduction

Debates about the nature of the global economy have become increasingly focused on the important role played by knowledge-intensive industries, and in particularly the professional business services sector (Hermelin 1997, Harrington and Daniels 2006). This category – professional business services – of course covers a whole range of industries and sub-sectors including financial services, ICT, advertising, marketing, legal services – to name just a few (c.f. Strom and Mattsson 2005). All are knowledge-intensive industries, although most attention has been paid within the social scientific literature to sectors like banking and management consultancy which are argued to be at the forefront of economic globalization (Sassen 2001, Wood 2002, 2006), both in terms of the transnationalization of business service firms themselves, and also their role in facilitating the development of 'corporate globality' in firms across all sectors (Aharoni and Nucham 2000). Whether it is the role played by investment banks in financing the global economy, or management consultants in advising firms how to invest overseas, business services are seen as playing a key part in enabling global economic interconnectedness (Jones 2003, Roberts 2006, Aslesen et al. 2008).

It is in this context that debates about mobility in professional business services have been framed. Given the apparent centrality of business service activity to economic globalization, it has been argued that the professionals employed by business service firms are amongst the most mobile workers in the global economy. From this perspective, they represent a key component of a developing and highly mobile transnational business class (c.f. Castells 2001, Sklair 2001). Driving this mobility is the knowledge-intensive nature of the business service work process where face-to-face contact is crucially important (Grabher 2002, Glückler and Armbruster 2003, Jones 2005). In combination with the key role played by business service firms in facilitating the transnationalization of other firms, this has led to the proposition that business service professionals are arguably amongst the most mobile workers in the contemporary global economy. Furthermore, as economic globalization develops further, various theorists have suggested that more and more of these professionals are having to spend more of their time engaged in business travel (Beaverstock 2004, Faulconbridge and

Muzio 2008). Business service professionals are thus argued to be increasingly mobile in response to transformations in the both the role and market for business services in the contemporary global economy (Jones 2003, Beaverstock 2004).

However, these arguments have largely been based on limited empirical evidence from specific industries within the broad range of activities classified as 'business services'. The mobility of business service sector employees has thus become widely acknowledged without the benefit of extensive or wide-ranging empirical enquiry. This chapter thus sets out to examine the nature, form and function of mobility in the professional business service sector. In so doing, it will also assess the extent to which claims about the high degree of mobility amongst business service sector employees are generally applicable. One of the key questions in this respect is the extent to which arguments about employee mobility are relevant for the business service sector as a whole, and for which types of employees within different business service industry sub-sectors. To do this, the chapter draws on a range of empirical research into different business service industries. In relation to the wider concern of this book with business travel, the central proposition which emerges from this analysis is the concept of 'business travel' – when applied to the business service sector – seeks to capture what is in fact a complex phenomenon involving a range of different forms of mobility which fulfil different functions within the operations of business service firms. It further explores how certain forms of mobility within business service industries are bound into the work process in business services, and how specific forms of employee mobility play a crucial role in the success or failure of globalization strategies in different professional business service industries. In addition, I suggest that the case of professional business services is illustrative of some of the conceptual difficulties in both defining and theorizing the nature and role of business travel in the contemporary global economy.

These arguments are developed in a series of stages through the chapter. The next section begins by providing a brief overview of the business service sector, and examining recent trends across the sector as a whole as well as its constituent industries in the contemporary global informational economy. It moves on to examine how existing theoretical and conceptual arguments concerning business travel and mobility are of significance to business services industries. In so doing, some of the more general claims that have been made by theorists thus far about the nature and role of business travel in business services are considered. The third part of the chapter then proposes a conceptual approach for understanding the nature and function of employee mobility in professional business services. Drawing on both the existing literature and empirical research into professional business service industries, it proposes a two-pronged theoretical framework addressing the form and function of mobility in professional business services. The fourth part of the chapter illustrates the utility of this framework by considering the nature and role of business travel in two distinct business service sub-sectors: management consultancy and legal services. In so doing it examines how different forms of mobility fulfil different functions essential to the ongoing operation and continued competiveness of professional business service firms. Finally, the fifth section draws together the implications that this analysis has for future business travel and mobility trends in professional business services, and also in particular what kinds of mobility are more or less likely to be substitutable in future with new and improved forms of ICT.

Business Services, Globalization and Mobility

Whilst there is a growing social scientific literature spanning management studies (Lowendahl 2005, Roberts 2006), economic geography (Wood 2002, Beaverstock 2004, Jones 2005, Daniels 2006) and organizational sociology (Flood 1999, Empson 2002) which seeks to both conceptualise and understand the development of professional business services in the contemporary global economy, the category is itself a problematic one. Although theorists such as the sociologist Manuel Castells and the urban theorist Saskia Sassen have argued at length that advanced business services are central features of contemporary economic globalization, most particularly in the their role in developing global city networks and facilitating 'command and control' in the global economy (Sassen 2001, Castells 2001), such general arguments pay little attention to either the diversity of business service activity or the complexity of functions that such industries perform. It is therefore necessary to consider some of the definitional issues around the concept of professional business services. At least two points are important in this respect.

First, there is a need to distinguish between the wider category 'business services' from the more specific 'professional business services' (c.f. Alvesson 2004, Lowendahl 2005). The former covers a much wider and more diverse set of industries and industry sub-sectors than theorists such as Castells are referring to. In most advanced industrial economies (and many developing ones), a growing proportion of the economy corresponds to 'service sector activity' (Dicken 2007). And within that, 'producer' or 'business' services are also a growing proportion of all activity. However, many of these business services are neither professionalized nor globalized. Business services in general includes a whole range of low skill, low value added services such as, for example, catering, cleaning or property maintenance. Such industries often include many small firms operating in national or sub-national market places and their work process often involves highly immobile forms of co-presence. They are not the subject of the discussion in this chapter.

Second, within the 'professional' category of business services there is enormous diversity. There is a tendency for the literature to blithely refer to 'professional business services' as a common grouping, suggesting that financial services such as investment banking have much in common with sectors like advertising or marketing. Whilst there is certainly some commonality, this should not be overestimated and different industries within the category exhibit major differences in the nature of the work process, the organization of firms and the size and scale of market within which they operate (Lowendahl 2005, Wood 2006). These considerable difference between different industries need to be understood in the following discussion about the globalization of these sectors.

The Globalization of Professional Business Services

Over the last couple of decades, research has indicated that in common with other industries, professional business service activity has become increasingly globalized. Broadly speaking, since the late 1980s industries such as banking, management consultancy, insurance, legal services, advertising and, accountancy have begun to move out of national-based markets and operations to transnational ones (Enderwick 1989, Aharoni 1993, Daniels 1993). This process has been a progressive and uneven one, varying between both industry sectors and national economies (Bryson et al. 2004, Jones 2007). A range of theorists have argued that the major drivers behind this shift are at least threefold. First, as TNCs have developed in all industry sectors, business activity has escaped national economies and moved into new markets at the global scale (Dicken 2007). TNCs represent the major clients (i.e. the market) for professional business services, and thus professional business have followed their market and transnationalized their activity (Bryson et al. 2004). In this respect, professional business services have had to respond to the needs of their clients for global-scale services (Majkgard and Sharma 1998, Nachum 1999, Strom and Mattsson 2006). Second, within many professional business service sectors such as banking, the globalization of markets has also been accompanied by the development of larger transnational professional service firms (Jones 2003, Faulconbridge and Muzio 2007, 2008). Organic growth and acquisition of overseas firms has produced a growing number of professional service firms that are themselves transnational. These service TNCs are at the forefront of the production, distribution and consumption of services in the global economy (Bryson et al. 2004). Clearly this is entwined with the globalization of markets for these services in a complex ways (Roberts 1999, Warf 2001, Miozzo and Miles 2002). Third, many professional business service firms are embedded in economic globalization as key actors who have developed informational products whose purpose is to facilitate the globalization of markets and firms in other sectors (Roberts 2006). This driver varies between different industries but certainly investment banking and management consultancy are heavily involved in providing advisory services to clients firms on how to transnationalize their operations and do business in markets at the global-scale. An important component of much professional business service advice in a range of sub-sectors is thus concerned with helping other firms develop, for example, effective *organizational globality* (in spheres such as operations, ICT, human resources and information management) as they transnationalize which is essential for them to compete effectively at the global-scale (c.f. Jones 2005). Contemporary TNCs are complex and disparate organizations that are trading in numerous differentiated environments and consequently face enormous logistically challenges (Morgan et al. 2001). A growing related literature here has examined how professional service firms thus play an important role in cross-border knowledge transmission and innovation (Andersen et al. 2000, Bryson 2002, Werr and Stjernberg 2003).

Existing approaches to mobility in professional business services

All three of these wider drivers of globalization in professional business service industries are linked to a transformation of business travel and mobility. The existing research within the social sciences on this issue is limited and itself diverse. Part of the core issue here is the contrast between the longer standing and more specific concern with 'business travel' present within transport studies, planning and tourism studies (e.g. Swarbrooke and Horner 2001, Bannister 2002, Hankinson 2005, Hall 2007) and the more recent literature within organizational sociology, management and economic geography concerning with globalized work (Beaverstock and Boardwell 2000, Faulconbridge 2006, Jones 2008) and mobilities paradigm (c.f. Urry 2007, Knowles et al. 2007). In terms of research data, whilst economic geographers span both groups (Derudder et al. 2007, Taylor et al. 2007), the former literature tends to make use of a more quantitative methodological approach that analyses, for example, measures of the numbers of air travellers for business purposes (Abdelghany and Abdelghany 2007) or the requirements for airport capacity (e.g. Irandu and Rhoades 2006). The latter literature, however, draws more on qualitative research that offers insight into corporate strategies for mobility, the function that business travel plays and the role that it plays in the work process. An important example of recent work is Millar and Salt's (2008) study of how TNCs source expertise and move highly skilled employees around in the extractive and aerospace industries, showing how different types of mobility play distinct roles within transnational firms. It is also within this second strand of the literature where what little engagement with business travel and mobility within professional business services has occurred. However, it is reasonable to argue that current understanding of the nature and role of business travel and mobility in professional business services is partial at best. I identify at least three major arguments that are present in the existing literature and which will be used to inform the discussion I develop in the rest of this chapter.

First, firm and market globalization has led to a growing volume and frequency of both national and international business travel across professional business service industries. This of course varies between firms and sectors but in general business-service firms increasingly need employees who are willing and prepared to travel and who have a global outlook. There has also been a transformation in the nature of work travel. For example, in sectors such as accountancy, existing research suggests a complex growth in short-term and long-term business travel (secondments) overseas. In research conducted for the Corporation of London, Beaverstock (2007) found that accountancy firms used 'international assignees in conjunction with local staff and cross-border commuters and business travellers to add value by servicing clients in close physical proximity either in the office environment or directly liaising with the client' (Beaverstock 2007: 7). Moreover, in accountancy the research found widespread increases 'in short-term assignments of one year or less' leading to 'very high incidences of very frequent and very short term forms of transnational mobility' (Beaverstock 2007: 7). Previously, Beaverstock (2004) identified very similar patterns of developing mobility to these in legal services.

Second, a considerable volume of research has emphasized the centrality of face-to-face contact as central to the work process in professional business services (Beaverstock 2004, Jones 2005, Faulconbridge 2008, Millar and Salt 2008) and a greater proportion of roles within professional business service firms require business travel mobile. For example, research that examined the relationship between London and Frankfurt as world cities found that across a range of professional business service industries, the globalization of firms had increased the need for business travel through the global city network. Whilst the specific 'nature of flows and interactions' varies between firms and industries, firm integration and the international nature of client projects means that contact is increasingly continuous and this involves it being increasingly 'usual' to have employees from one city in the other on a day to day basis (Beaverstock et al. 2001: 34). It is clear that the transformations associated with globalization are producing new working practices and patterns of working across professional business-services. Furthermore, it is becoming clear that the relationship between this globalization of working practice – what I have termed 'global work' elsewhere – and the physical mobility of employees themselves is a complex one since not all global working involves the mobility, although it may involve the movement of objects or knowledge (c.f. Jones 2008).

Third, and following on, there exists a complex relationship between new forms of ICT, employee mobility and working practices (Daniels 2006). Corporate globalization in professional business services is much more than simply a firm opening new offices in more countries or across the global city network. There is evidence that the places and spaces in which professional service work takes place – along with way in which it is mediated by information and communication technologies – has reconfigured the location of professional business service work. For example, in several sectors research suggests growing use of 'intermediate' workspaces (airport meeting spaces, conference centres, hotel) and work during travel (on train and aircraft) (c.f. Jones 2009).

Fourth, the literature suggests that increasing business travel and requirements for mobility is also likely to have negative impacts on business service professionals. Employees in this sector need to be receptive to increasing mobility in order to succeed (Jones 2003, Beaverstock 2004) and there is evidence that this generates a range of problems in terms of work-life balance. Long-haul international travel is especially demanding on employees seeking to balance family life with their careers (c.f. Greed 2008).

Theorizing Mobility and Travel in Professional Business Services

In seeking to advance understandings of mobility in professional business services, I want to outline an approach for better conceptualising its nature and function than has yet emerged from the existing social scientific literature. In part this draws upon existing research discussed across the social sciences, but it is more directly a consequence of number of research projects I have undertaken over the last decade or so examining the nature of globalization in several professional business service sectors. I want to propose a two-pronged theoretical framework that seeks to understand mobility in professional business services around form and function.

With regard to the form, there are at least four aspects to employee mobility in professional business services. First, a distinction needs to be made between intra- and inter-firm mobility – that is employees moving within their firm as opposed to between their firm and another (or multiple others). This relates to a second issue – the distinction between mobility associated with clients (the market for services), and that with suppliers to professional business service firms. Third, there is the issue of *which* employees are mobile in professional business services. Existing research suggests that mobility is differential between employees in different roles and at different positions in the hierarchy within professional service firms (Jones 2003, Beaverstock 2004). In short, not all professional service employees are equally mobile. For example, within consultancy and legal services the most highly mobile employees are senior manager and partners who lead in management of the firm and in the acquisition and retention of new business (Jones 2003). This issue of which employees are mobile also has a gendered dimension to this, not least because women continue to remain in the minority in many of these senior roles within professional service firms (c.f. McDowell 1995, Jones 1998, 2003). Fourth is the issue of the temporal form (i.e. the frequency and duration) of business travel and mobility. The existing research clearly points to the fact that there is significant variation in the length of business trips, from short-term travel of one or two days to long term secondments of months or years (Beaverstock et al. 2001, Beaverstock 2004, 2007, Jones 2007). This latter form of mobility is a point of debate.[1] The frequency of mobility also varies enormously within professional business services with, for example, some working practices in some firms shifting towards highly frequent daily national and international travel where in others mobility is more infrequent (Beaverstock et al. 2001, Jones 2007).

The second 'prong' to my theoretical framework concerns the functions of mobility. I want to propose four key dimensions, each of which relates to a different aspect of the function of employee mobility (and also why it is increasing) in

---

1   Millar and Salt (2008) define business travel as being up to a thirty day trip, whereas the UK Office for National Statistics (ONS) include secondments of up to one year. In professional business services, some secondments last longer than this and I would argue there is a need to include secondments of longer than a year in theorizations of mobility.

relation to the role it plays for business practice in this sector of the economy. Clearly, these concepts are 'mid-level' generalisations that seek to capture key commonalities in the nature of mobility, and they do not represent universal truths about the mobility so much as sector-wide trends. They cross the boundaries between different forms of mobility in terms of whether it is 'intra-' or 'inter-firm', as well as mobility associated with both suppliers and clients. Furthermore my aim is to transcend the existing division between the 'business travel' literature and the newer mobilities paradigm to try to draw insight from both approaches into one framework. Their utility of this approach will be examined, however, in the subsequent sections of this chapter which draws on research into mobility and travel in two specific professional business service sector – management consultancy and legal services.

The first dimension is *business acquisition and retention.* This is primarily inter-firm mobility associated with firms' client relationships. As the market for business services has transnationalized, professional business service employees have had to become increasingly mobile to undertake practices associated with acquiring new business. Business acquisition in professional business service has always been heavily reliant on face-to-face interaction, personal contact networks, firm reputation and trust between a firm and its client (Aharoni and Nachum 2000, Storper and Venables 2004, Jones 2005). In the context of globalization where firms are increasingly marketing their services in international markets and the global city network, mobility becomes an essential requirement for key employees in attempts to gain new business. This function tends to fall on senior managers at the level of, for example, a divisional director in an investment bank or a partner in a law firm. Acquiring new business involves employees in this role travelling to meet with potential clients, developing contact networks across a range of global cities and constructing and maintaining personal relationships with key gatekeeper employees in client firms. Furthermore, research suggests that for many professional business service firms much business is 'repeat business' (Jones 2003, Beaverstock 2004), and thus the need for ongoing business travel to maintain existing client relationships and social contact networks.

Second, and related, in the context of industry globalization, mobility in professional business services is unavoidable in the practices involved in *doing business* with both clients and suppliers who are not in the same location. The centrality of face-to-face interaction, trust and personal relationship in the work process is now well established in many business service sectors (Faulconbridge and Muzio 2007), with the consequence that once business has been acquired, professional service firm employees will need to travel repeatedly to undertake that work. Clearly not all practices in professional business service work require face-to-face interaction and meetings, but a large proportion of practices do. The mobility associated with the work process however involves a wider group of workers than for the first dimension. This mobility involves not just members of senior management, but also mid-management and the core professional layer of employees in a professional business service firm – the lawyers and trainee lawyers in a law firm. It is largely, but not exclusively, inter-firm mobility. Whilst new forms of ICT have altered and reconfigured the nature of which tasks in business service work will require face-to-face interaction and thus mobility, this represents a modification rather than a substitution of the need for mobility to undertake professional business service work itself.

The third dimension of the need for mobility in professional business services concerns the nature of *corporate control* in the context of sector globalization. As with developing transnational firms in all sectors (Morgan et al. 2001), transnationalization involves a series of significant organizational challenges around issues of management. As firms set up operations outside their original home national economies and develop scattered office networks across the globe, senior managers need to spend an increasing amount of time travelling to undertake managerial practices of control. In short, whilst senior managers in professional business service firms are becoming more mobile in order to acquire non-local client business, they are also becoming more mobile in order to undertake effective control of the internal operations of their firms. As with client contact, effective management practice can only very partially be undertaken at distance using ICT. Key decisions and strategic discussion, as well as problem solving, requires face-to-face contact. In a globalizing firm, this inevitably means greater senior management intra-firm mobility.

Fourth, and again following on, as with firms in other industries and in fact any kind of transnational organization, mobility is bound into practices associated with the (re)production of *organizational coherence* and *corporate culture* (Jones 2003). As professional service firms have expanded their operations across the globe, it is not just the managerial practices of control which require senior managers to be mobile but more general mobility that is required of employees at a much wider range of organizational layers across the firm in order that the firm remains *coherent* as a scattered transnational network. As the organanizational and management literature has discussed, transnational firms face significant challenges in generating a sense of common organizational identity, standards of behaviour and consistent corporate culture as they seek to operate at the global scale (Jones 2003). Mobility is thus essential for employees at all levels in business service firms to provide forms face-to-face contact that maintain internal networks, share knowledge, facilitate learning and develop common sense of identity and behaviours.

Mobility in Management Consultancy and Legal Services

Thus far in this chapter I have argued that in the context of the globalization of professional business service industries, employee mobility is increasing as a consequence of the need for face-to-face interaction and co-presence in order for transnational professional service firms both to 'do' business in the contemporary global economy and to operate as increasingly extensive firms. The latter certainly does correspond to an increasing transnationalization of business activity, but mobility is also increasing at the sub-national level as the extensification of professional service firm markets occurs within nations and between city-regions. The two-pronged framework outlined in the previous section holds general relevance for many professional business service sectors, but in order to develop this argument further I want now to consider two specific case study industries in particular: management consultancy and legal services.

The research presented in this part of the chapter draws on several research projects conducted within the last decade which have examined the nature of transnationalization in these sectors. These research projects all to a greater or lesser extent addresses the issue of mobility and business travel, although not necessarily as a primary rationale for the research. However, in bringing several sets of findings together from diverse projects on these sectors, I present here what in effect represents a cumulative analysis of the nature and role of mobility in these professional service industries that develops a series of theoretical insights in light of the mobilities turn in the social sciences. This research draws on three projects undertaken by the author which investigated the globalization of a range of professional service industries over a period from 1999 to 2008. In total, aside from a wide range of secondary sources, the primary data amounts to over 150 in-depth interviews with professional business service practitioners. The majority of interviews were undertaken in London and New York, with a smaller proportion in UK and European regional cities. Whilst the data has been anonymized, all the interviews were conducted with employees in firms that were ranked in the largest twenty five UK and US legal service and management consultancy firms ranked by fee income at the time when each project was conducted.

As professional service industries, management consultancy and legal services have much in common in terms of the nature of the industry, but also important differences. Management consultancy emerged as a distinct professional service industry since the late 1960s, initially in the US and arising as a 'spin-off' activity from the accountancy industry (Beaverstock 1996). In auditing other firms' books, accountants moved into the business of offering advice on how to run their business more effectively. The management consultancy industry now spans what can be broadly divided between more day-to-day operational advice to longer term strategic advice, with firms in the industry often specializing in a given sub-area. The knowledge such firms sell is essentially based on industry experience and business modelling techniques which require no specific vocational or technical knowledge from employees. In contrast, legal services (law) is a much older industry sector with several more distinct sub-specialisms (corporate, tax, litigation, intellectual property, etc.) and a geography of national jurisdictions that has made transnationalization more challenging and complex than in other professional business service sectors (Beaverstock 2004). Legal services clearly extends beyond the dimension of a business service, with the focus of 'business legal services' being on corporate law.

Whilst the issues concerning form of mobility run through the discussion, the rest of this section takes as its focus the function of mobility in these professional business service industries. I consider each of the four functional dimensions I outlined in the previous section in turn.

Business acquisition and retention

In both management consultancy and legal services, the research indicates at least five features of mobility in relation to its role in client acquisition and retention. First, the heavy dependence on reputation, trust and social contact networks for business acquisition and retention means that firms rely on key individuals to be mobile. These key individuals in both sectors are normally experienced (senior) managers – partners and senior partners – who take the lead in 'pitching activity' through face-to-face interaction:

> In this industry, it doesn't matter where you're trying to do business ... it's a lot about knowing people, building relationships ... and that means a lot of travel in today's world. Especially in my area [logistics] where clients are by their very nature scattered ... (Partner [Logistics] US Consultancy 2)

> We never get business "cold" in the UK, let alone elsewhere ... people come to us, we talk to them, there is an exploration of what we can do ... and that will obviously involve us getting out of the office and going to see them. (Partner, UK Law Firm 3)

In the context of firm transnationalization strategies, this mobility is key to breaking into new markets:

> We sent a guy to Tokyo a few years ago who did very well. It's very hard to get a network but he succeeded ... lots of seeing people, time and again ... working on them. (HR Director, UK Law Firm 7)

> Whether we are viewed as competitive is about perception ... clients form a view about quality that you build up through a series of interactions ... law is highly subjective in that sense ... (Partner, UK Law Firm 1)

Second, there is strong evidence in both industries of *increasing levels of mobility* amongst this employee group over the last decade as sector transnationalization has changed the geographies of client location:

> As we become a global firm, travel is inevitably becoming part of everyday working life. (Partner, US Consultancy 5)

> As we try to move into Europe, inevitably people are going there more often. (Senior Partner, UK Law Firm 8)

The frequency of this kind of travel has also increased, although respondents perception of greater mobility may be greater than the reality (few firms studied in these research projects collected quantitative data on business travel to corroborate this). Nevertheless, on balance the evidence supports increasing frequency of business travel and for a growing number of shorter duration business trips as transport connections have become easier and cheaper:

> With budget airlines, European travel has changed. It used to be overnight, in a hotel … now you get up at 5am and do a day trip. (Partner, UK Law Firm 2)

> Ways of working have changed here a lot with a lot of people travelling on a daily basis to clients … certainly to near continental Europe … .better air connections and lower fares have certainly helped with that. (Partner, Retail, US Consultancy 2)

However, a distinction appears between the two sectors in terms of which employees are travelling. Whilst in management consultancy, business acquisition appears to focus on senior staff, there is some evidence in legal services that a wider group of professional employees at all professional levels are involved:

> I would say qualified lawyers in this firm travel 2 or 3 times a week … it is not just the Partners. (HR Manager, UK Law Firm 4)

> … in gaining a new client, this is often a team effort … I would certainly take qualified lawyers and maybe trainees with me if we go to talk to a certain kind of client … it very much depends … (Partner, UK Law Firm 2)

Third, not all travel is of course international. Increased mobility in both sectors is associated with travel across a range of scales. The research suggests that in both sectors, a significant proportion of employee travel is associated with short trips to client offices within a city region or national economy:

> In last five years or so, we have seen an increase in UK as well as EU travel by lawyers in this firm … as we move into European markets, we have also been doing more work outside London and the south-east … it's the way the business is changing … (Partner, UK Law Firm 4)

> we have regional offices … Manchester, Leeds, Cardiff, Glasgow, Belfast … and a lot of travel from the London office is between those for project meetings or internal meeting. (Partner, UK Consultancy 3)

Fourth, whilst the work of maintaining social contact networks can in part be done through ICT, the major part is through face-to-face contact. Mobility is thus crucial in the process of trust-building and client firms having an ongoing understanding what firm can offer:

> ... part of it is maintenance. Making sure the guy feels you are investing in him [sic], in the relationship ... so you have to take the time to go see him [sic] ... (Senior Consultant, US Consultancy 1)

> He [senior partner] is very good at conveying how we work ... how we deal with people here ... how we will represent them. (Partner, UK Law Firm 8)

In both management consultancy and legal services, as in other professional business services, firms rely heavily on 'repeat business' with existing clients. As transnationalization of firms and sectors developed, this reinforces and maintains the higher levels of mobility found over the last decade:

> We work closely with our clients and team with them as a partner. The key element to success is long-term clients ... so inevitably that means our teams travelling a lot ... (Partner, UK Consultancy 2)

> I reached a point the year before last when I was making more than 200 flights, mostly to maintain relationships ... that is tough, and you can't sustain it forever ... .but that is the world we are now operating in. (Senior Partner, US Consultancy 2)

Doing business

As with business acquisition and retention activities, the work process involved in delivering management consultancy or legal services itself requires significant amounts of co-presence. Sector and firm transnationalization thus means that employee mobility amongst professional level employees in these firms has become a central and inevitable part of working practice. This is well established in the literature, yet the more specific factors that lead to employee travel as opposed to ICT-mediated forms of communication are less well understood. In the context of these two professional business service sectors, the research identifies at least three common features of the work process in these sectors that appear to produce employee mobility.

First, in both professional service industries, many work practices relate to information gathering and knowledge generation. Management consultancy firms have been characterized as knowledge 'engines' that gather and adapt knowledge in innovative ways (Czerniawska 2002). The work process in law firms is similar, although it is framed by a more codified set of legal knowledges (Faulconbridge 2008). For both professional service sectors, the research indicates clearly that face-to-face interaction requiring employee mobility is a central feature of this aspect of working practice:

> There is no substitute in corporate law for working through what the client wants. You can only do that by being there, which means if we globalize, the people will have to travel more and more. (Senior Partner, Law Firm 2)

> A lot of the business of consultancy is about gathering information, understanding the client's business. That is the core of it, because only then can you help them develop a way forward ... so [firm] globalization means going to wherever they are located, and doing that. (Senior Partner, UK Strategy Consultancy Firm 1)

Second, with ongoing firm and sector transnationalization, the work process in both sectors increasingly involves patterns of employee mobility dictated by clients being based and operating in multiple locations within and beyond nation states. Consultants and lawyers have to travel to meet with people in different branch offices of client firms that are themselves increasingly distributed through offices spread across the national and transnational scale:

> I think in general as law firms are looking to European and Asian markets, more travel becomes inevitable. We are opening offices in Europe and elsewhere, but clients are also globalizing their operations ... that means we have to follow wherever the clients are doing business ... (Partner, Law Firm 1)

Furthermore, the simple division of professional business service firm 'supplying' a service and client 'receiving' this service conceals the complex role of a range of other stakeholders in the professional business service work process:

> It's often complicated ... I mean, it is not just the client ... the client may have their bankers at a meeting, or we may need to go and meet with a subsidiary or their insurers ... all of this means makes the issue of why you travel to a meeting variable, and down to the specific transaction or deal being done. (Partner, Law Firm 3)

Third, mobility appears to be closely linked to providing face-to-face interaction when problems arise in the work process, and in particular 'crisis' management. Both consultants and lawyers suggested that co-presence was an essential component when dealing with a significant problem in delivering the service, or when a client was 'unhappy' with as aspect of the service.

> If a client gets the jitters in Poland or Slovakia for example, then Partners will go out there and see them. Sit down with them ... that is important. (Senior Partner, UK Law Firm 2)

This was especially evident in the case of a serious problem or 'crisis':

> If it all goes wrong, then someone is going to have to there and sort it ... and these days that might mean someone senior getting on a plane the following morning ... that is the best option when something goes really wrong, although it is not always possible ... (Senior Consultant, US Firm 2)

Innovation and learning

A third driver behind mobility in these professional service industries is the need for innovation and to develop a learning organization (c.f. Faulconbridge 2006) – crucial in strategies to retain firm competitiveness in the context of industry globalization. In both management consultancy and legal service firms, the research suggests that what constitutes innovation is in effect the development of both new service products and new ways of working (process innovation) that are reliant on intense face-to-face interaction with clients, other client-related stakeholders and within firms itself. Given the scattered nature of clients already discussed, employee mobility thus represents an essential requirement for fostering successful innovation:

> ... developing a new service, a new way of dealing with a client is impossible without spending time with them face-to-face, learning their needs and problems ... innovation then is something that comes from that ... you can't develop something new in this a service industry like by sitting on your own in an office. (Senior Partner, US Management Consultancy 5)

> The problem operating in a new country is expectation. Different cultures expect different styles of service. Our lawyers have to learn how to adapt as they deal with clients on the ground ... (Senior Partner, UK Law Firm 2, paraphrased)

A second facet of innovation is the way in which employees within professional business services learn from each other. In knowledge-intensive sectors such as legal services and management consultancy, learning is a complex process with a heavy emphasis on tacit and experiential knowledge. Lawyers more than management consultants have in theory a stock of codified knowledge about the law, but in terms of providing legal services, the value-added for clients comes from contextualized knowledge based on experience. The research suggests in both sectors that in the context of firm transnationalization, employee mobility has become an essential strategy to foster such learning. Trainees in both sectors, for example, travel to come together for training courses, conference and other meetings from across transnational office networks:

> We get these guys together in Chicago and they go to programmes, lectures
> ... important in fostering global relationships within the firm. (Partner, US
> Consultancy 2)

In the legal service firms, new trainee lawyers are also engaged in a more long term form of short-term secondment mobility, with several of the largest UK firms reporting that trainees spent two of their four training positions (each lasting six months) on placements in overseas offices:

> Secondments are becoming just part of life for lawyers in the big firms ... that's
> changed from say 5 years ago. We encourage all our new trainees to take a seat
> abroad. (HR Director, UK Law Firm 2)

> I had two "seats" overseas. One in Madrid, the other in Singapore ... to see how
> different offices have to work differently and relate that to how the firm does
> things. (Trainee, UK Law Firm 5)

The evidence suggests that this mobility – both in its short and long duration forms- aims to develop learning amongst employees that is impossible without extensive periods of co-presence in an overseas working environment. In this sense, mobility is an essential strategy for these professional service firms to develop a workforce that can effectively deliver business services outside their origin market:

> As we become a global operation, there is a need for people in this firm to
> learn how other local markets work ... you can only do that by going there,
> meeting people, working in that environment ... so we have to be more and
> more prepared to do that [travel]. (Senior Consultant, US Consultancy 2)

Corporate coherence and culture

Mobility is also an important factor in maintaining the organizational coherence of professional business service firms. Regarding coherence, in professional business services where the product is constituted through employee behaviours and working practices, it is important that employees in a transnationalizing firm behave in a similar manner and deliver services to a similar quality. This is a major challenge for firms in both industries, and the research suggests that mobility is playing a key role in enabling sufficient face-to-face interaction between employees within the firm for organizational coherence and consistency to be generated:

> We do make a conscious effort to try to get a group of people to get to know each
> other before they scatter to the four corners ... this is crucial if you are going to
> develop a common sense of identity and purpose in a firm like ours. (Head of
> HR, UK Law Firm 2)

Oh, everybody faces this ... all the major global firms. How do you get these scattered people talking to each other ... you have to bring them together as often as possible ... of course that is often easier said than done. (Partner, US Consultancy 6)

A further aspect of this issue of coherence is the idea of 'corporate culture', with the research suggesting that firms in both sectors seeing the development and maintenance of a common corporate culture as key – albeit difficult. Mobility is again a necessary strategy in practices that aim to promote a common culture, whether at the national or transnational level:

Generating a common culture is the big challenge ... a really big one as you try to create a global firm ... we do this in a number of ways. Training events, yes, but also get-togethers, conference ... and simply bringing people back from Tokyo or wherever so they spend some face time with their counterparts here ... (HR Director, UK Law Firm 4)

Conclusion: The Complex Nature of Mobility in Business Service Work

Business travel and employee mobility in professional business services has increasingly become a central feature of the work process. Through this chapter, I have outlined the findings from a number of research projects undertaken over the last decade or so which shed some light onto the multiple functions that employee mobility fulfils for professional service firms in the contemporary global economy. It should be clear that the evidence suggests that increasingly mobility is at root being driven by globalization of these industries. Firms are transnationalizing in order to seek new markets, but also equally because in business services, their clients are themselves globalizing and require a new kind of globalized business services. Professional service firms are thus increasingly providing services to firms with operations scattered across multiple countries, and who need new forms of service geared to addressing their needs as transnational firms.

The aim of the framework proposed in this chapter is to provide a starting point for better theorizing mobility in business service industries, but clearly this approach has wider relevance beyond professional business service firms. Many of the drivers behind increasing business travel, as well as the functions it service for firms, apply to firms outside the professional business service sector. Many functions in industries from manufacturing to pharmaceutical equally require co-presence (c.f. Gertler 2004), and as firms and markets transnationalize in these sectors, the same kinds of drivers are producing greater need for employee mobility.

However, as the more detailed analysis of the different dimensions to this mobility in management consultancy and legal services illustrates, the nature of business travel and employee mobility is complex. For a start, whilst this chapter has focused largely on the role and function of mobility, it should be clear that the nature of mobility and travel itself varies hugely. In the professional service firms discussed, employee mobility ranges from short-term, (relatively) short distance travel on a daily or part-daily time-scale to long-term employment secondments to offices on the other side of the planet. Whether or not all of these forms of employee mobility amount to business travel is debateable, but more significant it is also problematic as to whether current theories of mobility provide an adequate conceptual framework to understand the diversity of this phenomenon in the professional business service industries discussed.

This raises a second and related issue which is whether business travel and employee mobility can be effectively demarcated from other forms of globalized working practice. Many of the working practices undertaken by employees in professional business services are bound into distanciated relations and connections at distance that only partially are constituted through physical employee mobility. ICT technologies now enable work to be 'global work' (cf. Jones 2008), without employees necessarily leaving their office. Such globalized working practices appear to be enmeshed with employee mobility and business travel in a complex manner. Separating pure 'business travel' from these wider forms of global working thus remains a problematic issue. Whether or not new forms of ICT can be a substitute for business travel remains however unclear since the research continues to emphasize the key centrality of face-to-face interaction in the work process. ICT may substitute for some forms of business travel, but the evidence also suggests it may also lead to an increased level of mobility as it increases the capacity of professional service firms to deliver existing and new services to global client markets.

Third, and finally, there is the question of whether this trend in increasing employee mobility will continue and whether in subjective terms it is desirable. There is certainly evidence that increasing demands for employee mobility are placing great demand on employees in relations to the issue of work-life balance (c.f. Uteng and Cresswell 2008), and career development (c.f. Schiebelhofer 2008). Furthermore, in the context of current debates about global environmental change, increasingly physical travel has significant implications for greenhouse gas emissions. It may be, for example, that in future that rising costs may curtail some forms of business travel in these business service industries.

None of these issues has been within the scope of this chapter, but in terms of where future research into business travel and mobility needs to be directed, they represent key areas in need of further investigation. Certainly with ongoing globalization in professional business service industries, the nature of mobility is likely to continue to change in the near future in a manner that – given the central role played by these sectors in the global economy – has significant ramifications for firms, employees, government policy and the environment.

References

Abdelghany, A. and Abdelghany, K. 2007. Modelling air-carrier's portfolio of business travel. *Journal of Revenue and Pricing Management*, 6(1), 51-63.

Aharoni, Y. 1993. *Coalitions and Competition: The Globalization of Professional Business Services*. Oxford: OUP.

Aharoni, Y. and Nachum, L. 2000. *Globalization of Services: Some Implications for Theory and Practice*. London; Routledge.

Alvesson, M. 2004. *Knowledge Work and Knowledge Intensive Firms*. Oxford: OUP.

Andersen, B. Howells, J., Hull, R., Miles, I. and Roberts, J. 2000. *Knowledge and Innovation in the New Service Economy*. Cheltenham: Edward Elgar.

Aslesen, H., Isaksen, A and Stambol, L. 2008. Knowledge-intensive business service as innovation agent through client interaction and labour mobility. *International Journal of Services Technology and Management*, 9(2), 138-153.

Irandu, E. and Rhoades, D. 2006. *World Review of Entrepreneurship, Management and Sustainable Development*, 2(4), 362-374.

Bannister, D. 2002. *Transport Planning*. London: Routledge.

Beaverstock, J. 1996. Subcontracting the accountant! Professional labour markets, migration, organizational networks in the global accountancy industry. *Environment and Planning A*, 28, 303–326.

Beaverstock, J. 2004. 'Managing across borders': Knowledge management and expatriation in professional legal service firms. *Journal of Economic Geography*, 4, 1-25.

Beaverstock, J. 2007. Transnational work: Global professional labour markets in professional service accounting firms, in *The Handbook of Service Industries*, edited by J. Bryson and P. Daniels. Cheltenham: Edward Elgar, 409-432.

Beaverstock, J. and Boardwell, J. 2000. Negotiating globalization, transnational corporations and global city financial centres in transient migration studies. *Applied Geography*, 20, 277-304.

Beaverstock, J., Hoyler, M., Pain, K. and Taylor, P. 2001. *Comparing London and Frankfurt as world cities: A relational study of contemporary urban change*. London: Anglo-German Foundation.

Bryson, J. 2002. 'Trading' business knowledge between countries; consultants and the diffusion of management knowledge, in *Trading Services in the Global Economy*, edited by J. Cuadrado-Roura, L. Rubalcaba-Bermejo and J. Bryson. Cheltenham: Edward Elgar, 175-190.

Bryson, J., Daniels, P., and Warf, B. 2004. *Service Worlds: People, Organizations, Technologies*. London: Routledge.

Castells, M. 2001. *The Rise of the Network Society*. Second Edition. Oxford: Blackwell.

Czerniawska, F. 2002. *Management Consultancy: What Next?* Basingstoke: Palgrave Macmillan.

Daniels, P. 1993. *Service Industries in the World Economy*. Oxford: Blackwell.

Daniels, P. 2006. Internationalization, technology, services. *Journal of Economic Geography*, 4(4), 475-476.

Derudder, B., Devriendt, L. and Witlox, F. 2007. Flying where you don't want to go: an empirical analysis of hubs in the global airline network. *Tijdschrift voor Economische en Sociale Geografie*, 98(3), 307-324.

Dicken, P. 2007. *Global Shift*. Fifth Edition. London: Sage.

Empson, L. 2002. Introduction: Knowledge management in professional service firms. *Human Relations*, 54(7), 811-817.

Enderwick, E. 1989. *Multinational Service Firms* London: Routledge.

Faulconbridge, J. 2006. Stretching tacit knowledge beyond a local fix? Global spaces of learning in advertising professional service firms. *Journal of Economic Geography*, 6, 517-540.

Faulconbridge, J. 2008. Negotiating cultures of work in transnational law firms. *Journal of Economic Geography*, 8, 497-517.

Faulconbridge, J. and Muzio, D. 2007. Reinserting the professional into the study of globalizing professional service firms. *Global Networks*, 7(3), 249-270.

Faulconbridge, J. and Muzio, D. 2008. Organizational professionalism in globalizing law firms. *Work, Employment and Society*, 22(1), 7-25.

Flood, J. 1999. Professionals organizing professionals: Comparing the logic of US and UK law practice, in *Professional competition and professional power: Lawyers, accountants and the social construction of markets*, edited by Y. Dezalay and D. Sugarman. London: Routledge, 154-182.

Gertler, M. 2004. *Manufacturing Culture: The Institutional Geography of Industrial Practice* Oxford: OUP.

Gluckler, J. and Armbruster, T. 2003. Bridging uncertainty in management consulting: The mechanisms of trust and networked reputation. *Organization Studies*, 24, 269-297.

Grabher, G. 2002. The project ecology of advertising: Tasks, talents and teams. *Regional Studies*, 36(3), 245-263.

Greed, C. 2008. Are we there yet? Women and Transport revisited, in *Gendered Mobilities 0*, edited by T. Uteng and T. Cresswell. Aldershot: Ashgate, 243-256.

Hall, M. 2007. *Tourism Planning: Policies, processes and relationships*. Harlow: Prentice Hall.

Hankinson, G. 2005. Destination brand images: A business tourism perspective. *Journal of Services Marketing*, 19(1), 24-32.

Harrington, J. and Daniels, P. 2006. *Knowledge-based Services, Internationalization and Regional Development*. Aldershot: Ashgate.

Hermelin, B. 1997. *Professional Business Services – Conceptual Framework and a Swedish Case Study*. Uppsala: Dept of Social and Economic Geography.

Irandu, E. and Roades, D. 2006. Challenges of sustaining growth in African aviation: The case of Jomo Kenyatta international airport. *World Review of Entrepreneurship, Management and Sustainable Development*, 2(4), 362-374.

Jones, A 1998. Reproducing gender cultures: Theorizing gender in investment banking recruitment. *Geoforum*, 294, 451-474.

Jones, A. 2003. *Management Consultancy and Banking an Era of Globalization*. Basingstoke: Palgrave Macmillan.

Jones, A. 2005. Truly global corporations? The politics of organizational globalization in business-service firms. *Journal of Economic Geography*, 5, 177-200.

Jones, A. 2007. More than managing across borders? The complex role of face-to-face interaction in globalizing law firms. *Journal of Economic Geography*, 7, 223-246.

Jones, A. 2008. The rise of global work. *Transactions of the Institute of British Geographers*, 33(1), 12-26.

Jones, A. 2009. Theorising global business spaces. *Geografisker Annaler B: Human Geography*, forthcoming.

Knowles, R., Shaw, J. and Docherty, I. 2007. *Transport Geographies: Mobilities, Flows, Spaces*. Oxford: Blackwell.

Lowendahl, B. 2005. *Strategic Management in Professional Service Firms*. Copenhagen: Copenhagan Business School Press.

Majkgard, A. and Sharma, D. 1998. Client-following and market-seeking strategies in the internationalization of service firms. *Journal of Business-to-Business Marketing*, 4(3), 1-41.

McDowell, L. 1995. *Capital Culture: Gender at Work in the City*. Oxford: Blackwell.

Millar, J. and Salt, J. 2008. Portfolios of mobility: The movement of expertise in transnational corporations in two sectors: Aerospace and extractive industries. *Global Networks*, 8, 25-50.

Miozzo, M. and Miles, I. 2002. *Internationalization, Technology and Services*. Cheltenham: Edward Elgar.

Morgan, G., Kristensen, P., and Whitley, R. 2001. *The Multinational Firm*. Oxford: OUP.

Nachum, L. 1999. *The Origins of International Competitiveness of Firms: The Impact of Location and Ownership in Professional Service Industries*. Cheltenham: Edward Elgar.

Roberts, J. 1999. The internationalization of business service firms: A stages approach. *The Service Industries Journal*, 19(4), 68-88.

Roberts, J. 2006. Internationalization of management consultancy services: Conceptual issues concerning the cross-border delivery of knowledge intensive services, in *Knowledge-based Services, Internationalization and Regional Development*, edited by J. Harrington and P. Daniels. Aldershot: Ashgate, 101-124.

Sassen, S. 2001. *The Global City*. Second Edition. Princeton: Princeton University Press.

Schiebelhofer, E. 2008. Gender still matters: Mobility aspirations among European scientists working abroad, in *Gendered Mobilities*, edited by T. Uteng and T. Cresswell. Aldershot: Ashgate, 115-128.

Sklair, L. 2001. *The Transnational Capitalist Class*. Cambridge: Polity.

Storper, M. and Venables, A. 2004. Buzz: face-to-face contact and the urban economy. *Journal of Economic Geography*, 4, 351-370.

Strom, P. and Mattsson, J. 2005. Japanese professional business services: A proposed analytical typology. *Asia Pacific Business Review*, 11(1), 49-68.

Strom, P. and Mattsson, J. 2006. Internationalization of Japanese professional business service firms. *The Service Industries Journal*, 26(3), 249-265.

Swarbrooke, J. and Horner, S. 2001. *Business Travel and Tourism*. London: Butterworth Heinneman.

Taylor, P., Derudder, B. and Witlox, F. 2007. Comparing airline passenger destinations with global service connectivities: A worldwide empirical study of 214 cities. *Urban Geography*, 28(3), 232-248.

Uteng, T. and Cresswell, T. 2008. *Gendered Mobilities 0*. Aldershot: Ashgate.

Urry, J. 2007. *Mobilities*. Cambridge: Polity.

Warf, B. 2001. Global Dimensions of US legal services. *Professional Geographer*, 53, 398-406.

Werr, A. and Stjernberg, T. 2003. Exploring management consulting firms as knowledge systems. *Organization Studies*, 24(6), 881-908.

Wood, P. 2002. *Consultancy and Innovation*. London: Routledge.

Wood, P. 2006. The regional significance of knowledge-intensive services in Europe. *Innovation*, 19(1), 51-66.

Chapter 12

Face-to-Face by Travel or Picture – The Relationship between Travelling and Video Communication in Business Settings

Jon Martin Denstadli and Mattias Gripsrud

Introduction

Business communication is influenced by the rapid development of information and communication technology. Traditionally, travel and face-to-face meetings have been recognized as the most effective ways of doing business, seeking out new markets, exchanging ideas and communicating with colleagues and customers alike. The significance of personal meetings is particularly observed higher up in the organizational hierarchy. Boden and Molotch (1994) quote research showing that some managers may spend up to half of their time in face-to-face contacts. The emphasis put on co-presence in business settings is in part due to the content of the information being exchanged. Business communication is often characterized by ambiguous information requiring complex discussions and understandings. More than any other medium, face-to-face meetings have been considered as having the capacity to transmit equivocal information and build a personal atmosphere, qualities judged important in these settings. Urry (2002) emphasizes the ability to access the other participants eyes, since eye contact enables the establishment of intimacy and trust, as well as fear, power and control. Co-presence also signals commitment – by travelling and meeting face-to-face one is investing time and money in the relationship. Thus, business meetings are multifunctional, they are arenas for decision making, executing procedures, building and strengthening friendship, judging commitment and so on (Urry 2002).

However, sophisticated communication technologies, in particular video conferencing facilities, provide many of the same features as personal meetings. Polycom, Tandberg and LifeSize, the big players in the video conferencing market, offer flexible communication services for conference rooms, desktops, and mobile terminals for different groups and usage situations. These fixed and mobile solutions seamlessly encompass voice, video, and data collaboration, and are now able to cater for a range of business needs. The video conferencing industry has also to a large part been integrated into computer networks, and has enjoyed a steady influx of innovative services from the internet and computer industry. Thus, the potential for replacing business travel with virtual communication should be greater than ever, and industry analysts have found a steady growth in the adoption and usage of video conferencing in businesses (First Securities Norway 2008).

Substitution is particularly attractive in the light of the growth in air travel. Today, there are four million air passengers each day and 1.9 billion air journeys each year (Urry 2007). According to the World Tourism Organization (WTO) work related travel counts globally for about 20 per cent of all international travel, and forecasts predict faster growth in business than in leisure passengers (Patterson 2008). This trend is also seen in Norway where for the first time air travel growth rates are higher for the business segment than for leisure trips (Denstadli et al. 2008). In 2007, business travel constituted 56 per cent of the domestic market (up from 52 per cent in 2003) and 41 per cent of international air travel (40 per cent in 2005).

The purpose of this chapter is to assess the qualities of video conferencing as a communication technology and evaluate how it fits in with modern business practices. We also review the transportation literature and summarize empirical evidence on the travel-video conferencing relationship. The chapter is organized as follows. Next, the market development of video conferencing technology is presented. In section 3, some theoretical perspectives on video communication in business settings are discussed, while section 4 provides empirical evidence of the travel-telecommunication relationship. Section 5 presents some of the latest developments in video conferencing technology, and finally, section 6, prospects on technology development and its future impacts on business travel.

Video Conferencing – Market and Development

The current video conference market

The video conferencing market has shown a remarkable growth during the past 15-20 years. In 1991, the total equipment market was estimated at USD 210 million (Kraut and Fish 2006:708). Fifteen years later, figures from one of the leading players in the market, Tandberg, estimate the global video conferencing market at USD 1.06 billion (Figure 12.1), i.e., five times bigger than in 1991 (not taking inflation into account). In particular, sales have boosted in recent years with an annual growth rate of 17 per cent in the period 2003 to 2006, and further growth is expected both in the US, in Europe, and in Asia.

As seen in Figure 12.1, growth has been stronger for infrastructure (i.e., bridges, gateways, and management tools) than for endpoints, which reflects the costs of the ongoing standardization and convergence between video conferencing, computers and computer networks. However, the total market for endpoints is still 3.5 times bigger than the infrastructure market, and is forecasted to reach a total of 1.1 billion USD in 2009, with 275,000 units sold worldwide (Source: Tandberg).

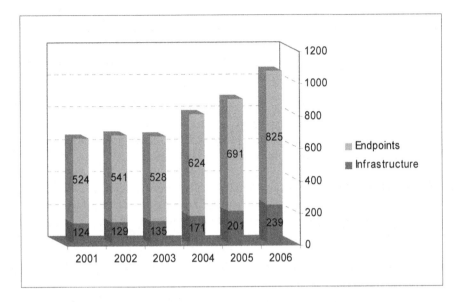

**Figure 12.1 Global market value for video conference equipment
(value in million USD)**
Source: Tandberg.

The market leaders are US-based Polycom and Norwegian-based Tandberg, with approximately 40 and 30 per cent market share respectively, and the newcomer LifeSize. Their product portfolios are to a large part overlapping, all three offering solutions for the desktop, the conference room and for the mobile user. Market shares for smaller manufacturers have diminished in the last 10 years, except for those who do specialized applications (e.g., telemedicine, teleeducation, etc). The largest region for endpoint sales is currently North America, accounting for 42 per cent of the total revenue, but the growth has been strong both in Europe and Asia.

Several factors have contributed to the growth seen in recent years. First, investments costs and the operational cost per minute (kilobit price per second) has been significantly reduced due to the development of more efficient broadband technologies and improved techniques for compression of live video. Second, the development of smaller-scale systems has enabled more frequent and easier use of video communication. Third, as we shall see, the actual range of services offered in video conferencing solutions is much greater, more versatile and better adjusted to a range of modern business practices. Finally, user groups beyond the executive management of large corporations and government have been targeted. For instance, market leader Polycom identifies the following groups as the most important markets in their 2006 annual report: government and public sector, education, justice system, health care, financial sector, oil/gas, manufacturing and remote monitoring.

Historic development of video communication

The possibility for simultaneous audio and visual communication by electronic means has a rather long history. From an analytical point of view, the history of video communication can roughly be divided into three stages based on the technology, characteristics of services and levels of diffusion.

1. *The pioneering era* – lasting from its technical conception in the 1960s until the mid 1980s. This stage was characterized by a crude level of technology and quite limited possibilities for communication.
2. *The telematic era* of the late 1980s and the 1990s, characterized by moderate levels of diffusion and proprietary technical solutions of the telecommunication industry.
3. *The era of integrated collaboration* – starting with the Internet revolution up till now, and is characterized by a rich influx of ideas and services from the computer and Internet industry, and a corresponding proliferation of video-based communication solutions and possibilities.

The pioneering era   The pioneering phase began in 1964 when the first commercial video telephony system, Picturephone, was demonstrated by AT&T (Kraut and Fish 1995:699). The Picturephone was technologically far ahead of its time and made the transition from field trial to a commercial service.[1] AT&T intended to turn their product into a success both in the home and in the office, and also offered add-ons specifically for businesses. Among these were features that enabled Picturephone to connect to an enterprise mainframe, and even possibilities for showing documents by utilizing a mirror (Lipertito 2003: 62).

Nevertheless, its success as commercial system was another story. It was considered more a curiosity than a useful tool in business life. Summing up the pioneering era, Noll (1992:308) states that '*[...] these early efforts were impressive for their time, but were also considered little more than novelties and failed to catch on with the consumers*'. Lipertito, in his in-depth analysis of the Picturephone, also agrees that it was a commercial failure (2003: 52). On the other hand, Kraut and Fish (1995) claimed that several experimental studies, other than the commercial Picturephone, proved that video conferencing had values for its users, and that users would prefer audio-video communication to audio-only when they had the choice. In hindsight we can say that this might well be true, but as long as these trial services were not launched commercially they were not able to prove their real potential outside the labs and field trials. It is perhaps ironic that at about the

---

1   Some of the experiments and trials of video conferencing are described in Kraut and Fish (1995: 701).

same time a discourse emerged about how telecommunications could help save the environment and maintain productivity by replacing travel. Forecasts made at the time also indicated that there was a large potential for substitution.

The telematic era   The telematic stage began in the 1980s and lasted until the internet revolution. *Videophone* by AT&T was one typical example of video conferencing in this stage. The video conferencing now offered somewhat more communicational flexibility by offering both (1) traditional point-to-point systems, which enabled video conferencing between two locations, and (2) multipoint systems, which allowed for video conferencing between more than two locations (thereby also requiring more than two screens, a video producer, or a split screen system).

During these years several manufacturers offered systems for video communication for businesses, and video conferences began to enjoy widespread popularity. However, most of the systems in enterprise settings shared some important disadvantages that slowed diffusion:

- High costs and dedicated rooms (some of them even required a conference host and/or a technician to set up and host the conference);
- Required proprietary technologies (meaning that users with systems from different vendors could not communicate);
- Low bandwidth (ISDN or even lower bandwidth technologies caused video lag and low resolution video).

The aggregated outcome of these characteristics was a high user threshold and a technology that took limited advantage of the video feature. A certain level of popularity notwithstanding, video conferencing in the telematic era did not become the breakthrough success that many captains of the video conference industry had hoped for (Lipartito 2003).

Even more troubling was that the value of video itself was called into question. For instance, Boyle et al (1994) reported no differences in problem solving skills between groups that could see and hear each other and groups that only had audio communication. Many industry commentators and academics expressed disappointment with the entire concept of video conferencing. The debate between Noll (1992) and Kraut and Fish (1995) is interesting from a principle point of view. Noll's position was that the *video* element of video conferencing solutions did not really provide extra value for the user; its value was incremental, or even negative. Kraut and Fish agreed in part with Noll in that: '*The visual channel does little to improve conversation when the main goal is the exchange of information*', but also added that '*[...] video telephony seems more valuable for complex, ambiguous or conflictful tasks and for tasks in which the social component is the key*' (Kraut and Fish 1995: 706).

This debate was important because it provided an impetus for more useful ways of using video. Kraut and Fish's response suggested ways this could be done. Other early suggestions of how the video channel could be further exploited was made by Watanabe (1980), who suggested that office functions could be directly integrated into solutions for visual communication. In other words, the industry had to leave behind the static 'talking head' concept, and make video conferencing a more dynamic means of communication. Early research by the US telecommunication company AT&T had also suggested that video was more valuable when it showed the *object* of the conversation rather than the participants in it.

Video conferences up to the mid-1990s were also hampered by the issue of standardization, or rather lack thereof. Since the theoretic value of a network increases exponentially with the number of users of the systems, standards had to be developed that enabled users of a system from vendor A to have a video conference with a group using a video conference system from vendor B. This is for instance how the mobile phone business succeeded by establishing common standards (GSM in Europe) that enabled users of say Motorola phones, to call users of Nokia phones. This was in general not possible in video conferencing until 1996, with the introduction of the H.320 standard (Muller 1998), and was one important prerequisite for renewed growth.

The era of integrated collaboration   Probably the single most important factor during the past decade has been the integration of video conferencing with PCs and computer applications over computer networks, moving video communication into the third stage of collaborative integration. The modern video communications solutions has transformed the way the video channel is used, and also offer much more flexibility, both in terms of range of services and modes of communication by offering a virtual activity space that is much better aligned with the full range of work practices in modern businesses.

Important features of modern business practice are project organization, processing and annotating of digital material and content, like memos, presentations, spreadsheets and other material relevant in a business context. Modern video communication systems have to a large degree accommodated these practices. This started with the need for live display of presentation material (Power Point slides, spreadsheets, etc), and developed further into the need for live and collective processing of data files and information. It has now evolved even further by integrating web conferences, project cooperation tools, chat, access to archived work material, databases etc. Davis (1999:5) explains the concept of integrated collaboration as: '*[...] a process that allows two or more users to interact with audio, video, and/or data streams in both real-time and non-real-time communications modes across packet and circuit switched networks*'. The participants are not just able to exchange information, but are also able to process and share all kinds of digital information.

The debate between Noll and Fish and Kraut revealed that including video elements in communication did not automatically improve communication. We will now examine in some more detail the theoretical arguments in favour of integrating video into telecommunication. Without an explicit understanding of how video conferencing compares with other modes of communication, it becomes even harder to understand the relationship between video conferencing and travel. So, how sound is the concept of video conferencing?

Travel or Video Conferencing – A Media Choice

Travel and telecommunications can be seen as subsystems of a communication system (Salomon 1985). This perspective implies that personal contact and video conferencing both fulfil some basic communication needs, and that a person, when faced with a particular communication need, goes through some kind of decision process in which various ways of communicating are evaluated according to some criteria. One important rationale for video conferencing has been the replacement of travel. The same purpose can be achieved both via the physical activity of travelling and by the virtual activity of a video conference. Hence, the individual(s) faces the problem of how a virtual conference compares with a physical meeting (and other communication means), and next, how the choice of communication media will affect the quality of the communication itself and the status of the participants taking part in the communication process.

One approach has been to model communication media according to their level of 'authenticity'. The idea of adding visual information to audio communication is based on this line of thought. Visual cues are supposed to attach more depth to the information, transmit natural language, make participants able to read each others body language, etc (cf. the debate between Noll and Kraut/Fish referred to above). Some proponents of this view can be found within the theory of 'media richness', a theoretical direction originally developed by Daft and Lengel (1984, 1986). According to the media richness theory, media can be characterized as 'rich' or 'lean' based upon their ability to (1) produce instant feedback; (2) transmit multiple cues; (3) use natural language; and (4) create a personal atmosphere. Face-to-face meetings are considered the richest medium since these fulfil all the criteria, i.e., allows immediate feedback, has the capacity to provide multiple cues, communicates in natural language, and can be highly personal. On the other hand, written media such as reports and bulletins are regarded lean sources of information, since these only provide limited cues and are particularly slow to generate feedback. One implication of this theory is that the participants in the communication process should choose the richest possible medium to communicate the desired message. As a video conference is a richer medium than for instance an audio conference, according to this theory, performance should increase when using the former (Dennis and Valacich 1999).

This line of social-psychological research has been criticized for being at odds with the reality of media use. The communication scholar van Dijk discusses media richness theory, and concludes that: '*A large number of media phenomena could not be explained using its objective approach*' (van Dijk 1999:16). Other researchers have also pointed out that the empirical evidence of media richness theory is lacking (Dennis and Valacich 1999, Dennis and Kinney 1998).

A quite different approach can be found in mainstream media and communication theory (Holmes 2005, van Dijk 1999). One basic premise in most communication research is that *all* communication is mediated (even a face-to-face meeting is mediated by the voice and the verbal medium of language), and that there can be no general model for 'authentic' communication. Consequently, a face-to-face meeting is not in principle 'richer' than a telephone conversation or a video conference, but it is *different*. It is these differences that offer possibilities for choosing appropriate media. To a certain degree, mainstream media theory turns the media richness theory up-side-down. The attraction and effectiveness of media to a large extent depend on them (1) *suppressing* complexity judged irrelevant to the purpose of the communication situation at hand (i.e., making the message as 'poor' as possible, but not poorer!); (2) *enabling* modes of communication and forms of interaction that are unique to each specific medium (Holmes 2005). The debate between Noll vs Kraut and Fish regarding the usefulness of video conferencing can be reframed in this theoretical light. Noll adhered to pragmatist media theory, while Kraut and Fish leaned toward a version of media richness theory.

The theory of media synchronicity (Dennis and Valacich 1999) represents a refinement of the media richness theory and is more or less in agreement with standard media theory as they conclude: '*We believe that the key to effective use of media is to match media capabilities to the fundamental communication processes required to perform the task*' (Dennis and Valacich 1999:8). In this light the use of video can not be seen as an improvement per se, as predicted by media richness theory, but depends on how the video channel is used and in what context. On the other hand, as long as the video capacity is used in order to match the task at hand, the use of video will be perceived as adding value to the communication task.

The choice of using video communication must therefore take into account exactly *what* can be achieved by using video and visual elements, and how this compares to alternate means, either other media or travelling. One severe limitation of the telematic era was that it only allowed information exchange among the participants, and had not really found a way to integrate *collaboration* that in turn would increase 'constructive interaction'. We will later see how the internet and the computer industry introduced new ways of using the video and visual elements of video communication, thereby moving video communication from the telematic era into to the era of integrated collaboration by aligning the use of video to a broader array of tasks in business life.

The Relationship between Business Travel and Telecommunications

Theories about the relationship

The interaction between telecommunications and business travel has been discussed in the transportation and communication research literature since the first video telephony systems were introduced in the early 1960s. Much of the discussion is characterized by anecdotal and suggestive arguments without any empirical evidence, and even today, one has not been able to draw unambiguous conclusions about the relationship between the different media. One reason for this is the complexity of the problem and difficulties with respect to controlling for the numerous factors that can potentially influence the relationship. Few interactions are simple in the sense that teleconferencing has a direct, well-defined impact on business travel. Characteristics of the communication activities and business connections, individual and organizational characteristics, and time and costs are some of the factors that may determine the relationship (Fischer et al. 1990, Moore and Jovanis 1988).

A number of studies have discussed the potential relationships between travel and different forms of telecommunications (e.g., Batten and Thorn 1989, Bennison 1988, Mokhtarian 1990, Salomon 1985, 1986). Four possible impacts of telecommunications on travel have been suggested:

1. *The substitution hypothesis* suggests that the use of telecommunications eliminate trips that would have been taken if the technology was not present.
2. *The complementarity hypothesis* implies that telecommunications have a generating effect on travel causing additional trips that would not have occurred in the absence of the technology.
3. *The modification hypothesis* proposes that telecommunications may change the time, mode, destination, etc of a trip that otherwise would have occurred.
4. *The neutrality hypothesis* suggests that there is no impact of one on the other, meaning that travel and telecommunications in effect operate as independent communication systems.

In the business travel literature, discussions have primarily concerned the two first effects, with a special focus on the potential for replacing travel and personal meetings with teleconferencing. The substitution hypothesis is an appealing one for several reasons. At the aggregate level, replacement of travel will contribute to less energy use, congestion, air pollution, accidents, etc, while at the disaggregated level individuals and companies would benefit from more efficient time use and reduced costs. Toffler (1980) also mentions greater societal stability, less stress, and less temporary relationships as positive side effects of increased use of telecommunications. The substitution hypothesis assumes that the total amount of interactions (including both travel and communication) is not affected by the specific assignments to either mode (Plaut 1999). However, an implicit assumption behind the substitution hypothesis is that the relative competitiveness of telecommunications will increase with technology improvements, price reductions, and greater accessibility.

On the other hand, the complementarity hypothesis suggests that there is a dependency between the two, that telecommunications are likely to induce more travel. In the context of business travel, trip-generating effects may be due to:

- Telecommunications increasing labour efficiency which frees time for additional (and more desired) business travel. For example, having a business meeting over video can free time to attend a conference at a nice location.
- Telecommunications allowing for more geographical dispersion of organizations, increasing travel between the dispersed offices/plants.
- The globalization of markets which implies more international business travel and communications.

As discussed next, evidence for both effects are reported in the literature.

Evidence of the relationship

During the pioneering phase in the 1960s and 1970s, it was widely held that the traditional way of doing business by meeting face-to-face would gradually be replaced by more time-efficient virtual communication. Geels and Smith (2000) refer to a number of studies conducted in this period where the potential for substituting business travel was assumed to be substantial, up to 66 per cent in a German estimate from 1974/75 (Petersen 1977). Likewise, Coddington (1993) refers to a study released by the US Department of Transportation in 1978 which claimed that video conferencing could reduce company travel by approximately 50 per cent over the coming decade, and Bennison (1988) reported on an evaluation of a British Telecom trial where 87 per cent of the respondents using video conferences expressed anticipations of travel reductions due to virtual conferencing. Although some authors pointed to more modest effects (e.g., Kahn 1987), beliefs in substitution were widespread in the pioneering era of video conferencing, which in turn caused the airline business much concern.

However, by the end of the 1980s, video conferencing had had no noticeable impact on business traffic. Thus, going into the telematic era of the 1990s, a more nuanced view of the business travel – video conferencing relationship emerged. In 1993, Arthur D. Little Inc. launched an oft-cited study commissioned by the Massachusetts Aeronautics Commission in the US. This study predicted that video conferencing would replace about seven per cent of total US business air travel by 2010. In other words, substitution effects were expected to be more modest than previously anticipated. The study emphasized that the substitution level would vary significantly depending on the purpose of the trip, with intra-firm travel most likely being replaced. The study further showed that replacement effects increased significantly with trip distance, and had greater impact on domestic flights than on international travel. Smaller effects on international travel are due to the importance of building trust and confidence when meeting with business partners from different cultures. Kraut et al. (1998) emphasize the still important role of personal relationships and linkages in modern global business, and maintain that electronic communication must be supported by 'personal linkages'.

Roy and Filiatrault (1998) estimated the substitution rate for Canadian business air travel to be 9.4 per cent for companies using video conferencing, and an overall effect of 1.8 per cent (companies not utilizing video conferencing included). This is a relatively limited effect, but replacement was expected to increase. In the relatively short term, the authors calculated that substitution rates would rise to 14.5 per cent for users, 70 per cent of this due to less intra-firm travel. The total substitution effect including organizations not utilizing video conferencing was estimated to be 4.3 per cent. Another relative conservative scenario presented in this period was that from Appogee Research Inc. (1994, quoted in Roy and Filiatrault 1998) which estimated business air travel substitution to be about two per cent.

Although some authors still claimed that video conferencing could replace large proportions of business travel (e.g., Stephenson and Bender 1996, Bender and Stephenson 1998), the relationship between telecommunications and transportation went through considerable rethinking in the 1990s. In particular, complementarity effects were more investigated. Anecdotal remarks were presented by Saffo (1993) who emphasized the significance of relationships in business life, claiming that people who become acquainted by wire would inevitably want to meet in person, and, as a result, that travel would increase. Likewise, video conferencing extends spans of collaboration, and this too would generate more travel than video conferencing could possibly replace. Saffo's conclusion was that video conferencing would catch on, but that the consequences would actually be more business travel than ever.

It has been argued that many of the studies which have found support for substitution have been short-term and small scale, and have had a narrow focus on the impact of one specific telecommunication application, e.g., video conferencing, on travel (Choo and Mokhtarian 2007, Mokhtarian and Meenakshisundaram 1999). By applying a disaggregated perspective, one may underestimate complementarity effects by failing to consider the more indirect and longer-term relationships. On the other hand, aggregate analyses examine the relationships between industrial uses of transportation services with those of communications services at the national level, using economic input-output indicators.

Plaut (1997) studied industries' demand for transportation and communication services in nine European countries. For all nine countries correlation coefficients were predominantly positive, indicating a complementary relationship between transportation and communication. That is, industries requiring large amounts of transportation service inputs tended to require large amounts of communication service inputs. Results were stable across six different transportation sectors. For air transport, coefficients ranged from .19 (Belgium) to .82 (Denmark). Later, Plaut (1999) repeated the study in three non-European countries and found similar effects. For instance, the correlations for direct input-output coefficients for telecommunications and air transportation in Israel, Canada and USA were .62, .68, and .59 respectively. Thus, a strong pattern of complementarity seemed to exist in all countries examined. More recently, similar conclusions have been drawn by Choo and Mokhtarian (2007) and Lee and Mokhtarian (2008), and the latter concludes that in an industrial context, it is not realistic to expect telecommunications to substitute for travel. Taken together, the overwhelming optimism with respect to travel substitution characterizing the pioneering era of video conferencing has been replaced by a more nuanced picture of the relationship.

The Norwegian experience[2]

Video conferencing use in Norwegian trade and industries was rather modest in the 1990s, but experienced a strong growth at the beginning of the millennium. Estimates by Denstadli and Julsrud (2003) indicated a 50 per cent increase in the number of users from 1998 to 2003, and that about eight per cent of Norwegian enterprises with 10 employees or more made use of video conferencing technology in 2003. According to statistics available from Tandberg, sales of video conferencing equipment to Norwegian enterprises have continued to grow in recent years.

Two trends describe the development of the video conferencing market in Norway. First, the strongest growth is seen in small and medium sized companies. Previously, video conferencing was primarily a communication tool for large companies with geographically dispersed offices and production plants. However, standardizations, lower user thresholds, and reduced prices have opened new markets for video conferencing. In 2003, companies with less than 100 employees constituted 44 per cent of the users, compared to only 28 per cent in 1998. Second, video meetings are increasingly used in firm-client relations. The 2003 survey showed that 40 per cent of the responding firms used video conferencing in their customer relationship, up from 28 per cent in 1998. However, intra-firm contact is still the main area of use – 70 per cent state that they regularly use video conferencing for intra-firm meetings. Results from these surveys show that video meetings are primarily subject to clear, informal and unambiguous communication. Discussion of on-going projects, 'information exchange', and 'brainstorming' dominate use. A great majority of users report that these kinds of meetings are regularly done by video in their organization. On the other hand, communication with a high level of ambiguity and emotional content, e.g., negotiations and sales/marketing, is rarely done over video.

---

2   The following discussion is based on three surveys conducted in 1998, 2003 and 2007 (reported in Denstadli and Haukeland (1999), Denstadli and Julsrud (2003), and Denstadli et al. (2008) respectively).

Time saving has been the leading motive for implementing video conferencing equipment. In the 2003 survey, 9 out of 10 respondents stated that this was an important reason for use (Figure 12.2). Nearly all were therefore concerned with efficiency gains to be made from video conferencing. Time-savings can be accomplished in the areas of travelling and/or more effective decision-making. Figure 3 indicates that reduced travel was an important motive when the decision to implement video conferencing was taken: 81 per cent stated that reduced travel costs were an inducement for use. Many were also concerned with the positive effects of video conferencing on the traveller. Nearly half stated that they wanted to reduce travel fatigue among employees. Better contact between the different parts of the organization was also important to many, while environmental aspects, internal training/upgrading and improved contacts with customers and suppliers were of less consideration.

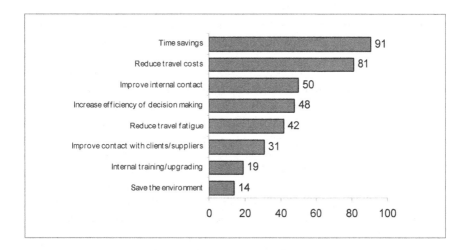

Figure 12.2 Reasons for adopting video conferencing
Note: 5-point scale (1=not at all important, 5=very important); Proportion stating that the motive was important (i.e., ticked 4 or 5).

Norwegian business air travel has experienced significant fluctuations during the past 10 years (Figure 12.3). After a steady growth in both domestic and international business travel in the 1990s, a five year period with considerable decreases in air traffic followed. In 2003, the number of business trips undertaken was down by 1.78 million (19 per cent) compared to 1998. As pointed out above, this period corresponded with a significant increase in the number of enterprises investing in video conferencing equipment, and it is reasonable to assume that some of the drop in air travel was caused by video conferencing substitutions.

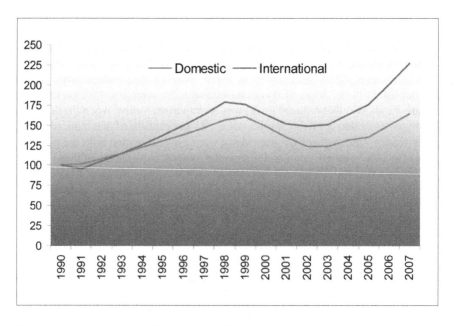

Figure 12.3 International and domestic business air travel in Norway, 1990-2007 (1990 = 100)

Research has shown that substitution effects are most likely to occur within domestic intra-firm travel (Arthur D. Little Inc. 1993, Denstadli and Julsrud 2003, Roy and Filiatrault 1998). However, intra-firm travel only represents about 7-8 per cent of business air travel in Norway. In the period 1998-2003, the number of domestic intra-firm travel declined by 37 per cent, or about 170,000 trips (Table 12.1). It is difficult to say exactly how much of this was due to video conferencing substitution, but there is reason to believe that a majority of these trips were replaced by video meetings. Most likely a small share of 'Other business trips' relating to customer contact was also replaced by video conferencing. For other purposes, substitution is expected to be minor. Much of the reduction in travel to/from work between 1998 and 2003 was caused by workforce cuts in the oil industry. It is also doubtful that the decline in travel associated with courses and conferences was caused by increased use of telecommunications. Denstadli and Julsrud (2003) showed that video conferencing is rarely used for these purposes in Norwegian enterprises. The decline was mainly a result of cost-cutting in industry and commerce.

A rough estimate would be that between 150,000 and 200,000 domestic business trips were substituted for video conferencing between 1998 and 2003. This represented 12-16 per cent of the total decline, and comes to an overall substitution rate of 2.5-3.5 per cent for domestic business air travel over the 5-year period. Thus, despite anticipations of substitution, Norwegian enterprises have only to a limited extent been able to replace business travel, and in 2007 Norwegian business air travel was all time high, both domestic and international.

Table 12.1 Domestic business air travel in Norway, 1998, 2003, and 2007 (million trips)

	1998	2003	2007
To/from work	1.10	1.00	1.46
Courses, conferences	1.71	1.50	1.89
Intra-firm	0.46	0.29	0.38
Other	2.50	1.76	2.32
Business travel total	5.77	4.55	6.05

The Most Recent Developments – From One Size Fits All Towards a Plurality of Integrated Collaboration

New platforms for video conferencing

In recent years, new platforms in video conferencing have emerged. In particular, the US corporation *LifeSize* has released some interesting systems. One if these is the desktop solution *LifeSize Express* which includes a high definition camera, a microphone (or optional audio conference phone), a highly efficient codec, and a wireless remote control. With this very simple system one is able to share documents, objects and multimedia, and it can be installed any place with a broadband connection. Hence, with this system video conferencing does not have to be fixed to a dedicated video conferencing room.

Video conferencing solutions targeted against distributed teams have also emerged. *LifeSize Team* is a solution worthy of note because it is really *not* a conference in the normal sense, meaning a pre-scheduled meeting involving exchange of information. Rather, it is a benign form of monitoring that is always on, and it is placed at the desk of the team members. The point of this solution is to promote a kind of telepresence: spontaneous and informal contact and possibilities for collaboration among a geographically distributed team.

Mobile video conference solutions require dedicated mobile terminals, like *Fieldwire* from Tandberg. This system is intended for technical field use and site inspection. Mobile video enables real-time, remote collaboration between centrally located experts and personnel in the field. The typical use of this technology takes place within the fields of engineering, construction, insurance etc. Besides this, the potential for the use of video on 3G mobile phones and appliances has led to the inclusion of a video screen in many new mobile phones for the consumer market from Nokia and SonyEricsson, which now offer simple portable video telephony for personnel in transit. Video conferencing has made the transition out of the office locales and the home, and can also be used as a tool for monitoring and collaboration in the field. New and advanced handsets like iPhone and other PDA's will most likely make video conferencing viable also out of office.

Sheer technical improvements aside, modern video conferencing offer a range of new possibilities: data display, group and project collaboration, the possibility of video display of both physical object and 'information objects' alike, chat among participants, etc. Some systems also allow archiving the entire video conference. This makes the video conference available for later use by employees that did not attend, for instance by making the sessions available as downloads on the corporate intranet. The filing of entire video conferences expands the media characteristics, it is no longer exclusively a *live* phenomenon among a limited group of participants, but can be accessed later by anyone. The addition of services, new interfaces, and increased flexibility of use and the accommodation of other symbolic forms than verbal communication have greatly increased the versatility of video conferencing.

New services from the web and computer industry

In the current era, the computer industry and the Internet serve as the main engine for experimenting with new forms of communications and services. Some of the most substantial innovations in video communication that has been integrated into mainstream video conferencing solutions from the Internet and the computer industry the last decade are:

Web conferencing   It was introduced by WebEx at the industry conference Telecon in 1999 and represented a new form of collaboration. Web conferencing employs the Internet to allow users to collaborate with one another using their PCs. Meeting participants can share presentations and other contents of their PC desktop, and it offers options such as web-based chat, tools for presentations, streaming audio and video, and other tools. Web conferencing can be particularly effective for applications such as remote training or presentations to large, dispersed groups. Microsoft's Live Meeting is one such web conferencing tool, and Adobe Acrobat Connect combines web conferencing with multipoint video conferencing. Many new laptop PCs are now also equipped with cameras and are provided with software than enable spontaneous video conference on a peer-to-peer basis.

Instant Messaging (IM)   IM is a synchronous alternative to e-mail where the idea is to turn collaboration through messaging into a remote meeting with video. As video were added to instant messaging, the video conference industry added instant messaging to their own products, and forms of instant messaging have been integrated in many video conference systems, for instance making possible two-way messaging within a multipoint conference without interrupting the multipoint dialogue, thus increasing the parallelism of communication within a video meeting. This is an example of a general trend: the communication opportunities within video communication have been made more *scalable* and *flexible*.

CSCW and project portals   Project organization is a defining feature of modern businesses. Several video conference systems have incorporated features from so-called *project software* that allow archiving and access of project material, project schedules, and digital means of communication (live chat, project blog, message board, shared whiteboard for producing ideas etc.). These features are particularly useful when project personnel are located in different places. Another inspiration for group collaboration and academic field is Computer Supported Cooperative Work (CSCW). It addresses how collaborative activities and their coordination can be supported by computer systems, and has inspired a range of applications that support group cooperation. Video conferencing is in its essence a remote-synchronous communication form. CSCW has a much broader scope, also including modes of communication that are asynchronous (project management software, shift work groupware, team rooms, bulletin boards, blogs, wikis etc) and/or are co-located (shared tables, wall displays, group decision systems etc) (Baecker et al. 1995). Many of the innovations which can be found in modern video communication are to a large part inspired by CSCW and the computer industry at large. Historically, video conferencing has evolved from its legacy in remote interaction of the pioneering and telematic era. In the era of integrated collaboration video conferencing solutions also incorporate features and services that have asynchronous and co-located characteristics.

The last three factors emphasize a key point: the video conferencing industry was heavily influenced by the computer and internet revolution during the 1990s. It could not develop in isolation as it did previously when the low-bit telecommunication standard ISDN was used as technical carrier. Video has become an important part of digital communication, and innovative ways of using video are being developed for computer networks and the Web. From the IT industry, innovations in *Computer Supported Cooperation Work* (CSCW) paved the way for new concepts that could be integrated into the existing video communication industry. In parallel with the video conferencing industry integrating the innovations from the Internet, the computer and Internet industry developed its own video solutions and integrated video-conference-like functionality to their own applications. Video communication has now become a part of the rapid development of web services that often are characterized by the term *social media*. Today, even the IP-telephony service *Skype* offers video conferencing, now also joined by by Google's *Gmail Video Chat* and other web services.

Conclusions and Further Prospects

Video conferencing and integrated collaboration have now reached a level of utility and user-friendliness so that it can be integrated into everyday business practice. As we see it, the use of video conferencing in business settings will most likely follow two tracks; one based on the traditional idea of the video conferencing, and one based on the ongoing experimentations with communication services on the Web. This last kind of usage is likely to emphasize the collaboration aspect of video conferencing.

Sporadic users of video conferencing will likely continue to use it in a customary way, more or less like an audio conference with picture and with the face-to-face conference as an (implicit) model. This traditional way of using video conferencing is strongly supported by the ongoing development in screen and aural technology and other technical improvements that now quite convincingly can remediate a face-to-face meeting without the technical problems associated with earlier solutions.

However, the fastest growing type of video conferences is the type in which the participants can communicate with each other while viewing and interacting with digital material (Ward 2002). This kind of video conferencing is more about using the technology as a direct working tool for processing digital objects, not just a means of information exchange or decision making. The video conferencing industry for enterprises is still likely to exist and provide services for the business community, but their long term survival is probably dependent on the rich experimenting with and influx of new ways of communicating on the web.

The borders between video conferences, web conferences and the field of Computer Supported Cooperation Work have been increasingly blurred, and the phenomenon of video conferencing has also been profoundly changed over the last fifteen years. The intensive users of video communication are likely to be users of integrated collaboration, and their line of usage has to a far extent merged with CSCW and all the flexible opportunities for cooperation and communication made possible with these solutions. Products from big players like Microsoft Live Meeting and Adobe Connect are two examples thereof.

How do these developments impact business travel? As shown previously, research indicates that video conferencing so far only have had minor impacts on travel. Disaggregated substitution effects can be found, and from the individual or company perspective there is clearly a question of travel replacement. Video conferencing also has a green side. By substituting travel by wire, emissions from cars, planes and other modes of transportation can be reduced. Although environmental benefits of video conferencing have not been high on the business agenda up to now (c.f. Figure 12.3), increased awareness of the global crisis can change these attitudes. On the other hand, aggregate analyses are fairly conclusive in that industries demand for transportation and telecommunications follow parallel tracks, and that the net effect for the economy as a whole is complementarity. When respondents in the Norwegian surveys pointed out future developments in the use of different media, they predicted increased use for seven of the 11 listed media, only for the fax machine a significant decline was expected. This is a strong indication of continued growth in the total amount of communication in business life.

Although video communication might curb some of the rise in business travel, the overall substitution effects appear rather minor. First, business travel develops in line with business cycles, and the main driving force in this market is economic growth. Historically, slowdowns in the economy, like the current financial crisis, have triggered tighter control of travel and more focus on alternative ways of communicating, but these effects have remained temporary. Second, to understand the interaction between video communication and business travel, it is important to grasp the social basis for travelling and why there is a desire to travel (Urry 2003). Modern work life is organized around different networks where travel and face-to-face contacts are crucial. Lassen (2006, 2008) points out that the social need of co-presence and face-to-face contact is determined by the individual's desire to travel, the time available for travelling, external demands and expectations, and the content of the specific interaction (formal/informal). Global workers construct a need for 'co-presence' and 'face-to-face' communication which is not a stable function of work tasks; instead it is dynamic and changeable, and different for each individual. Virtual communication systems have an advantage over physical travel when the working task contains a high degree of formality. However, business travel very often includes an informal element, not only attached to the traditional work life (Denstadli 2004, Lian and Denstadli 2004, Gripsrud 2007). A number of investigations dealing with the possibilities of increased use of video communication are characterized by an idealization of the advantages attached to saved travel time, neglecting a number of mechanisms and social patterns of meaning which affect the level of travel in the opposite direction.

Travel and personal contact is still regarded as the most effective way of conducting business, and there are aspects of business life that hardly seem to be replaced by video conferencing, or any form of telecommunication technology. Although new technologies can create 'virtual rooms' giving the participants a sense of co-presence, video conferencing can never replace the genuine aspect of personal meetings: the direct face-to-face contact.

References

Appogee Research Inc. 1994. *Making connections: How telecommunications technology will affect business and leisure travel*. Prepared for the federal Aviation Administration, Office of Aviation Policy, Plan, and Management Analysis. As quoted in Roy and Filiatrault 1998.

Arthur, D. Little Inc. 1993. *Strategic assessment report: Report to the Massachusetts Aeronautics Commission*. Cambridge, MA: Arthur D. Little Inc.

Baecker, R.M., Grudin, J., Buxton, W.A.S. and Greenberg, S. 1995. Groupware and Computer-Supported Cooperative Work, in Baecker, R.M., Grudin, J., Buxton, W.A.A. and Greenberg, S. 1995 (eds) *Readings in human-computer interaction: Toward the year 2000*, 741-753. San Francisco: Morgan Kaufmann Publishers.

Batten, D.F. and R. Thorn 1989. *Transportation for the future*. Heidelberg: Springer Verlag.

Bender, A.R. and Stephenson, F.J. 1998. Contemporary issues affecting the demand for business travel in the United States. *Journal of Air Transport Management*, 4(2), 99-109.

Bennison, D.J. 1988. Transport/telecommunication interactions: Empirical evidence from a video conferencing field trial in the United Kingdom. *Transportation Research Part A*, 22(4), 291-300.

Boden, D. and Molotch, H.L. 1994. The compulsion of proximity, in R. Friedland and D. Boden (eds) *NowHere Space, Time and Modernity*, 257-286. Berkeley: University of California Press.

Boyle, E., Anderson A. and Newlands, A. 1994. The effects of visibility on dialogue and performance in a cooperative problem-solving task. *Language and Speech*, 37(1), 1-20.

Choo, S. and P.L. Mokhtarian 2007. Telecommunications and travel demand and supply: Aggregate structural equation models for the US. *Transportation Research Part A*, 41(1), 4-18.

Coddington, P., 1993. The impact of videoconferencing on airline business traffic. *Journal of Travel Research*, 31(2), 64-66.

Daft, R.L. and R.H. Lengel 1984. Information richness: A new approach to managerial behavior and organizational design, in Cummings, L.L. and B.M. Staw (eds) *Research in organizational behavior*, 6, 191-233. Homewood, IL: JAI Press.

Daft, R.L. and R.H. Lengel 1986. Organizational information requirements, media richness and structural design. *Management Science*, 32(5), 554-571.

Davis, A. 1999. *Integrated collaboration: Driving business efficiency into the next millennium*. Tempe, AZ: Forward Concepts.

Dennis, A.R. and J.S. Valacich 1999. Rethinking Media Richness: Towards a Theory of Media Synchronicity. *Proceedings of the 32nd Hawaii International Conference on System Sciences – 1999*.

Dennis, A.R. and S.T. Kinney 1998. Testing Media Richness Theory in the New Media: The Effects of Cues, Feedback, and Task Equivocality. *Information System Research*, 9(3), 256-274.

Denstadli, J.M. 2004. Impacts of video conferencing on business travel: The Norwegian experience. *Journal of Air Transport Management*, 10(6), 371-376.

Denstadli, J.M., Gripsrud, M. and Rideng, A. 2008. *International and domestic air travel in Norway 2007*. Oslo: Institute of Transport Economics, report 974/2008 (English summary available).

Denstadli, J.M., Ø. Engebretsen, A. Gjerdåker, and L. Vågane 2008. *Person travel in Norwegian trade and industries*. Oslo: Institute of Transport Economics, report 938/2008 (English summary available).

Denstadli, J.M. and T.E. Julsrud 2003. *Video conferencing in Norwegian industry and commerce: Increased use, less travel?* Oslo: Institute of Transport Economics, report 670/2003 (English summary available).

Denstadli, J.M. and J.V. Haukeland 1999. *Videoconferences – a new meeting place for businesses?* Oslo: Institute of Transport Economics, report 426/1999 (English summary available).

First Securities 2008. *Videoconferencing – continued momentum*. Internal report, First Securities, Oslo.

Fischer, M., R. Maggi and C. Rammer 1990. Context specific media choice and barriers to communication in universities. *The Annals of Regional Science*, 24(4), 253-269.

Geels, F.W. and W.A. Smith 2000. Failed technology futures: Pitfalls and lessons from a historical survey. *Futures*, 32(9-10), 867-885.

Gripsrud, M. 2007. *Interplay between Transport, Personal Mobility and Information and Communication Technology*. Oslo: Institute of Transport Economics, report 844/2007 (English summary available).

Holmes, D. 2005. *Communication theory: Media, technology and society*. London: Sage.

Kahn, A.M. 1987. Sociotechnical factors in air travel: Some new insights into telecommunications interactions. *Transportation Research Record*, 1147, 6-14.

Kraut, R.E, and R.S. Fish 2006. Prospects for video telephony. *Telecommunicatons Policy*, 19(9), 699-719.

Lassen, C. 2006. Work and Aeromobility, *Environment and Planning A*, 38, 301-312.

Lassen, C. 2008. A life in corridors – Social perspectives on aeromobility and work in knowledge Organisations, in Urry, J. (ed.) *Aeromobilities*. London: Routledge.

Lee, T. and P.L. Mokhtarian 2007. Correlations between industrial demands (direct and total) for communications and transportation in the U.S. economy 1947-1997. *Transportation*, 35, 1-22.

Lian, J.I. and J.M. Denstadli 2004. Norwegian business air travel – segments and trends. *Journal of Air Transport Management*, 10(2), 109-118.

Lipartito, K. 2003. Picturephone and the Information Age: The Social Meaning of Failure. *Technology and Culture*, 44(1), 50-81.

Mokhtarian, P.L. 1990. A typology of relationships between telecommunications and transportation. *Transportation Research Part A*, 24(3), 231-242.

Mokhtarian, P.L. and R. Meenakshisundaram 1999. Beyond tele-substitution: Disaggregate longitudinal structural equation modeling of communication impacts. *Transportation Research Part C*, 7(1), 33-52.

Moore, A. and P.P. Jovanis 1988. Modelling media choices in business organisations: Implications for analyzing telecommunications-transportation interaction. *Transportation Research Part A*, 22(4), 257-273.

Muller, N. 1998. *Desktop encyclopedia of telecommunications*. New York: McGraw Hill.

Noll, A.M. 1992. Anatomy of a failure: Picturephone revisited. *Telecommunicatons Policy*, 16(4), 307-317.

Patterson, P. 2008. *High fliers: Business leaders' view on air travel*. London: Institute of Directors, Policy paper (ISDN: 978 1904520 634).

Petersen, H. 1977. Telekommunikation und verkehr. *Internationales Verkehrswesen*, 1977: 224-228. As quoted in Geels and Smith 2000.

Plaut, P.O. 1999. Do telecommunications reduce industrial uses of transportation? An international comparison of Israel, Canada, U.S.A. & Europe. *World Transport Policy & Practice*, 5(4), 42-49.

Plaut, P.O. 1997. Transportation-communications relationships in industry. *Transportation Research Part A*, 31(6), 419-429.

Saffo, P. 1993. The future of travel. *Fortune Magazine*, 128(7), 112-119.

Salomon, I. 1985. Telecommunications and travel. Substitution or modified mobility? *Journal of Transport Economics and Policy*, 19(Sept.), 219-235.

Salomon, I. 1986. Telecommunications and travel relationships: A review. *Transportation Research Part A*, 20(3), 223-238.

Stephenson, F.J. and A.R. Bender 1996. Watershed: The Future of U.S. Business Air Travel. *Transportation Journal*, 35(3), 14-32.

Kraut, R., C. Steinfield, A. Chan, B. Butler, and A. Hoag 1998. Coordination and virtualization: The role of electronic networks and personal relationships. *Journal of Computer- Mediated Communication (on-line)*, 3(4).

Roy, J. and P. Filiatrault 1998. The impact of new business practices and information technologies on business air travel demand. *Journal of Air Transport Management*, 4(2), 77-86.

Toffler, A. 1980. *The third wave*. New York: Bantam Books.

Urry, J. 2002. Mobility and proximity. *Sociology*, 36(2), 255-274.

Urry, J. 2003. *Global Complexity*. Cambridge: Polity Press.

Urry, J. 2007. *Mobilities*. Cambridge: Polity Press.

van Dijk, J. 1999. *The Network Society*. London: Sage.

Ward, L. 2002. The rise of rich media and real-time conferencing. *Business Communications Review*, March, 2002.

Watanabe, T. 1980. Visual communication technology: Priorities for the 1980s. *Telecommunications Policy*, 4(4) 287-94.

Index

Lightning Source UK Ltd.
Milton Keynes UK
UKOW01n2031290917
310142UK00010B/81/P